Dichotomy Between Science and Religion? A Lived Experimental Research Journey

Science and Religion Intertwined Human Endeavors

by

Jerome V. Scholle

Assisted by

Savvy Book Marketing

New Jersey

Dichotomy Between Science and Religion? A Lived Experimental Research Journey
by Jerome V. Scholle

This book is written to provide information and motivation to readers. Its purpose isn't to render any type of psychological, legal, or professional advice of any kind. The content is the sole opinion and expression of the author.

ISBN: 978-1-0880-1388-5

Printed in the United States of America

Acknowledgments are made to the following for permission to quote:

Material excerpted from *Parallel Myths* by J.F. Bierlein, copyright © 1994 by J.F. Bierlein. Used by permission of Ballantine Books, an imprint of Random House, a division of Penguin Random House LLC. All rights reserved.

For eBooks, excerpt(s) from *Conversations with God: An Uncommon Dialogue* by Neale Donald Walsch, copyright © 1995, 2002, 2003, 2005 by Neale Donald Walsch. Used by permission of G. P. Putnam's Sons, an imprint of Penguin Publishing Group, a division of Penguin Random House LLC. All rights reserved.

For hardback and paperback books, excerpt(s) from *Conversations with God: An Uncommon Dialogue, Book 1* by Neale Donald Walsch, copyright © 1995 by Neale Donald Walsch. Used by permission of TarcherPerigee, an imprint of the Penguin Publishing Group, a division of Penguin Random House LLC. All rights reserved

Material excerpted from God and Consciousness (we are one) © Matthew Webb used with permission of The World Mind Society, http://www.ipher.org/~visionquest/World%20Mind%20Society%20Disclaimer.htm [Accessed 210726]

Material excerpted from Hunter-Gatherers and the Origins of Religion © 2016 Hervey C. Peoples, & Pavel Duda, & Frank W. Marlowe used with permission from Open Access: This article is distributed under the terms of the Creative Commons Attribution 4.0 International License http://creativecommons.org/licenses/by/4.0/.

Material excerpted from *Physics and Beyond: Encounters and Conversations* © 1971 Werner Heisenberg used with permission from HarperCollins Publishers.

Material excerpted from *Something There, The Biology of the Human Spirit* © 2006 David Hay used with permission from Templeton Foundation Press, Conshohocken, PA www.templetonpress.org.

Material excerpted from *The Case for Religion* © 2004 Keith Ward reproduced with permission of the Licensor through PLSclear.

Material excerpted from *The God Theory* © 2006 Bernard Haisch used with permission from Red Wheel Weiser, LLC Newburyport, MA www.redwheelweiser.com.

Scriptures taken from the Holy Bible, New International Version®, NIV®. Copyright © 1973, 1978, 1984, 2011 by Biblica, Inc.™ Used by permission of Zondervan. All rights reserved worldwide. www.zondervan.com The "NIV" and "New International Version" are trademarks registered in the United States Patent and Trademark Office by Biblica, Inc.™

Material excerpted from *Why Religion Is Natural and Science Is Not* © 2011 Robert N. McCauley. Reproduced with permission of the Licensor through PLSclear.

Material excerpted from Wikipedia articles; text is available under the Creative Commons Attribution-ShareAlike License https://creativecommons.org/licenses/by-sa/3.0/.

Table of Contents

List of Tables

List of Figures

Acknowledgments

Deep appreciation is felt for all those who have gone before me over the millennia as you have simply recorded your observations and experiences in your journey of life on this planet earth. From these records and those writing today in their various fields of study, I am able only to sample an iota of all the writings past and present. From this sample, I have synthesized and integrated ideas into my own thoughts and observations documented in this writing of my journey.

Thanks to all those with whom I have had an interconnectedness in my journey. You also affected my life's observations and experiences. Thus, during my life journey, you have influenced the expressions in this autobiographical research documentary letter to the reader of my high school quest on the 'dichotomy between science and religion.' As I view my life, it has been a first-hand living experimental and experiential research project. My career and avocation were a direct involvement in the physical sciences, various levels of different religious sects, and studies of philosophy, astrology, and other metaphysics.

Thank you, friends, for reviewing earlier versions and especially those giving comments and edits on this work: Ray Bass, Kyler Bruton, Eleanore D'Andrea, Shelley Firestone, Sylvia Gonzalez, Stephanie Jones, Matthew Kaemerer, Nicholas Kilzer, Marilyn Parsons, Guy Rowley, and Edwin Westbrook.

Notable comments are:

Ray Bass: "Thank you for this highly fascinating book! I finished reading and was very impressed by it. I think it's the first time I ever saw such an exhaustive analysis of the different states of beliefs throughout history! What this taught me is a greater consciousness of who I am as a human being and a greater sense of belonging through not just spirituality but science. I feel that your book is like a fuller picture of life which exposes areas that were untapped before by religion and science alone. I am thankful for it and have no doubt a lot of people are about to benefit from it."

Marilyn Parsons: "What can I say.........it takes a lot of guts to make your life an open book as you did. This is the kind of paper that really requires a lengthy discussion, so I am only going to discuss a few aspects of it. I read it twice as I do all readings with some real 'meat' in them.

I agree with much of what you wrote and disagree with other things you said.

When I was a student at McCormick Seminary (over 35 years ago), I researched the story of creation of several other cultures to write a comparison of them to the Bible's story of creation. Much to my shock, they were similar. I had no idea as I had thought that the Bible was "the truth". How naive I was. It was like learning there is no Santa Claus. I started to read Joseph Campbell, and it was then that I realized that all peoples and cultures have the same longings and that the religions and beliefs of each culture come about to satisfy these longings. This is why religions and stories of creation are so similar.

You talked about how much alike we large animals are. We all have a language that enables us to communicate with others. But humans are different in our language in that we can create fiction, and we can gossip unlike other animals. If it were not for both of these, there could not have been a Bible.

I have returned to a church after many years absent. I do believe that religion can lead to spirituality and that they are not separate (I do know you showed a Venn diagram). I also believe that there are churches that the leadership is not into power or greed...as mine is not but is into serving (it is a large church with a congregation of 1000). It took me a long time to find this church, but they are there.

Anyway, that is it. I am grateful for the opportunity to read this paper as it has made me think about many issues."

Guy Rowley, MD: "It was a pleasure reading your manifesto.

Wow, have you done a lot of work!

It's always agreeable to share opinions with others whose beliefs overlap your own.

Art and poetry: necessity of knowing the context or intent of the art is? I think it's desirable to interpret without this knowledge, then reassess after knowing. Robert Frost advised that you should 'never disillusion your admirers with the tale of your sources and processes.'

They infused your work with your personal life, which I find interesting and important.

Janitor versus higher-up's equality. My high school class chose to include in our yearbook all of the various support staff in our school, and we continue to be proud of doing so.

'No' hurting people. I try to use the 'philosophy of Yes.' Always start with 'Yes.' My patient is in restraints, 'Let me out of these restraints right away.' 'Yes, we'll release you as soon as you're not raging on toxic drugs.' A little sloppy, but it's usually fairly effective.

Arrogance: Liked your mentioning this tendency in our world, foisting one's own beliefs on others.

Sylvia Gonzalez: Let me begin by thanking you for the opportunity to read thru your work! I am an avid reader, but admittedly, not on your scholastic nor professional level. This being said: I still was able to retain many of your ideas, which either enlightened me, or explained away many doubts I have had about "self" and existence.

As I began reading, may I respectfully say, that your writing seemed so detached, which became clear to me as to why, when you related you grew up with no emotional attachments, friends, nor hugs. I am glad the universe compensated you with a partner into your life. Now, I better understand your "style" of writing.

There was a moment which took my breath away...you explained "significant other" and that we were reincarnated from being past partners to this new life to bring this someone joy. My hubby of 30 years passed away, and I always felt as though we had been together before!

I so enjoyed your explanations of "living spirit"," and why it allows us to suffer.

Your admittance that not one god or religion is better than another is not usually verbalized; I tire of this ignorance. I also agree that all religions have a general order of things, we may worship differently, but with the same pleas in mind.

Thank you, kind sir, for very well researched trip thru religion and science...your friend now.

Thanks for sharing."

Thanks to the Savvy Book Marketing design team for expanding the author's concept into an interesting book cover.

Thanks to Michelle Mulheron of Savvy Book Marketing for editing of the manuscript in a mutually benefitting process and the ability to work together quite interactively.

Thanks to Isaac Levine, the Project Manager at Savvy Book Marketing, for guiding the publication of the author's unique presentation.

Prologue

A central theme undergirding my life is that I am, among others, with many similarities but also many differences, pondering what many before me have done. Human beings have pondered, "What is the purpose of his/her spirit, an iota portion of the universal energy and universal consciousness?" This spirit keeps the body functioning for what is termed living and ceases to be expressed in this plane in the body when it changes functionality in what is termed death. It is with this spirit came my talents, abilities, and psychological disposition with limitations so that I need others for sustaining life. Likewise, others being limited need others throughout their spirits' sojourns on this universe stratum, earth. So, what are the observations to be made about this entity termed a human being?

- The environments show a wide variation within extremes which the human entity has been formed to live within. The human entity adapts to living within these environmental differences.

  - What is the source of this planet with its polarities of extremes within the diversified environments found in various regions on this planet?

  - How did this planet come about?

  - How did human beings come about with the ability to live in this environment?

  - Why is the environment constantly changing?

- Human beings are gifted to create and speak sounds that are termed languages to communicate with their other like human beings. Although different human groups have the same basic body structures with myriad variations, they speak different languages, which are unintelligible to those outside the groups.

  - How did this come about and why?

  - What source is behind this behavior?

- The human entities are endowed with thinking and observation skills, resulting in the development of divergent thought patterns having polarities and all variations within, not unlike that of the environment. One of these polarities comprises theism (one god or many gods) and atheism (no god). Recent centuries have brought about another polarity, science-religion, or a more pronounced seen-unseen perspective.

  - Why these variations often leading to conflicts between opposing thought patterns?

  - What is the human entity to learn beyond his/her adaptations within this physical plane he/she finds his/her spirit?

- Observations show that both higher animals and human beings have varying personalities. Human beings have unique talents and drives of life careers that are independent of family origins. Within families, we observe each child having distinct personalities starting from birth.

  - Why and what is this source of differences?

  - Is each of us one small part of a universal consciousness comprising all living beings? Such that our interactions with each other are necessary to understand this plane and learn how to be in harmony with divergent ideas.

  - How are we to be in harmony with the environment and its effect on our personalities?

- We come into this plane with nothing, needing others to care for us until we are capable of caring for ourselves, unless we have disabilities. Then, after using goods to sustain our life and interacting with others of this plane and maybe other unseen planes, we need others to care for us as we pass from this plane, taking nothing with us.

  - What are we to have learned spiritually by living in this plane, called earth, of the universe?

  - Where did this spirit come from that inhabited our bodies to have caused it to function in the way it did?

  - Where does the spirit go when it passes from the body?

- Everything observed exhibits a birth-growth-reproductive-death cycle in varying forms for the myriad of species. Within these species, many different cycles exist for balancing planet earth's species' lives. For example, some species feed on capturing other living species, whereas other species feed on a deceased form. When the environment can no longer sustain a specie, diseases ravage the specie reducing the group size.

  - Because of the human desire to live forever, are we missing this birth-to-death cycle, and how we should live life differently?

  - Are we humans missing that ravaging diseases and wars are about reducing the number of humans that the earth may support?

  - Are ravaging diseases and wars part of the unknown universal energy and universal consciousness in its balanced operation of the created universe?

Humankind has been addressing these questions as far back as recorded history goes and even further back through reasoning from observations of past events uncovered in archeological and anthropological finds. Today we are still addressing these questions and modifying recorded thoughts with newer information. After all, all learning and expression of our thoughts build on what has gone before, whether living now or having lived millennia ago. Newer insights are modifications to that learning guided by our perceptions of what is happening. In what follows, I will endeavor to give insights from my observations and experiences, both as a scientist and a religionist, as well as from readings of materials related to the origins of religions, religious systems, and spirituality. The writing has been evolving over the past seventeen years in retirement from the physical sciences, so to concentrate on my lifelong avocation of the dichotomy between science and religion. Since there is extensive literature that I might read, the sense is the universal consciousness guided me in some unknown way to what I cited for meaningfulness in this writing.

I have lived eighty-some years on this planet named earth, as an entity named Jerome, however, more frequently known as Jerry, in a form designated a male human body. I hold a worldview of coming into this plane with talents and abilities to support myself and, more importantly, for the benefit of others. The view has had both positive and negative effects on my life so that I may experience life as a human being and not as a robot. This view has been colored by my childhood emotional abandonment as well as psychological and spiritual development in journeying through the stages of life. These personal factors interweave throughout this work since they affect my fact-driven intertwinement of philosophy, physical science, and religion.

To help the reader through this fact-based, highly detailed work, I instructionally wrote it using bullets, footnotes, and other formatting. As an educator, where we often state explanations in three different ways for students' understanding, I repeat some experiences related to the topic. There are many references noted by superscript numbers and many additional informational footnotes noted by superscript bracketed numbers, especially for the references within quoted referenced materials.[1] Thus, this work details the author's journey personally through life in five chapters and a closing commentary about the entire work:

1. I, a Human Being: Characteristic of being human described by aspects of being human and the quest determining "Who am I?"

2. Science Journey: The development and primary career journey in physics, mathematics, and chemistry.

3. Ministry Journey: The development and secondary journey while participating in religious systems, including ministering for a while as a priest in the Western Orthodox Church of America.

4. Avocation: Origins of Religion: The lifelong studies of the origins and comparison of religions and conclusions drawn from these four chapters.

5. Recent Concepts: Covers the work about what others have said concerning these concepts from research within the last two years of this writing.

Closing Commentary: This expresses thoughts drawn from the entire work

---

[1] Respecting the author's humanness of imperfection, times, and culture, all quotes were not edited for grammar or spelling.

Chapter 1

I, a Human Being

Searching for Identity in the Universe

I am the product of all that has gone before me, but within me stirs a need to express new understandings. These are built on intuitions, past observations, experiences, and studies in living each moment now. These new understandings provide food for thought for future development for myself and next generations as to understanding "the why do I exist and for what purpose." For many, the answers to these questions are found in a religious system, often the one's birth family.

The quest is to comprehend the universal consciousness and universal energy. This is often expressed as an entity named Creator, a term being passed down to me for the founder of this universe and my being. Journeying through life in this quest, I have what is like a sea of boxes before me, all labeled "GOD," a moniker for the entity, Creator, from my childhood religious training. In the quest for relationship and thus knowing the "GOD," I have opened some of these boxes without my spirit resonating long term to this so-called Creator. All the boxes were like being in a relationship with another person, but only through a book, not a one-on-one relationship. In fact, the leaders and participants of these boxes seemed to be more interested in maintaining their belief systems and the power it gives them in controlling others. There was minimal help to one's development in navigating this plane in harmony with the environment and other human beings. Although my original religious system, Roman Catholicism, had encouraged a personal relationship with the Creator through dogma and rituals, this method came to make no sense since I was seeing myself as part and integral with the universal energy with an iota of the universal consciousness.

As the quest has evolved, the name for Creator has changed to Living Spirit or Creative Force. This rename removes the confusion with the term God, which has many connotations depending on which religious system one is reviewing. If I am a resemblance of this Living Spirit as expressed through my ability connoted by free will to think and act independently and thus experience life, then the Living Spirit must have the same ability to create everything in the universe.

As a human being, I am generally functioning independently as an adult, depending on others to meet some needs for existence. Thus, as a child, I learned from others to do things, and some things were beyond my talents and abilities, so finding myself being limited. This learning from others continues throughout life, as well as my teaching others until one's spirit passes from this earth. Thus, for this to happen, forms of communication between individuals are needed to fulfill the needs of others.

Human Communication

Human beings are created with remarkably varied physical and mental abilities that do not appear to exist in any of the other parts of the observed universe that human beings find themselves occupying. Let us look at one of these, the communicative ability. At birth, human infants express oral sounds that the surrounding persons begin to interpret the infant's meaning, and these persons make similar sounds back. The infant's visual expression shows connection. As the infant grows, the caring persons train the infant in the recognizable sounds for items and concepts in their culture. Barring physical or mental disabilities, the infant progresses in physical and mental abilities, learning the oral and written communication of his/her culture.

From the sounds made by the people of a given culture, a visual system was developed as a code for their sounds. The code is then used in both oral and written communication to describe ideas, things, events, etc. Examples of these systematic symbols are hieroglyphics of ancient Egypt, letters of Western European languages, characters of Far East Asian languages, and the scripts of the Arabic language groups. For example, the English word *man*, designating a human of the male gender, is in the codes of German *Mann*[1], of French *homme*[2], of modern Greek *'άντρας*, antras[3], of the original Biblical Greek *ANEP*, aner[4], and of Biblical Hebrew אִישׁ, 'îysh, eesh.[5][2] The code also has an order in reading the symbols: in the above languages, the words are read left to right, except in the Hebrew language, where the words are read right to left. Thus, all aspects of the code system by a given people are known as people's language. Here a few major world languages are noted, yet there are thousands of languages throughout the world. Many are being lost through declining populations or assimilation into the larger surrounding culture or through worldwide usage of the major world languages.

As a code is continually used, changes of meaning and methods of writing the code occur. For example, English poet Chaucer (1340-1400) wrote:

> "Whan that Aprille with his shoures swote
> The droghte of Marche hath perced to the rote..."

In modern English this reads:

> "When April with his sweet showers has
> struck to the roots the dryness of March..."[6]

Another example is Figure 1, the title from a 1611 book page.[7]

In this title, the modern "s" looks like "f" without the crossbar. Also, note the additional "e" on brief and learn, which we do not use in modern English.

Since any language is a systematic set of code or symbols for vocalizations, then all human communication is an interpretation of these vocalizations. First, the originator of oral or written communication interprets his/her thoughts in words that cannot convey the total nuances engendered in the thoughts. And secondly, the hearer or reader then further interprets what he/she hears or reads based on what the words mean in his/her own experiences in life. They will understand each other if both have similar shared experiences. However, within this

Figure 1. The title from a 1611 book page

---

[2]The English transliteration and pronunciation are read left to right.

2

culture, if one does not have similar shared experiences, one will not be able to communicate with another on a specific topic. For example, a person not versed in nuclear physics terminology will often not understand the discourse of a nuclear physicist on subatomic structures. Another example, a person not versed in the many literary forms used in poems may miss the sophisticated nuances and possibly the whole meaning that the poet is conveying.

When you are speaking, you have at your disposal: tone, inflection, facial expression, and body language besides words to convey the interpretation of your thoughts to another person or persons. Likewise, these hearers are using body language to convey what they are hearing and feeling. Whereas in written communication, a writer lacks non-verbal factors and uses words to paint a picture that the reader formulates with his/her imagination to understand the message the writer intended to convey. In literary writing, the emphasis is on the emotional and psychological aspects of the subject in contrast to technical writing, where the emphasis is on reasoning and logic leading to a conclusion from data.

Besides the literal meaning of words, this picture painting uses many literary figures of speech that convey a message different from the actual literal meaning of the words. Some examples of figures of speech are apostrophe, euphemism, hyperbole, idiom, irony, metaphor, metonymy, paradox, personification, play on words, simile, and synecdoche. All languages use these, and they may not be directly translatable into another language to convey the meaning in the original language. Idioms are challenging as they are understood only by the people living in a specific area and have a sense vastly different from the literal meanings of the words. This difference from the literal meanings is true in any culture, as idioms have different meanings to a localized group from others, not within that group. Figures of speech are then used in larger language structures, such as axioms, hymns, legal codes, legends, letters, oration, poetry, prayers, proverbs, sermons, short stories, etc. In these structures, the same word may again take on different shades of meaning.

The challenge to the reader is first to understand the message of the writer to its intended audience, then to interpret it for application, if applicable, to one's life. This process is usually easier with scientific writings than with literary ones. In literary writings, you are encouraged to enter the world that the writer has created to send his/her message. The same is true for the ancient writings, such as sacred writings of the various religious systems in the world, only more complicated because of the times, people, cultures, and languages, which are all vastly different from modern times.

You often better understand an author's message if you know something about the author's life and interactions with others, both in relationships and circumstances that the author experienced. Most often, this occurs after reading an article or viewing a piece of art when one desires a deeper understanding of what the author or artist is trying to convey. Thus, it is crucial to read not only what the author wrote but also the history of others of that same time and circumstances, if available. Therefore, you are encouraged to read what else is written about peoples and cultures during the times of ancient authors. Furthermore, since there is difficulty in being truly objective without imposing one's own worldview in describing an event, it is vital to read many others, especially with differing viewpoints, to understand the event entirely. For example, in today's reporting of current events, you have both liberal and conservative contrasting views for the same event.

The challenge for me has been discerning the truth from both views as I consider neither to have the whole truth. By stating one's views using words of persuasion and selective information, authors make an effort to entice the reader to accept their view. In so doing, the author or its group then has power over others. Nowhere, except in politics, is this more common than the interpretations leading to dogmas and doctrines from sacred literature of religions—both within and outside reporting what is authentic in each religion. Thus, over time many different versions of a subject, such as religion, emerge, often leading to ostracizing those not agreeing to a given version and/or violence against those ostracized by the group having more power for one version. We see this today in the Sunni-Shiite conflict in Iraq, the Catholic-Protestant conflict in Northern Ireland, the liberal-conservative political conflict around the world, and the physicalists-panpsychists[3] conflict in science.

Aspects of Humans

I discarded the religious system of youth, as my spiritual needs were unfulfilled. Being a person with an innate talent for research, I set out on a new journey to understand my relationship to the universal consciousness and universal energy, also termed Living Spirit or Creative Force. In the process, wholeness was found to be expressed as an inner void centered among five primary aspects interacting with and being influenced by each other.

Before discussing these aspects, it is essential to understand how I see myself and others exhibiting similar traits constructed. Observations show a class of entities called human beings that, when alive, have three interrelated and interacting faculties termed: body, mind, and spirit:

- **Body is the physical structure that:**
  - Is limited and differentiated from other living organisms and aspects of its environs.
  - Functions in the environs of this region of an observable expanse that is called a universe. This region of the universe is termed earth, with a unique set of characteristics in which the body can function. The body is made of substances in the universe that have been broken down into atoms that arrange themselves in molecular structures of varying degrees of complexities. These atoms are currently understood to follow specific physical laws that humans have determined from observation. These observations show an extensive set of biological variations. Some are common to all, and some are characteristic of what is termed sexes of male and female for reproduction and continuance of life following a birth-death cycle.
  - Compared to an ideal, one observes that many physical abnormalities exist. Some are understood enough to be restored to a near first condition, and others are not even understood.
  - Invites the question, "What causes the body to function as it does in this realm of limitations, cause and effect, and time in forwarding motion?"

---

[3]Defined in Chapter 5.

- At what is termed death, the body of complex molecules ceases operation and deteriorates into the substances from which it is composed. What caused the body to have functionality? If it was just the chemical configurations, then they should be able to continue.

- Houses the only entity that I can conceive is one invisible and having an unknown origin. I will term this entity "spirit," being an integral part of universal energy that is the life force in all things classified as living or showing life-death cycles. This universal energy is also present in inanimate objects as their atoms are known to be in motion. For example, if a stone is placed on a gold leaf, gold spots will be seen on the stone when separated after an extended time, like a high school year physics course.

■ **Mind is the mental/emotional mechanism seated in the brain that:**

- Controls the automatic bodily functions, such as the heart pumping the blood throughout the body, the nourishment of cells through the digestive tract enzyme interactions, and the purification system to remove deleterious compounds from the body.

- Is continually in a decision-making mode to act between two situations, i.e., to do or not do a specific task, to go or not go to a particular place, to act now or later, etc. If there are more than two options, then a process of repeated choices of two things at a time is done. This human mind functionality is behind the design of the computer to use only 1 or 0 for whether to do or not an operation.

- Learns new things by building stepwise on previous learning. For example, I learned mathematics by first having learned arithmetic in elementary school, algebra, geometry, trigonometry in high school, and calculus and higher mathematics in college.

- Expresses various emotions in varying degrees (often thought to be centered in the heart, sometimes equated with the soul).

- Has the ability to think and express the thinking in various communicative forms describing rational[4] and irrational[5] actions towards oneself, others, and the environment.

- Records in memory for later recall as needed in new experiences and learning. In some views, the cognitive portion of the mind is equilibrated to the soul, which may partake in out-of-body[8] or mystical[9,10] experiences and remains along with the spirit after death.

- Has the complexity and wide variation of communication and the ability to adapt to widely varying conditions that differ significantly from other animated life forms. The functioning of the mental mechanism is not well understood. Still, progress has been made over centuries in finding when certain brain areas

---

[4]Logical reasoning leading to an understanding of reality.

[5]Imaginations leading to the fictionalization of the relationship to understood reality.

are not functioning correctly. There is a loss of control in one or more physical and mental areas. Similarly, it is observed that many mental abnormalities exist with even less of an understanding than with physical abnormalities.

- **Spirit or part of universal consciousness is a mechanism that:**
  - Gives function, called life, to the physical and mental mechanisms (sometimes equated with soul).

  - Appears to be centered more in the physical heart area, although it probably encompasses the entire body and maybe also a short distance outside of the body. This short distance outside the body emanation is termed aura, which some are said to observe in different colors, indicating the person's psychological state.

  - Is also an unexplained and undefined mechanism from which one experiences dreams and other sense influences. These are not explainable through understood physical or mental mechanisms. Some of these different influences are intuition, Déjà vu[6], extrasensory perception (ESP), visions, clairvoyance, all-in-oneness with the universe, etc.

  - Is the least understood of these three faculties of life. Since spirit has not been adequately explained scientifically and appears as another dimension in the universe, many scientists show resistance to accepting its existence because it cannot be physically measured or experimentally tested. Thus, there are the questions:

    - Where did the spirit come from?

    - Where does it go on physical death?

    - What is its relationship to the Living Spirit?

    - Is it a separate entity from the Living Spirit, or is it part of the Living Spirit—like cells in the human body?

Humankind has been attempting to understand the variations and interrelationships of the body, mind, and spirit for centuries. It permeates throughout the sacred literature and other systems, such as the chakras[11], which attributes energy flow for certain characteristics related to one's life to specific nodes in the body, or astrology, which attributes the person's attributes under the zodiacal sign and planet alignments at one's time of birth. We are still doing this today through various psychological tests to provide guidance for potential careers or determine how one operates with given sets of conditions. A couple of these are:

1. Kuder Preference Record Vocational Form BB[12] taken as a 1958 senior in high school.

2. The Myers-Brigg Type Indicator[13] taken while employed by Motorola Automotive Division in 1990.

---

[6]Experiencing or feeling that one has lived this previously during a first-time encounter.

Body, Mind, Spirit Relationship Paradigm

Observing my own life and other humans in their functioning in earth's environs, I see humans having six fundamental aspects within these three interrelating faculties. One could define more aspects; however, they would be subsets within these six. The six aspects are inner void, mental, spiritual, companion, economic, and political. The most straightforward representation of the six aspects is as a sphere (the inner void) in the center of the triangular pyramid inside a sphere (mental aspect). The pyramid points: spiritual, companion, economic, and political, touch the surface of the sphere, thus interacting with the mental aspect. The interconnecting lines show influence and interaction between the aspects, i.e., all aspects influence and interrelate to all other aspects. The complete representation shown in Figure 2 depicts all that one is.

The meanings, followed by application to me, for the individual aspects in this expression are:

1. Inner Void

It is in the center of the triangular pyramid. It is defined as the drive or sense for the relationship with something more significant in the non-physical or unseen universe. Thus, it is the realization that there is a source invisibly greater than the visible universe

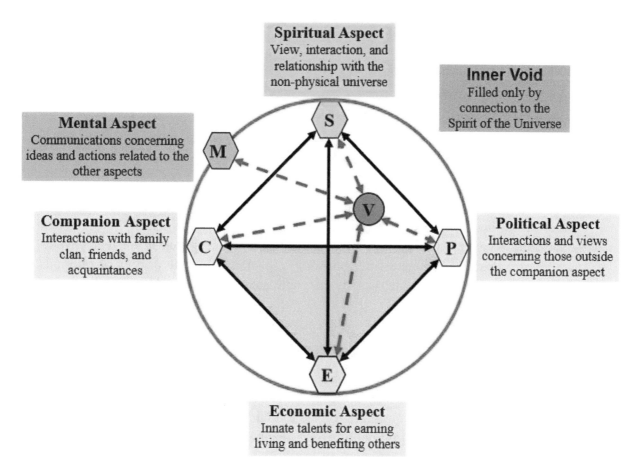

Figure 2. The representation of the aspects and interactions in a human being

in which one is a participant. It may be termed the seed-of-faith that one tries to fulfill by materialistic pursuits or power over others, usually unsatisfactorily.

For me, this is the source to explore my connection with Creative Force or the Living Spirit. I have tried unsuccessfully to fill the void through my worldview of using talents and abilities for others at the expense of my own needs.

2. Mental Aspect

It is the consciousness that is a small part of the universal consciousness. The human consciousness is the psychological, emotional, thought, and memory processes that one uses to relate in understanding and communicating ideas to others about one's observations and experiences of interactions within all six aspects.

In experiencing life, three successive facets govern living:

a. **Awareness:** first, one has a thought about something to do or an observation that may require action. For example, do I write a portion of my life's journey and am I a workaholic?

b. **Acceptance:** is one going to act or not act on the thoughts or is one acting or not acting on the observation. For example, I did not discard the ideas expressed about writing or the process of recovery but accepted that action was required.

c. **Action:** experiencing the acceptance by living the flow of life with its ongoing changes. For example, this book is the culmination of the writing thought, and I am continuing daily the recovery program from workaholism.

The identical process is followed in response to a situation from an outside source to one's being when encountered. These actions may be internal as well as external, giving rise to one's total humanity.

In school, I observed myself to be more adept in intellectual activities, particularly mathematics and the physical sciences. In contrast, my classmates were more adept in other areas, and some not as well as others in any subject or activity. I continued education, receiving a Master of Science in Physics concentrated in nuclear physics with a strong scientific interest in philosophy, theology, and the origins of religious systems. Literary works such as novels and movies have had minimal interest throughout my life.

3. Companion Aspect

It is the strengths and weaknesses in interactions within one's inner group that comprises one's parents[7], other members of the family, close associates, friends, acquaintances, and others that one comes in contact to meet the needs to live effectively and wholesomely without controlling others to their or one's detriment. There may be individuals who are controlling in this group, leading to problems in living effectively and wholesomely. These situations may lead to addictions, where recovery is to get

---

[7]Those providing guidance in the early years of life, whether after birth, or by adoption, or by foster care, or by orphanages.

back to living effectively and wholesomely. This group is constantly changing as some move out, and others move in. There is a variety in expression from those who need many people around them to those who are more satisfied with very few people in their lives, like the hermits.

I was born into a Roman Catholic farm family in the Midwest United States in which each member existed individually and pleasantly with each other with little closeness during childhood. Even as adults, there was little communication amongst my family. This lack of closeness appears to result from suppressing emotions, as they were not to be expressed but buried within oneself. Being an introvert and a researcher in the physical sciences and religious systems, I tend toward a tiny social group. This minimal social group may have been my coping mechanism as I had no playmates of my own age through high school because of my parents being ostracized out of their families because of their mixed religions. They then bought a farm in another community where the next house was at least a quarter of a mile away. In addition, they were not socializing with many others and seldom with those who had children of my age.

4. Economic Aspect

It is the limited talents and abilities one is endowed from birth to earn the means for sustaining life[8] and for benefiting others[9]. No one has been observed to be endowed with universal capabilities to meet all one's necessities without others. Instead, it appears that everyone exists in a universe of limits and dependency on others, who, like me, have been endowed with selected mental and physical abilities for other specific tasks that benefit others. One only needs to look at infants or a severe illness to realize the need for others to aid one in these times.

From my teens, mathematics, physics, and chemistry were of significant interest for the career path of my life until retirement. Although I had considered a Roman Catholic priesthood as a career until shown in a dream that it was not for me. The spiritual interests then were channeled into my avocation, studying the whys and wherefores of religious systems.

5. Political Aspect

It is the system of governance and worldview concept that defines how one's Companion Aspect group interacts with other groups outside and beyond it, such as the region, country, and the world at large.

My basic instinctive governance was to respect people for who they are and to treat others like I wanted to be treated. It is from this basis that I believe laws governing society should be based. However, observation is that a vastly different mentality is working in society as the majority of people are being exploited for a few people's greed (money or power). I am a pacifist more than a fighter. In my professional career, the janitor was viewed as equally important as the company executive.

---

[8]Necessities of life, such as food, housing, medical, etc.
[9]Employment, charities, support of family and friends, etc.

6. Spiritual Aspect

It is one's approach to one's relationship with the unseen world and one's ethics of what one considers right and wrong in the treatment of others and the environment. This aspect of the unseen world is the apex of the triangular pyramid and polar to the seen world represented by the triangular base of the pyramid, i.e., the companion, economic, and political aspects. Notably, in this aspect, are one's answers to the following fundamental questions. How do they shape the operation in the other aspects, the communications, and the benefits towards others?

a. **How did the universe come into being that one is experiencing?**

b. **What is the origin of life in this universe and thus also one's life?**

c. **What is the source of one's consciousness, disposition, talents, etc., that makes one the unique person that he/she is?**

d. **What is one's purpose in life?**

e. **How does one best interact with others, as observation and study show that this may be one function of religious systems?**

f. **Why is there suffering and mistreatment of people by others either individually or nationally or ethnically or religiously?**

g. **Where does one's spirit go when one dies, as observation shows all die?**

The answers to these questions give rise to one's expression of the inner void, i.e., spiritual life. Some find corporate religious systems fulfilling one's spiritual needs, whereas others meet their spiritual needs outside any religious systems. Each person's answers to these questions significantly influence how one expresses the other aspects; thus, it is the pyramid's apex.

This aspect has undergone the most change in my life. I was strongly drawn to the Roman Catholic priesthood until becoming disillusioned in monastic life the second time between my freshman and sophomore years of college. This disillusionment further commenced the quest to know the Creator of the universe. Having gone from agnosticism to a belief in a Christ outside organized religious systems and walking through many other religious systems, I returned to the atheism end of the theism-atheism polarity of being an integral part of the universal energy and universal consciousness.

Here, a paradigm was shown that might help explain the complexity of human faculties and how one lives life. It is a key concept throughout this work, especially the pyramid aspects. Although the sphere is shown as a perfect circle, for each person, the representation would be a highly distorted spheroid depending on the ranking of one's influence for each aspect of the pyramid. For example, the sphere for me would become an ellipsoid with the spiritual and economic aspects creating the longer axis.

Who am I? The Personal Application

Having mentioned that it is helpful to know something about authors in this paper, it is proper to include something about myself.

Since I did not choose my parents, birth date, name, or environment upon entering this plane, earth, Possible sources of my talents and personalities that gave rise to my career and journey in this life are:

- **Universal consciousness**

  For what I was to learn and help others to learn in our journeys during these times of our life spans.

  - **Family and Early Life**

    Because we are created imperfect, a necessity for experiencing life, our family structures are dysfunctional in one way or another. My parents had married in mid-life for the first time. Because of a Lutheran-Catholic marriage, their families ostracized them. Dad had to agree to raise us Catholic for the marriage. Because of the mixed religion, dad lost his right to his home place. They bought a small farm in another rural southern Indiana community where they were outsiders. They showed no emotional affection towards each other because mom, at least, felt that this was wrong. Dad was very distant and independent, with minimal interaction with his sons. Since my parents did not live near their siblings, there were few extended family interactions. If they did, there were no children of my age except the rare visits of mom's siblings. The siblings were years apart on dad's side, e.g., his oldest sibling was twenty years older than himself, resulting in first cousins older than dad or near dad's age. They had few friends who just came for some assistance.

    I was the oldest child born prior to World War II to workaholic parents who raised their children with the mentality that children were to be seen but not heard. If they were providing for their children physically, they were doing their duty. Even as we got older, there was little time spent with board games or card playing. Thus, with no affection and inability to express emotions, I have had suppressed emotions that I have spent my life slowly undoing.

    Already by the age of five, I started functioning independently in my play. My lack of social skills resulted from no playmates my own age through high school for better taking care of myself with the help of others. Another aspect of the home environment was experiencing childhood trauma when I was four with my sister's death at eight months following surgery for cleft palate. She had rolled over and choked on her blood. I have often wondered how this has been manifested in my life.

    I was two years older than my oldest brother and more of a loner because my interests were considerably different. Thus, there was little mutual interaction as kids, even though the younger brothers were more interactive—this lack of interaction carried through into our adult lives as well. Then later in life, with the birth of my two daughters, each had different personalities at birth.

A life-changing incident was my third-grade teacher saying that I could be whatever I wanted to be. This encouragement changed my expressed scholastic abilities from a C student to an A-B student. My parents never seemed to care how I did. As I desired to learn to play the piano, they were all right with that but never tuned the old player piano. I could participate in chorus, band, and scholastic contests in high school, but there was an underlying resentment that this was taking away from the farm. This resentment was most notably expressed when I wanted to go to college and was told that I was taking away from my brothers for wanting that for myself.

A little insight into me can be gathered from my classmates writing about me in our 1958 senior high school class yearbook (bound mimeograph pages). My nickname was "Professor," and their stanza was:

> "Jerome Scholle seems to have the brains,
> He gets his lessons without any pains,
> No matter if its rain or shine,
> He likes to enter contests any old time."

Another area that I have often wondered, "Why did I choose a given color over others, or one type of clothing versus another, or selected a specific seat on a bus when many are available?" These types of choices were observed in others as well. Thus, each person was given specific interests with their many different thoughts to work together in their fields of interests. As a working scientist, I saw this in my other scientist colleagues as we reached a consensus on how to proceed with a project. What appears is that all human beings are to work together for everyone else's wellbeing. For me, the only way that this makes sense is that each of us comes into this earth with a bit of the universal consciousness endowing us with the required personality and ability to learn specific fields to maintain our bodies, but more importantly, to use these personalities and interests for the benefit of others.

From hearing the stories of addicts and readings, children learn through observing one's parents' behavior. Then they apply it to themselves as to how to live. Thus, their recovery is about reprogramming themselves from these traumas. This reprogramming is true for my recovery work from workaholism and its associated alcoholism needing connectedness with other human beings at times from my preferred isolation in intellectual pursuits.

- **Sexuality**

It has been long recognized that human beings exhibit both feminine and masculine aspects as defined by a society. For example, American Indians speak of two-spirit people.[14] Today we speak about homosexuals and transgenders, who are viewed negatively by western religious thought as sexuality is only what the genitalia indicate. I often, in my early years, was showing feminine interests. However, as I became a teenager, I was more asexual as I had no sexual attraction to men or women. The internet provides tests to explore my lack of sexual attraction:

♦ **Bem Sex-Role Inventory**

It assesses how people identify themselves psychologically. Because my scores were masculine 27 and feminine 33, being below the 50% for each characteristic, I was defined as undifferentiated.[15,16]

♦ **Open Sex-Role Inventory**

This Inventory is based on the Bem Sex-Role Inventory but looks at just the large gender difference questions. Again, I was defined as undifferentiated as scores were masculine 70 and feminine 77. When graphed using the Bem topology, they showed again undifferentiated.[17,18]

♦ **Gender Role Inventory**

This inventory tests for immanent conceptions of gender (meaning that it does not theorize about whether gender roles are biological, cultural, or both). It is not to be confused with the Bem Sex-Role Inventory. My scores defined me as undifferentiated-androgynous as scores were masculine 33 (low) and feminine 44 (average). The Bem Androgynous classification occurs when a person's score is above 50% of the comparison group in both masculine and feminine categories.[19,20]

■ **Writings outside my science or religious fields**

A possible explanation to my quest may be in astrology, studies of paranormal activity, etc. These writings also reflect the inquisitiveness of humans from ancient times to understand themselves and the world they experienced. Thus, throughout my life, including today, as I write this, I have researched various writings to understand "Who I am." The aspects of "Who I am." include: (1) life goals, (2) home, (3) education and communication, (4) relationships, (5) motivation, (6) career and ambitions, (7) creativity and originality, (8) challenges in life, and (9) purpose and joy.[10]

● **Esoteric Studies**

Human beings have been trying to understand the aspects that make up the totality of the human experience for centuries. They have long recognized that they all have differences and similarities. From their observations of the seasons, from movements of the stars, planets, and sun in the sky, they were able to project when the seasons changed. These understandings led to observations of human behavior and abilities and to associate these with heavenly movements. Certain traits and behaviors were ascribed to the

---

[10]These are from the astrological birth chart referenced later.

astronomical systems when and where one was born, thus giving rise to astrology, numerology, and other esoteric studies. These foundations led to modern-day psychology, which does the same thing differently by the many different tests for learning about oneself. These esoteric studies are considered today as pseudoscience, yet our science systems today are based on the works of these early people who were the scientists of their day. It is pseudoscience because of the egocentricity of today's scientists who only think what we have done in the last 500 years is science. So, what do these esoteric studies say about me?

♦ **Eastern Astrology**[21,22,23]

This system is firmly rooted in the patterns of life. It is a sixty-year cycle composed of five elements (Water ruled by Mercury, Metal ruled by Venus, Fire ruled by Mars, Wood ruled by Jupiter, and earth ruled by Saturn) and twelve personalities ruled by a different animal (Rat, Ox, Tiger, Rabbit, Dragon, Snake, Horse, Sheep, Monkey, Rooster, Dog, and Boar). Each year is ascribed to one element and one animal. Only one of the animals is mythical, the Dragon. The time of day is also broken into 12 segments and is associated with one of the animals. To this is added the yin-yang (female-male polarity) and ten heaven stems.

I am a Yang Metal Geng-Chen (Dragon) with the Rat as an ascending sign. Geng (Mandarin Pinyin) was the 7th day of the 10-day week calendar of ancient China that is unused today and associated with the evening star. Chen is the Dragon.

◘ Strengths of the Dragon that I see in my life journey are a perceptive mind, hardworking, courageous, intelligent, honest, and craving to be of use. This latter craving is reflected in my worldview that I came into this plane with a set of talents and abilities that I was to use for the benefit of others.

◘ The Dragon's weakness observed in my life is perfectionism and not recognizing my own limits, resulting in over-working with psychosomatic illnesses. This weakness was later identified as workaholism. Because of frozen emotions from childhood emotional abandonment, I have struggled in applying the emotional terms in the reports to my life.

♦ **Western Astrology**[24]

This system has a one-year cycle composed of four elements (Fire, Earth, Water, and Air), and three qualities (Cardinal, Fixed, Mutable), and twelve signs (personalities) ruled by animals and three unique humans. The time of day is also broken into 12 segments called houses. In addition, the longitude and latitude of the birth location specify where the planets are located in the twelve signs and houses for giving information about what one's life will be.

I am a Fixed Earth Taurus (Bull) with Venus as the rising sign and Aquarius as the ascendant. At eighty, I ordered my esoteric astrological birth chart[25] to check my life journey against what it predicted. It has nine significant aspects of life with 47 subtopics concerning "Who am I?"

Key aspects from the chart as related to research herein are:

◻ My life was to be a journey to self-discovery with the purpose of humbly directing my service for the benefit of others.

◻ This was to be accomplished by being an independent, free spirit, and perceptive thinker seeking intellectual challenges on the subjects of science, religion, astrology, and metaphysics.

◻ The learning for living life involved how to be more assertive, to better express emotions, and to balance life between work, health, and relaxation. The latter has been my workaholism recovery work. Thus, the birth chart has fully predicted the significantly prominent aspects seen in my life.

♦ **Numerology**[26]

"The Pythagorean method uses an individual's name on the birth certificate and date of birth. The name number reveals the individual's outer nature. This outer nature is the personality that they present to the outside world." The determination of the outer nature uses my full name, Jerome Vincent Scholle, to give several specific numbers detailing aspects of life.

The numerology report[27] details me:

◻ A free spirit with many interests, adaptable to many life changes, and people with my forward-looking interests.

◻ The challenges were to learn to love myself by setting boundaries and learning to say "no" so that my sympathetic and compassionate nature was not abused.

Thus, my worldview was to use my talents and abilities for the benefit of others before taking care of myself. This view probably was a way to validate myself and have connections leading to my overcoming workaholism in the last quarter of my life.

♦ **Archetype**[28]

For the purposes here: "The concept of an archetype appears in areas relating to behavior, historical psychology, and literary analysis. An archetype can be a collectively inherited unconscious idea, pattern of thought, image, etc., that is universally present, in individual psyches, as in Jungian psychology."

My Archetype is the Jungian Hero.[29] "Heroes often have selfless goals that are directed towards improving the world and society. To achieve that, the Hero archetype invests most of its time into mastering skills and filling itself with relevant knowledge that will put it in a favorable position to make a difference. Because of this, the Hero archetype is often innovative when it comes to solving problems. Hero archetypes thoroughly enjoy exchanging ideas, opinions, and fiddling with the latest inventions."[30] This characterizes much of my life.

- **Modern Psychology**

  ♦ **Kuder Preference Record Vocational Form BB**[31]

  This test was first published in 1938 and was designed to measure the motivation of high school and college students. This form provided vocational guidance. As I can recall from my 1958 high school senior year, my scores were high in the thinking as in math and science, my main interest, and low in manual as mechanics. My majors when entering college were math and physical sciences (equal parts of physics and chemistry) for secondary education.

  ♦ **Myers-Brigg Type Indicator**[32]

  The Myers-Brigg Type Indicator was taken initially while employed by Motorola Automotive Division in the late 1980s or early 1990s. My results showed I was an ISTJ: where introversion (I) was significantly higher than extroversion (E), sensing (S) was nearly equal to intuition (N), thinking (T) was significantly higher than feeling (F), and judgment (J) was nearly equal to perception (P). Most of my colleagues were ISTJ as well. Retaking the test later, I recall the result as INTP but could not find a record of this in my files.

■ **Religious Ministry Gift Tests**

The closest that religions have helped me to discern "Who I am." is the Ministry Gift Tests. My files indicate that I took five of these over a period of probably two years (2000-2002); however, I had not recorded the internet references. Results are shown by rank from highest score to lowest. The equal sign indicates the same score. I have long recognized that the phrasing of questions is critical for how one will respond from their experience; thus, the variations in results are not unexpected.

- **Grace Gift Test**

  Teacher, Mercy Shower, Exhorter, Server, Giver, Ruler, and Prophet.

- **Spiritual Gifts Analysis**

  Teaching, Exhortation, Showing Mercy, Administration = Evangelism, Pastor/Shepherd, Giving, Serving, and Prophecy.

- **Motivational Gifts Test**

  Teaching, Exhortation, Serving, Mercy, and Administration = Giving = Prophecy.

- **Spiritual Gifts Questionnaire**

  Teacher, Exhorter, Mercy Shower, Shepherd, Prophet, Helper, Evangelist, Giver, and Administrator.

- **Spiritual Gift Inventory**

  Teaching, Mercy = Prophecy = Service, Exhortation = Giving, and Leadership.

As I reflect on "Who I am." throughout my journey from these writings, I have been primarily a Teacher in the broadest sense of the term, not the narrower sense of a classroom teacher, although I have done some. What do I mean by Teacher in the broadest sense? Everyone is a teacher in one way or another, but that is not their chief focus in life. For example, my parents were teachers enabling me to grow and live life, but that was not their life's focus. For me, the Teacher is one:

- Whose focus is a researcher, thinker, and conveyer of ideas to make changes in society by working with others:

  - To achieve their life activities.

  - To change their life through sharing experiences, such as ministry and 12-step work.

  - To provide educational-type writings to broader audiences that may help others to develop themselves further.

- Who expects no type of compensation other than the satisfaction of potentially seeing betterment changes in others.

The Life Cycle

From my farm life, I see that there is a life cycle to all forms of life in this plane, earth. We, humans, often fail to see this even though it is front and center to our lives. The cycle has the following segments for plants, birds, and animals:

- **Gestation**

  - For most plants, the flower consists of the stamen (male), which releases the pollen to be captured by the pistil (female) for the formation of seeds. There are some plants which have separate male and female counterparts, such as holly. The pollination takes place in different forms such as by the wind, birds, and bees. The gestation completes when the seed is in a soil condition that enables it to sprout.

17

- For birds, the male hops on the back of the female and releases the sperm, which travel over the feathers of both to enter the duct to the ovaries, where the sperm attaches to the yolk. The female forms the shell around the yolk and the fluid to be inside the shell and releases what is termed the egg. The gestation is then completed when the female body increases in temperature, and she sits on the eggs so that the chick forms inside the shell.

- For animals, which humans are part, copulation of the male with the female releases the sperm inside the vagina. The sperm then travel to the ovaries where one or more may join eggs, starting the formation of one or more animals. The gestation is complete when the female goes through contractions to expel the fetus when it can live outside the female body.

■ **Growth**

Each of these then grows according to its specie until it has aged that it may reproduce by the gestation process.

■ **Reproduction**

Each of these then reproduces new life according to its specie's reproduction span.

■ **Death**

Once the reproduction span has been completed, the specie starts the downward process leading to the death of the plant, bird, or animal. For humans, the reproduction span ends with the female going through menopause and the male having erection difficulties as the erection is no longer needed for reproduction. As seniors, we experience more health issues as our bodies are undergoing the shutdown process terminating in death just like the other parts of the biological world.

The following two chapters detail my journey in both fields of science and ministry. Since these are intertwined with Chapter 4, Avocation: Origins of Religion, I have chosen to write them separately for ease of understanding with some interactions expressed.

Chapter 2

Science Journey

The Seen World: Applying Sciences in Life Situations

Having grown up on a small forty-acre family farm, I had the opportunity to observe the life of plants and domestic animals. These experiences were invaluable in relating to other studies in my life.

My scholastic activities in high school laid the groundwork for me to be a workaholic. I had been taking piano lessons and making progress; however, my school load, farm work, and intellectual contest pursuits showed me I was limited in what I could healthily do, so I gave up my piano lessons. This experience was my first in starting to understand human limitations.

Since my small rural high school of fewer than two hundred students allowed students with high scholastic ability to take five courses rather than the usual four, five courses allowed one to maximize what he/she may need later in life. During the progression through the four years, specific courses were required, such as English, History, and Mathematics. Other courses were electives that students could take for the type of job they may be suited for or inclined to do. Thus, a student took one or more electives depending on the student's desire, whether carrying the usual four courses or a fifth course. At the Junior-Senior level, they offered some courses every other year, such as Physics and Algebra II.

I took five courses to maximize my mathematics and sciences courses and included Latin, Typing, and Bookkeeping. These latter two courses have been the most useful in my daily activities. I graduated salutatorian, rank second in the class. I had been together with most of my classmates through school for eleven years. For my freshman high school year, having a desire to be a priest, I attended St. Meinrad Minor Seminary, more about this in the chapter, Ministry Journey.

My high school extra-curricular activities were:

- Participating in mathematics contests, winning the district, and being in the state finals.

- Representing my high school with the Junior Red Cross along with students from other county high schools.

- Participating in the school chorus and band, playing either the glockenspiel or the bass drum.

- One of two winners representing the high school in the county spelling contest.

- Runner-up in a county speaking contest on a work topic of the United Nations.

I started college at Indiana State College in Terre Haute in the fall of 1958, where I had a tuition scholarship that was awarded to two students in each Indiana county. This scholarship was straightforward for me to get since I was planning to go across the state. My majors were mathematics and physical science (half physics and half chemistry) for secondary education. Yes,

I had intended for the dual major and not settle just for a simple minor in one of the physical sciences. I was able to get a loan through the 1958 National Defense Education Act for my college living. The 1958 National Defense Education Act was enacted to increase science studies because Russia had started space exploration with Sputnik in October 1957.[33] Additionally, I was also working part-time while living on campus. As a freshman, I initially worked for Arthur Murray Studios as a telemarketer and then as a dance instructor.

Between my freshman and sophomore college years, I had returned to priesthood studies as a member of the Conventual Franciscans. Upon leaving the order, as I had come to sense that this was not my life work from a vision of walking away from the college house across an empty field, I immediately went to summer school at Indiana State College, now Indiana State University. I was able to pick up where I left off, including requirements and tuition scholarship as when I had started two years prior. I was also able to get a loan under the National Defense Education Act. During this time, I mostly lived off-campus and worked in the college library.

During my undergraduate college years, I switched from secondary education to liberal arts, changing my major from mathematics, which was too easy, to physics, which was more challenging. During my junior year, I was considering doctoral studies in Chemical Physics, a new field at that time. When checking on the entrance requirements for graduate school in this field, it was recommended to have a major in one of my three fields of study and a minor in each of the other two. Thus, I finished undergraduate college studies midyear with a major in physics and minors in mathematics and chemistry. Unfortunately, this precluded continuing graduate studies, so I took a job as a physicist with Globe Union, a Milwaukee, Wisconsin manufacturer of lead-acid batteries and ceramic electronic components.

Since I finished undergraduate studies midyear, my degree was not awarded until the end of the college year. Thus, I started as a lab tech for specialty batteries and, upon receiving my degree, switched to being an analytical chemist for the quality of automotive lead-acid battery components and the manufacturing processes for the electronic components. During this time, a particular unreported study showed the lead-acid battery electrochemistry was not truly reversible as thought. Additionally, we started to replace destructive (wet) chemistry procedures with various non-destructive testing methods, such as x-ray fluorescent technology, for analyzing lead compounds. My colleagues and I presented a paper at the 7th National Meeting of the Society of Applied Spectroscopy (May 1968) titled, "Determination of Antimony, Tin and Arsenic in Antimonial Lead Alloys by X-Ray Fluorescence." This paper was published in Applied Spectroscopy in 1969.[34]

While working at Globe Union, they granted me an academic year to begin work on my graduate degree. After that year, I returned to work. I finished my degree at night school being awarded the Master of Science in Physics (MS) from the University of Wisconsin-Milwaukee with a concentration in nuclear physics. My thesis was: "Mössbauer Spectrometer Using a Variable Capacitor as a Velocity Sensor." This variable capacitor was an experimental instrument to measure the resonance fluorescence of ^{57}Fe[11]. I was advised not to pursue a doctorate.

---

[11]Fe is the chemical symbol for iron in the periodic table of elements; 57 is the specific isotope of iron that decays, emitting a gamma-ray for this resonance condition.

Upon earning my MS and desiring to pursue my interest in nuclear physics, I took a job with Westinghouse Electric Corporation who was managing the Department of Energy site, Bettis Atomic Power Laboratory in West Mifflin, PA, a suburb of Pittsburgh, PA. My initial work was in a testing facility for proving the design adequacy of the designing codes. Because of the security clearance, there was no discussion of my work outside of the site. During this time, I divorced my first wife. My supervisor asked if it was because of this work, and I said "no" without any further discussion.

While on jury duty, a mechanical failure occurred during a test. When I returned from jury duty, they assigned me to be the quality engineer for the facility, along with my other responsibilities for conducting experiments. Since this was a new field of work, I educated myself by reading and taking courses related to this field. This assignment then changed my career to analyzing processes for improvements and safety using all three of my undergraduate studies as well as my interest in teaching, which was my first college field of study.

Rounding out my career with Bettis Atomic Power Laboratory, I held three other positions:

1. I was promoted to supervisor of three engineers, four technicians, and a secretary for nuclear safety and fuel inventory of the Development Laboratory Section. Being poorly equipped emotionally and unable to get the needed help, I experienced the psychosomatic illness of feeling paralyzed on my right side when I stood up from my desk. CAT scans showed no signs of any brain damage to cause these episodes. When relieved of this position, a comment was made to me, "Did you see smiling Scholle walking around?" My outward demeanor had changed immediately.

2. I was then a Supplier Quality Assurance Engineer, writing and teaching training courses for government quality assurance inspectors and suppliers about nuclear plant operations and safety. These were:

   a. Nuclear Power Plant Theory and Operation

   b. Control Rod Operations and Safety

   c. Nuclear Valve Operations and Safety

3. I ended as a Naval Training Scientist writing training materials, maintaining exam databank, and engineering changes for training sailors operating nuclear reactors on boats and submarines.

Someone knowing me personally and my engineering achievements nominated me to be a member of the Engineering Honor Society, Tau Beta Pi. The Lambda (Pittsburgh) Chapter accepted me, and I made the presentation, "The Engineer's Role in Quality," at the January 1981 initiation ceremony.

Doing this scientific work, I realized that as humans; we are limited in knowing what deleterious effects we have created for the future. Nuclear power is wonderful; however, there is a significant drawback when the system is no longer usable to generate power. Either a catastrophic failure in the system occurs, such as the 1979 3-mile Island reactor system failure, or the nuclear fuel is spent (insufficient uranium to produce fission for energy). Most materials that were not reactive when the reactor was built had become radioactive with various half-lives from majorly short to millions of years, making disposal difficult and where to store. Burial underground has been the solution for some materials, but others needed to be secured, such as the area around the 1986 Chernobyl Reactor accident in Russia. A similar experience on the farm was the use of DDT, a pesticide; later, it was found to have weakened the shells of bird eggs, which was unrealized at the time of its introduction as a pesticide. Clinical studies for new medicines are an attempt to do better, yet many side effects are noted as possible since we cannot know how the medicine will react in everybody because we do not know their individual specific chemical variability.

While still doing the work above, I started teaching short courses at night for clients of the now-defunct American Technical Institute, Pittsburgh, PA. Their contracts and courses were:

- Chung-Shan Institute of Science and Technology, Republic of China (Taiwan)
  - Basic Quality Assurance
  - Design of Experiments
  - Reliability Engineering
- Volkswagen of America
  - Statistical Quality Control
  - Acceptance Plans
- Bureau of Weights and Measure of the Republic of China (Taiwan)
  - Theory of Measurements
  - Physical Calibration and Measurements
  - Leading a tour of measuring instrument companies in the Atlantic and Northeast States. This tour resulted from the person to teach Reliability Engineering backing out, leaving me with the total program.

Since I was a contractor for American Technical Institute, I formed my own Quality Consultant Company to do this work. Unfortunately, because American Technical Institute had financial troubles, they could not fully pay me, forcing me to close my company.

Then, I took the position of Manager of Quality Assurance at Basic Technology, Inc. The tasks were:

- Provide consulting services.
- Teach statistical process control short courses.
- Perform product liability and accident investigations, including courtroom testimonies.
- Manage three professional investigators.
- Market company services.
- Be a customer advocate.
- Approve nuclear calculations meeting nuclear code requirements.

Additionally, I was holding offices in the Pittsburgh Section of the American Society for Quality Control. Presentations made were:

- "Custom Quality Training Programs" presented at the May 1982 International Congress on Technology and Technology Exchange (ICTTE).

- "Reconstructing the Automobile Accident" at the April 1983 Northwest Claims Association meeting.

- "Quality Assurance Curriculum at Point Park College" at the October 1983 Pittsburgh Section American Society for Quality Control meeting.

- "Statistical Quality Control: What Is It?" at the February 1984 Pittsburgh Section Society of Plastics Engineers.

I now understood better my human doing, although not recognized when in the midst. The following activities were interwoven during this period and probably led to the psychosomatic illness described below:

- My living relationship with my significant other.

- Fulfilling weekly visitation time with my daughters.

- My job with Basic Technology.

- My leadership roles with the Pittsburgh Section of the American Society for Quality Control.

- Seeing an ad to become a priest, I joined the Servants of the Good Shepherd, priests within the Western Orthodox Church of America, and after finishing the at-home studies, was ordained a priest. This activity is in the Ministry Journey.

- Believing Quality Engineering should be at least a college minor, I worked with Point Park College, Pittsburgh, PA to establish a six-course (3-credits each) minor in Quality Sciences within the Business, Accounting, and Computer Science Department. A fellow Quality Assurance friend taught Reliability Engineering as he worked in that field. Unfortunately, Quality Auditing did not get taught. The four courses I taught until the program was rendered no longer viable with changes in curricula:

  - Quality Management (2)

  - Financial Principles for Non-Accountants and Engineers (2)

  - Statistical Quality Control

  - Vendor-Customer Relations in Quality Assurance

- After my divorce, contract duplicate bridge became a major activity because it was a communication and analytical game, fitting well with my mathematics and science interests. Upon being encouraged to be a director by fellow players, I became an American Contract Bridge League certified director, directing club and a few tournament games. Unfortunately, because of the psychosomatic illness of angina pain, this activity was dropped until retirement. During retirement, I returned to club directing and eventually became a Life Master.

In looking at all this activity now as a retired senior, it is no wonder that in 1983, I had a major psychosomatic illness: angina pain, resulting in a heart catheterization because I could not complete the stress test. The catheterization test showed no damage to blood vessels. Reviewing this illness years later, it was because I was a human doing rather than a human being. It was during this time I identified my weakness as workaholism at my 25th high school reunion. I knew nothing of how this was to be treated, nor do I know why I chose this term. Around this time, Workaholics Anonymous (WA)[35] was just forming with a group in California and a group in New York. They could not agree on proceedings, so the California group became the lead in establishing the organization.

With expanding my ministry work to the aged and infirm and realizing that I could not also do my science work, I quit my science work and devoted full time to my ministry. During this time, a significant interaction of the two fields occurred with teaching chemistry, calculus, and biology at a Christian High School for one year. This work is also detailed in my Ministry Journey.

The offer for next year was half-time, so I decided to look for work back in the sciences. During this time between school years, I worked for the Pittsburgh Post-Gazette, delivering morning newspapers on five automotive routes. I worked for Domino's Pizza in the evening, preparing food, taking orders, delivering food, and cleaning the store. For the start of the fall semester, I secured a one-semester job teaching Physical Science and Physics I, including labs for a professor on sabbatical at the nearby Community College of Beaver County. A one-semester job followed this job for a professor on sabbatical at Indiana University of Pennsylvania, Indiana, PA. Here I taught Physical Science at a satellite campus and Physics II labs on the main campus.

During the summer following and while clerking in a 7-Eleven store, I found a job as a Supplier Quality Engineer with Motorola Corporation, Automotive Industrial Electronics in Elma, New York. The product was automotive electronic ignition circuits on a ceramic substrate for mounting on the engine block. The suppliers were worldwide, involving chemical and physical properties. Thus, my science training allowed me to work with any supplier. We also interacted with three other sister plants in Austin, Texas; Stotfold, UK; and Angers, France.

One of the key quality initiatives at Motorola was the Six Sigma concept. "This is a set of techniques and tools for process improvement. A six-sigma process is one in which 99.99966% of all opportunities to produce some feature of a part are statistically expected to be free of defects."[36] To achieve this, Motorola had employees take many training courses; I took thirty-nine different courses. Being active in the American Society for Quality Control, I certified as a Quality Engineer, Reliability Engineer, and Quality Auditor.

Auditing of quality systems and processes was conducted to check the implementation of these techniques and tools. These audits were conducted internally of our systems, by the customers of our systems, and by us of our suppliers' systems. I traveled within the states and worldwide auditing suppliers and training suppliers, often traveling alone for two weeks, followed by staying at home for two weeks. The most extensive traveling alone was a five-week trip crisscrossing Europe, typically two days at a supplier, and traveling on Wednesday and Saturday or Sunday.

To help employees and suppliers to implement the Six Sigma techniques and tools, employees were asked to write chapters on various aspects of statistics for The Motorola University Press, The Six Sigma Research Institute Series to be published through Addison Wesley. I was not going to put my name in to be an author; however, one of my colleagues encouraged me to put my name in, saying, "Let them take it out." This writing was done during evenings and the typing the manuscripts on weekends using the secretary's computer because it had Word Perfect, which handled mathematical equation writing, whereas on my computer Microsoft Word did not yet have mathematical equation writing capability. I wrote one chapter a month for six months. Later, one more chapter was written. The final writing resulted in my book on "Metrology"[37] and two contributed chapters with two other authors on "Probability Distributions."[38] Receiving the reviewed copies back from Addison Wesley with minimal suggested corrections, I gained confidence that I was a reasonable technical writer. I donated these books to the University of Wisconsin-Milwaukee Library when I needed to downsize my library for living arrangements. In a previous downsizing, I had donated most of my science and related materials to this library.

Courses taught during this employment were:

- "Auditor Training for ISO-9000" for TAM Ceramics, Inc. at Niagara County Community College, Niagara Falls, NY.

- 3 sessions of "Certified Quality Auditor Refresher Course" for Buffalo Section of the American Society for Quality Control, Buffalo, NY.

- "Fundamentals of Auditing," an in-house course for Motorola Automotive and Electronics Group, Elma, NY.

Desiring still to do potentially a doctorate in Chemical Physics, in 1991, I enrolled for a night course in Organic Chemistry at the University of New York-Buffalo. This course was upgraded now, twenty-eight years from my undergraduate course for my Bachelor of Science degree. During my undergraduate studies, I had only taken the first semester of Organic Chemistry because I geared my studies to inorganic chemistries. While taking this course and being on a business trip, I read in the airline magazine "Workaholism: The Respectful Addiction."[39] Something in the article ended the desire for a doctorate and triggered me to get counseling for workaholism during the second semester of Organic Chemistry.

During the counseling, it was questioned as to whether alcoholism may also be an issue. The statement was that I could not overcome workaholism if I did not take alcohol out of my life. I met with several alcoholic addiction counselors who recommended that I could be an alcoholic, although I was not the usual type of drinking to suppress emotions. My only alcohol intake was when desiring socialization, as I was too busy with science and other activities. However, I now realize that the number of drinks, one or two, or many more, was my unknown emotional condition because of frozen emotions. To get help and understand this condition, I switched counselors and attended Alcoholic Anonymous (AA) meetings, admitting after a few meetings to be an alcoholic. AA was founded on a Christian background causing non-believers to struggle with its God emphasis from its inception.[40] My sobriety date is June 7, 1992. My primary association group was a gay-oriented group, which did not insist on sponsorship or working the twelve steps, although recommended. They also said, "Take what you need and leave the rest." This group was a high social group, and being an organizer, I fit in for the socializing part. Also, I was not relating to their type of alcoholism; however, they filled my need for socialization without alcohol. So, I stayed with the group as we attended other AA meetings during the week until changing cities because of a job change. In addition, I came to see alcohol as a significant toxin to the body, resulting in its transformation in a cell to an aldehyde, an embalming fluid. Thus, the cells are rendered non-functioning, and thus, they are needing to be excreted from the body.

Workaholism, a process addiction, was just beginning to be understood by psychiatry, and addiction counseling, focused only on substance addiction, was not understanding these two potentially interrelated addictions. This misunderstanding of interrelated addiction sidetracked me from my genuine need for workaholism help. This help first came to a head when the company nurse said that I might be suicidal and recommended that I see a psychiatrist. He did not think I was suicidal. Shortly after, I was meeting with a supplier representative, and a supervisor, overhearing our conversation felt I was not being firm enough for our company. He complained to my manager who asked me about it. I mentioned being somewhat suicidal and was immediately sent to see the psychiatrist. He prescribed the depression medication Doxepin, which I reacted to being up for 48 hours. I was then on medical leave for three months. This drug reaction led to thinking I had induced bipolar condition. Then, I was treated with lithium for several years. The depression medications were changed during this time to being finally taken off all medications after eight years with a new psychiatrist in the city of my next job. I have not had any depression episodes since.

Relieved of this position because of downsizing, they provided me with unemployment funds and counseling for getting a new job. This involved resume preparation, and that this effort was to be like a full-time job. After six months, I gained employment with Crown International in Elkhart, IN, as a Quality Assurance Engineer initially for magnetic resonance imaging (MRI) amplifiers being manufactured for GE until design changes in the MRI units resulting in GE changing supplier. I then did work for audio amplifiers and microphones.

The work performed was statistical analyses of data from automated test equipment to understand the chemistry and physics principles needed to drive continuous improvement in processes and products. Tasks also included performing reliability predictions, including mean-time-between-failures from field data, and maintaining ISO-9002 certification. A management position was offered and turned down, saying that I could do better work for the company as an engineer. In addition, there was the feeling that I did not want another episode as I had previously when at Westinghouse. Courses taught during this employment were:

- "Statistics Review Course for Thor Team" for Crown International, Inc., Elkhart, IN.

- "Variation and Problem Solving for Quality Specialists" two in-house sessions for Crown Audio, Inc., Elkhart, IN.

During this time, I felt led spiritually to move to Chicago, which I did, first staying during the week until that became too expensive and then driving daily back and forth. I retired in 2002 as I could now receive Social Security Benefits. This retirement ended my active work science journey, having encountered minimal negativity from religion affecting this journey. In retirement, I wanted to concentrate on my avocation of origins of religion, which may be more influenced by the companion Ministry Journey in the next chapter.

Today my science background is helpful in helping others deal with addictions and the current SARS-CoV-2 virus pandemic. I have tracked morning and evening my weight and blood pressure for several years. Near the end of March 2020, I started experiencing chest pressure under the breastbone. I immediately took a dose of NyQuil. This relieved the pressure for a short time before returning. I ended taking NyQuil within hourly recommendations for a month. I never had a fever, so I couldn't get tested for COVID-19 at that time, nor did my doctor want me to go to a hospital per phone call. After several months of the pandemic, I noted a shift in the blood pressure (BP) that indicated a potential mild case of COVID-19, the disease name from this virus at the beginning of the pandemic. This hump shift is most noticeably seen in the diastolic readings (Figure 3), and now after one year, the BP appears to be returning to what it was before the pandemic.

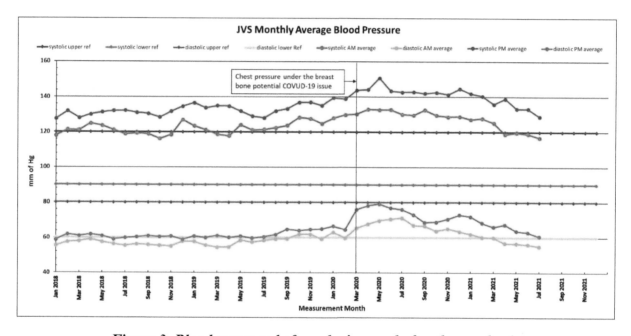

Figure 3. Blood pressure before, during, and after the pandemic

Chapter 3

Ministry Journey

The Unseen World: Experiences in Spiritual Activities

Roman Catholic rituals and prayer were a significant part of my family life. I identified with the Mass and the pageantry of it. I played saying Mass from memory as I had no book of prayer or Bible. During one of these times, I sensed an inanimate being enter my body and staying there, causing no harm. At that time, we were not to read the Bible or to have one, although we had dad's Bible since he had grown up in the Lutheran faith. At his funeral, we found he had been studying to be a Lutheran pastor.

During my school years, the Russian communist revolution was entering the eastern European countries following World War II. The Roman Catholic Church prepared pamphlets highlighting the fighting by the church against communism and how its leaders were being treated. These were available through my home church. These were impressionable in my mind.

Not having playmates of my age, I grew up being a loner and finding little acceptance, often being shunned, or bullied. As a loner, I became adept at making my own play alone and making my own decisions that did not affect anyone else. There was no communication with my parents about what I may need beyond the physical, resulting in childhood emotional abandonment. For example, I wanted to be an altar boy; however, my parents made no effort for me to participate. I was finally able to be an altar boy in the summer after 8th grade when at summer bible school, and ex-religious brother taught the boys how to be altar boys. If I had not had this training, I would have been at a disadvantage a few months later in the seminary.

During my 8th grade, I dreaded going through high school freshman initiation. Thus, I started to consider many ways to avoid that. These ways were suicide, running away from the farm, and studying for the priesthood, which I thought about as a life work. Since I was doing very well in school, I made known that I would like to be a priest. It overjoyed my mother that her son wanted to be a priest. I passed the test for admittance; thus, I went to study for the priesthood during my high school freshman year at St. Meinrad Minor Seminary, part of St. Meinrad Archabbey, St. Meinrad, Indiana near Evansville, Indiana, about 150 miles west from my near Cincinnati, Ohio home in Indiana. This seminary year allowed me to avoid freshman initiation at my hometown high school. The year at the seminary was a trying year for many reasons outside of scholastics, so I finished high school at my hometown, not dating because I was considering returning to priesthood studies at some point. In addition, I had no attraction to girls.

While at the seminary, my dad made the comment, "That the living experience encountered was worse than being in the military." I could not understand why this comment since he was not in the military as World War I ended before he was going to be drafted at 18. Since we had never talked about anything in my life, I did not ask him what he meant. I got the answer in my retirement when I met a fellow who had been in both fields. His experience was that the priesthood studies were about controlling your entire being, whereas the military was about discipline to work for cohesion in combat. Thus, no mind control in the military, which I have come to see as a problem in religious systems.

The Russian satellite, Sputnik, was launched in October 1957, the fall of my senior high school year. This launch started the space age. Although I had strong priesthood leanings and was planning on returning to those studies, I excelled in mathematics and physics. Chemistry was not offered. This science interest and my freshman seminary experience started my life quest as I finished high school to understand the dichotomy between science and religion.

During my freshman year at Indiana State College, I considered a mixed-race fraternity as all others were whites only. This vision was the beginning of my seeing that Christianity was being dominated by white race people. Because the white race was considered superior to the other four human races: black, brown, yellow, and red, these races were to be subjugated to the white race. I see the human races to have the same type of variations as we see in the animal world from my farm experience. Thus, none of the races are superior to others but are coequals. Western artists, being white skinned, have depicted Jesus Christ as white when he was more of the brown Near East feature. Only recently has there been better depictions of Jesus in his actual skin color.

Also, during this year, I was active in a Roman Catholic Church, pastored by a priest of the Conventual Franciscan Friars, and Pax Romana, an International Movement of Catholic Students. During this year, I again explored becoming a Roman Catholic priest. After considering the Jesuits, Holy Cross Fathers, and the Conventual Franciscan Friars, I applied to the Conventual Franciscan Friars. They accepted me to serve a postulancy at their major seminary in Chaska, Minnesota, which was outside Minneapolis. So, in the fall of 1959, my parents, dad's middle sister, and I made the trip to Chaska. This trip was the only time in my parents' life with a family that they were away from the farm for several days. They left my three younger brothers at home to take care of the livestock.

My family and I were taken on a tour of the facilities. While viewing the kitchen, my mother said that I knew cooking to the Rector. Thus, I became a cook with two Brothers[12] preparing meals for forty men three meals a day. Being a cook included menu planning, preparing all meals, cleaning the cooking utensils, and maintaining the kitchen-associated areas. In addition, the seminarians were responsible for washing the dishes used during the meals. I also did much of the meat preparation after slaughtering.

Those who were Franciscan Brothers, not priests, and the other postulants lived in a separate house. I practiced asceticism by sleeping on a board underneath the sheet on my bed. We partook in all the rituals of prayer service throughout the day. We had about an hour or so to relax after dinner and before evening prayers. This relaxation was usually spent with the other brothers in the house. Alcohol was free flowing, especially during the evening before evening prayers. Alcohol beverage trucks delivered beverages twice a week. I often drank two beers in the evening.

When it became time to enter the novitiate, I was accepted and transferred to the novitiate house in Angola, Indiana. This year was a time for reflection and spiritual development about whether

---

[12]Members of the order who were not desiring to be priests but who provided assistance in maintaining facilities and grounds.

he had a calling for monastic life either as a priest or a brother. Again, I had a period of practicing asceticism by sleeping on the floor. No alcoholic beverages were available to the novitiates. We also took a change in name to reflect our change in life, living who we were to be known as a friar. No two living men could have the same name. My chosen name was Cajetan; however, I have no recollection of why I chose that name. As I came to the end of that year, I had a vision of walking across a field away from the college house in Ohio. I honored that vision to mean that I was not to be a priest, much to my mother's chagrin. My parents never asked me why I left the priesthood studies.

During my latter undergraduate college years, I dropped the term God of my Roman Catholic years, becoming an agnostic and using Creative Force as the originator of the universe. I no longer attended religious services of any kind but did associate with some religious fellowship groups to manage my need for human fellowship. I rarely dated anybody as I was consumed with my studies as well as working part-time to put myself through school. An undercurrent thought since early high school, I was a homosexual. Not having anyone to talk about anything deep in life, it laid dormant, waiting to sprout.

Another undercurrent was my dread of serving in the military. I considered going to Canada as a conscientious objector and suicide if drafted. Another way was to be in ministry school because then you were classified 4F, thus part of my reasoning to return to the priesthood studies above. As reasons for draft deferments were changing during this period of my life, and the U. S. was moving towards a volunteer military. Marriage became an exemption, and then having children. When my girlfriend suggested that we get married, I thought it was a good idea, but a month later, I broke it off because of some homosexual thoughts which I could not express for fear of job loss. However, being co-dependent (a term that I did not know at that time, but since then I have worked to overcome), I agreed to it anyway, having a Roman Catholic ceremony. I went through the rituals of weekly church services but never having my heart in them.

Marriage was not about love, but something that I was supposed to do. I had met my first wife during one of my social group activities in college. I have no recollection of why there was any attraction except maybe that someone wanted me, as I felt no one really wanted me in their life. I have always been a serious, introverted person because of my childhood. Since I came into this plane with my talents and abilities for the benefit of others, the serious, introverted personality may have been a choice as well for this life's experience. Then, my parents' personalities enabled this choice and were not the cause.

My employment was highly classified, so there was no discussion of what I was doing. However, I participated in group activities sponsored by the company, such as baseball and bowling. During this time, I started reading principal philosophers, such as Hegel and Kant, to begin understanding why humans thought as they did. My next-door neighbor, who had advanced religion degrees, was a wonderful source to discuss my thoughts on religions contrasting with his.

I harbored a deep resentment towards myself for not standing firm against getting married, although the paperwork said we were married; deep in my spirit, I was never married spiritually or psychologically because of suppressed emotions. The marriage had been deteriorating for some years; however, that condition was not recognized, nor counseling sought. The marriage finally blew up in a nasty 10th wedding anniversary celebration after a couple of months of separation just prior. I left the house and only returned to take my belongings. From the shock of the end of the marriage, my wife ended up in the hospital. An attorney called me about the marriage, and I said no further. He wanted me to pay him for his services, and I told him, "No," as I had not contracted him. He told my wife to forget about me, and they began the divorce proceedings. Pennsylvania, where we were living, had a no-fault divorce law, so we went that route. The divorce settlement was such that she retained the house so that my two daughters, 7 and 3 years old, were not taken out of their environment, as I thought this was best for them. I saw my daughters weekly for about 6 hours on Sunday. Eventually, I was able to have a reasonably corrigible relationship with my ex-wife for a few years.

As the sexual liberation became more acceptable in the 1970s, I discreetly explored and learned what it meant to be a homosexual. Although I was more asexual in attraction to men and women, I wanted to experience the homosexual feelings that I had suppressed. With the separation from my wife, I discreetly entered the homosexual world. Discretion was necessary because of my classified job and the stigma attached to being homosexual. Also, I was able to express very slowly more of my emotions.

After a couple of short-term "gay" (a term that was becoming for homosexuality) relationships, I entered a deeper gay relationship with a church organist for a Lutheran Church. I started attending church with him. Since he had a house, I moved in with him, integrating my belongings with his. During this time, I was practicing astrology and reading on the paranormal. The astrology was primarily for understanding more about myself. During this relationship, I came across an announcement of becoming a priest. It was for the Servants of the Good Shepherd, priests within the Western Orthodox Church of America. The group wanted to form an American Orthodox Church as all the Orthodox Churches considered America a diaspora for missionary work. I made an application, was accepted, and after completing their curricula, was ordained a priest. We used the Roman Catholic Mass Liturgy, and we were free to choose what form of ministry we would provide. I chose ministry to the aged and infirm in assisted living and skilled nursing facilities. My significant other concurred with this and often provided the music for the services.

During this time, I became extreme in my practice of faith by destroying my books on astrology and others that did not align strictly with my newer concepts and beliefs of Christianity. In addition, I decided to work against my homosexuality because it also did not align with my concept of Christianity. I had become friendly with a widow who recently opened an assisted living home with two of her daughters. As a priest, I held weekly services for their clients. I separated from my significant other and eventually married the widow. Then, my children turned against me until the younger was graduating from high school and wanted me at her graduation. The older was also finishing her college undergraduate work. Today, there is no meaningful relationship with either daughter. The older decided to have no relationship with her birth family and associates only with her lesbian partner's family. The younger daughter married, and again there is no meaningful association as she is caring for her mother, who does not want my presence. I accept their decisions and allow them to follow their life journeys. I have learned that resentments and angers about the situation will not change them but only hurt myself. Resentments and angers are only hurting oneself, which is true in other relationships and interactions with people as well.

We stored my belongings in this wife's garage; thus, I had what was needed, if to live alone. To support me as a priest, I was relying on donations. Since this was not working, I started considering returning to the sciences. I wanted my wife to commit to going with me. However, she did not like the idea. This commitment was essential to me to feel she was committed to me. I had kept a letter from my previous significant other stating that I did not know how to love. My wife went through my personal files and found that letter. I moved out, having taken a job with a taxi company transporting special needs students to and from schools. I no longer held worship services at her assisted living home. I also had a short time as Prep Cook at a Denny's Restaurant. A few months later, I disbanded my ministry even though I felt I was doing good work; I was not finding spiritual or emotional satisfaction, as well as being unable to support myself. The marriage, having a Roman Catholic ceremony, was short-lived; however, the divorce was finalized three years later at the end of the statute of limitations for living apart three years with minimal contact.

I then became an active member of Faith Community Christian Church with a school attached to it. The need arose for a science teacher. Since the position was not being filled as the new school year was ready to start, I offered my services and became the Science Department chairman. My teaching load was heavy: AP Chemistry, Academic Chemistry, General Chemistry, Calculus, and Biology. I had not been active with these at the college or high school level for several decades. Although I had prepared many courses as an adjunct college professor and job-related in-house courses, I was ill-prepared psychologically and emotionally for teaching high school students, especially freshman Biology. During midyear, the school hired a teacher to teach Biology. I did reasonably well with the other classes. I do not remember whether I stayed with this church until I moved to Indiana, Pennsylvania.

My subsequent church association was with an Assemblies of God Church in Indiana, Pennsylvania. I had a job at the Indiana University of Pennsylvania teaching freshman college physics at a satellite campus and physics labs on the main campus during the spring semester for a physics professor on sabbatical. I have no recall of how I fit in that church.

My several years of short work jobs showed I was cared for by the universe as I did my part. The universe then provided a better job as a quality assurance engineer in Elma, New York. This town was a short distance south of Buffalo, New York. I chose to live on the south side of Buffalo and to drive to Elma. I never saw the Christian God as part of this journey, as I felt no relationship with Him. I have no recollection of any religious associations during this time.

With the move to Buffalo, I returned to being active in the gay community, feeling at home there. One activity was to man the AIDS hotline a couple of evenings a week when not traveling for work. Upon coming to grips with my addictions through counseling, I started with Gay AA meetings where there was no mention of God as they felt alienated from Him by the actions of society towards gays and especially most Christian churches. The AA meetings had a saying, "Take what you need and leave the rest." Since I did not drink to bury unwanted feelings and blacking out but for socialization, I did not easily relate to others' alcoholism. I was relatively happy being alone with my intellectual pursuits, except when I needed more human contact. The AA group I mostly identified with was a highly social group with activities outside of AA meetings. For the first time in my life, I encountered people who cared for me as a person and not someone to use because of my abilities. I finally came to accept that I did not have to suppress my needs for others. This acceptance was helped by the AA saying, "That we will help take care of you until you are more able to take care of yourself." One of the significant memories from this time of not drinking alcohol was my acceptance at the leathermen's annual party, where toasts of champagne were being made. Respecting me, the leader got me a shot of club soda, my drink of choice. Since alcohol was not an option for me, I was quite comfortable being in bars drinking club soda with this social group. The leather-oriented men's group was another one of my outreaches for acceptance.

Although AA was founded on Christian principles and refers to God in its suggested 12 steps of recovery, I worked my recovery outside of those concepts. For my 25th anniversary from alcohol, I wrote what my own 12-steps were. One does not need to believe in God to gain sobriety. This attainment is attested to by the many who attend Atheist and Agnostics AA meetings. Welcomely, the Atheist and Agnostics terms are now being replaced with the term Secular. AA is a spiritual program, not a religious one, because members support one another as each works his/her program of recovery. No one can change another person: only one can change him/herself, but they need support and connectedness with other like-minded people. For me, helping addicts change their way of living is a form of ministry, and to use my chemistry background on how alcohol is detrimental to the body.

Motorola, having moved closer to Buffalo, started downsizing, so I lost my job and was able to find one in Elkhart, Indiana. I chose to live nearby in South Bend, Indiana and compute the few miles to Elkhart, as South Bend had more to offer me. The AA meetings here were quite different, and the members were more spread out over a larger area than I had in Buffalo. So, I sought connections in Christian groups again without drinking any alcohol. One of these was the now-defunct Church of the Good Shepherd in Exile, a Gay Christian group founded by a gay ex-priest. I became active in this group. The church published the now-defunct Rainbow Gazzette, a monthly newsletter serving the Gay, Lesbian, Bisexual, and Transgender Community of Michiana. I thought it was appropriate to have a message of faith in the publication; thus, I wrote articles under the title, "The Bible Says Through Interpreting Itself"

1. Were Sodom and Gomorrah Gay Meccas (July & August 1999 issues)

2. God-Centered Homosexuals (September & October 1999 issues)

3. The Natures of God and Humans (November & December 1999/January 2000 issues)

4. Whom Do You Serve? Jesus or Self (February 2000 issue)

5. The Heart: The Mirror of Spiritual Health (March 2000 issue)

6. What Does God Hate? (April 2000 issue)

7. Whom God Seeks: Worshippers (May & June 2000 issues)

■ **Example: Bible interpreting itself**

As I look at the life of Jesus, I see a person following the call of the Hebrew prophets for the leadership to follow the commandment to "Love thy neighbor as thyself." However, human beings, especially leaders, fail to care for the poor and the less fortunate through greed and a quest for power. At the time prior to the Babylonian captivity and the destruction of Solomon's temple, Ezekiel writes what he heard from God concerning Jerusalem's abominations in Ezekiel 16:49-50:

> "Now this was the sin of your sister Sodom[13]: arrogance! She and her daughters were arrogant, overfed, and unconcerned; they did not help the poor and needy. They were haughty and did detestable things before me. Therefore, I did away with them as you have seen."[41]

And Jeremiah, writing about the prophets' and priests' behavior, states in Jeremiah 23:13-14:

> "Among the prophets of Samaria, I saw this repulsive thing: they prophesied by Baal and led my people Israel astray. And among the prophets of Jerusalem, I have seen something horrible: they commit adultery and live a lie. They strengthen the hands of evildoers; so that no one turns from his wickedness. They are all like Sodom to me: the people of Jerusalem are like Gomorrah."[42]

Unfortunately, these same unloving conditions happened again after the temple was rebuilt, and the later prophets cried out about these uncaring and unloving conditions. Jesus' message is the same to the leaders of his time. With no change, The Temple was destroyed by the Romans in 70 CE, effectively dispersing the Jews for centuries.[43]

These verses also contradict the Christian message that the fault of Sodom and Gomorrah was homosexuality. Thus, failing to live the message of love for those who are different psychologically.

I see much of the Torah, the first five books of the Hebrew Bible, contradicting the message of the Ten Commandments. These commandments are a message of love and how to live it.[44]

During this time, I founded Christ the Master Ministries based on my experience in the gay leathermen communities and the related study of the Judeo-Christian Scriptures showing that Christ is my Master, and I am his slave. I created an oval patch for the back of my leather vest stating, "My Master," above "Jesus, the open cross and open tomb, Christ," and below "his slave" on a bright red background (Figure 4).

To carry the message of loving one another to a larger audience, I created a website www.christianbear.org for Christ the Master Ministries, to publish writings. It continued until I could no longer afford it in retirement.

Figure 4. Leather Patch

I started writing tracts, including the artwork, using a trifold one-half sheet of letter-size paper. The first tract was for the church founded by two gay lovers, New Life Community Church of Hope in Laporte, Indiana, with which I had a connection but not as a member. The tract titled: "A Letter from Jesus Accepting His Gay

---

[13]The Hebrew Scriptures, Genesis Chapters 18 and 19, state the conditions that led to the destruction of Sodom and Gomorrah.

Sons and Daughters" was a handout for the 1998 Chicago Gay Pride parade. I did not participate as I was not out as a gay person in my employment.

I wrote a trifold full letter-size sheet tract before retiring to Chicago. It was "Jesus Christ, the Master, says to my beloved Leather People and Bears, "You're acceptable as you are. Come! Enter into my great love.""

Upon retiring to Chicago, I was active in gay-oriented churches, Good Shepherd Metropolitan Community Church, where I led a Bible Study and Grace Baptist Church, a member of the American Baptist Association.

Besides the above, the following writings were featured on the website and/or used within the churches:

A. Christ and Leather

1. Leather People and Bears 2001 (tri-folded, full sheet of letter-size paper

2. Leather Play Reflects the Walk with Christ 2003 (article)

B. Encouraging Words for Life Series: (tri-folded, one-half sheet of letter-size paper)

1. Is Jesus My Most Significant Other? (2002)

2. Whose Sin Is Worse Yours or Mine? (2002)

3. Am I My Own Idol? (2002)

4. Is Jesus My Role Model? (2002)

5. Am I Clothed but Naked? (2002)

6. Am I Loved and Accepted by Jesus? (2002)

7. Is My Soul Healthy? (2002)

8. Am I Reflecting Jesus? (2002)

9. Am I Spiritually Blind? (2003)

10. Am I Legalistic or Merciful? (2003)

11. Am I Bound or Free? (2003)

12. Who or What Is My Treasure? (2005)

13. Am I Intimate with Christ? (2005)

14. Am I a Willing Slave to Christ? (2005)

C. Studying the Scriptures Series (bi-folded, two full sheets of letter paper)

1. A Guide for Private Study of the Holy Bible (last revised September 2004)

2. Establishment of the Judeo-Christian Scriptures (last revised September 2004)

3. Translations of the Holy Bible for the Common Person (last revised September 2004)

4. Interpreting the Holy Bible for Spiritual Growth (last revised September 2004)

D. Aids for Communicating with God (bi-folded, two or three full sheets of letter paper)

1. Daily Devotions (last revised December 2004)

2. Living Forgiveness (October 2005)

3. Fasting (January 2006)

E. Other writings

1. The Belief (statement about Christ the Master Ministries, probably 1998)

2. My Journey in Christ (2000)

3. A Personal Experience of Jesus Quieting the Storms of Life (2003)

4. *Advent 2005* A Time for Hope and Spiritual Renewal (daily reflections from the First Sunday of Advent through Christmas Day)

5. A Prayer of Thankfulness for Roy (2007)

While also doing the above writings, a major four-year undertaking in early retirement was the inter-comparison and translation from Greek to English of the three primary Greek texts of the Gospels. This research was entered from noting the significant and nuanced meanings found in the twenty plus renditions of the Judeo-Christian Scriptures in English, Greek, Hebrew, German, and Italian accumulated in my library. A synopsis of the research process is stated in the bullet, Translation Effort, at the end of this chapter.

After finishing my Gospel work, I had contact with another translator of the Gospels who used Leo Tolstoy's writings as the basis for his work. Unfortunately, he was nearing the end of his life when I encountered him. I digitized his works to conform to Chapter and Verse as commonly used in the Biblical Scriptures since he wrote without this notation. These were also recorded on CDs in 2011 and made available to those who desired at his 12-step memorial service.

So, having completed the translations and observing how Christianity was not living and espousing Christlikeness, I could no longer be supportive of any of its forms, so I laid aside all associations. I still maintained my patch on my leather vest when associating with leather-wearing-oriented people. It appears now that a seed for a new activity change was being watered and nourished over these many years to sprout forth, bringing significant changes to my life at 70.

I finally was able to get help for my workaholism, my human doing, through Workaholics Anonymous (WA). This human doing was constantly giving myself for others by thinking that my talents and abilities were to be used for others without any caring for my own needs. Again, I did not relate to other workaholics who buried their emotions through work. I had experienced many psychosomatic illnesses over my career and into retirement. One of these was angina without any damage to the heart or arteries. Because of this psychosomatic illness, I stopped playing and directing competitive contract duplicate bridge games until returning in early retirement.

When an opening on the WA World Service Organization Board (WAWSO) occurred for a Communications Coordinator, I felt I could do that, but there was no time for me unless I gave up something else as I was learning to prioritize and under schedule in my WA recovery. The owner of the bridge club that I was directing got me a dealing machine in 2011, thus reducing the time to prepare the pre-dealt weekly boards from four hours to thirty minutes. With this new free time, I offered the WAWSO board my services for Communications Coordinator, and they accepted my offer. I attended the fall 2011 WA World Service Conference becoming a member of the WAWSO board. At one point, I was wearing my full leathers with the Christ the Master patch. A comment was made that the patch message did not reflect who I was. When I came home and mentioned this to my new significant other, he also said that it was not me. I removed the patch from my leather vest. This episode was then the final ending of my Christian expressions.

Another significant change earlier in 2011 was entering into a meaningful love relationship with another senior man who was also in addiction recovery but in different programs. Sixteen years before our meeting, he had been diagnosed with acquired immunodeficiency syndrome (AIDS) due to the progressive attack of the human immunodeficiency virus (HIV) on his body. He was taking multiple medications and walking with a cane. He held a Master of Divinity degree and had been a concert harpsichordist.

He grew up Jewish but had converted to Christianity. He studied to be an Episcopalian priest, but his preaching was considered divergent from the denomination's dogmas. Thus, he was denied ordination. He used this background to minister to those dying from AIDS-related illness during this epidemic of the late 1980s. Therefore, his background and mine had many similarities. One of the unusual aspects was his immediate recognition at our early meeting, "Where have I been all his life." This mention indicated that we possibly had been significant others in a previous life. I have felt that the universe brought us together at this time to give him joy and happiness as he was being prepared to transition from this life in about four years after our getting together.

Because I related to very few addicts' alcoholism, I did not consistently attend AA meetings over the prior years. However, I maintained my sobriety by choosing my associations. I started again attending AA meetings with a different heart of just stating my experience and finding acceptance that I could help other addicts live a new way of life. With the passing of the chair of the AA meeting that I was attending, I became the chair. As my significant other's health declined, we started having his meetings in the apartment on the same evening and time that I was chairing my AA meeting. Thus, I got to know his friends who would be invaluable to his care, as he insisted, I could not care for him 24/7. They came and cared for him so that I could attend my bridge management functions at the twice-weekly games and one of my two WA meetings; the other WA was laid aside until after his passing. I was not directing bridge games at this time because I had laid aside that duty to manage a WAWSO conference in Chicago two years prior. However, in caring for my significant other, I could not have done both bridge directing and caring for him. I had resigned from the WAWSO board the fall before.

After his passing, I went back to both WA meetings and continued his meeting in the apartment to handle grief and prepare for the next transition. I then added an Atheist Agnostic Alcoholics Anonymous (Quad-A) meeting where some attendees went to lunch after the meeting to increase my social connections. I have sponsees who have some recovery time; mainly, these are long-distance, out of the country. I am helping them maintain sobriety in everyday life, more than initially giving up their addiction.

In 2020, we started experiencing the worldwide effects of the COVID-19 pandemic resulting in shutting down in-person meetings of all types. The 12-step meetings are now handled by remote video. Bridge games are also by this format; however, after I fell in fall of 2018, breaking my right femur, I am unable to sit for the length of time for a game in front of a computer. Reopening of in-person gatherings started in the summer of 2021, and there are signs that in 2022 the pandemic may abate in some sections of the world, such as the United States.

The fall also changed me psychologically because my activities since the fall do not have the same meaning to me as before the fall even though I am again doing them. Circumstances in my roommate's life as well as in mine brought us together to share a two-bedroom, two-bath apartment. This arrangement has been an invaluable help with my healing from the fall breaking my femur. During this pandemic, he provides tremendous support by handling groceries and necessities requiring exposure outside the apartment as he is an essential worker in a hospital.

Throughout my life since high school, while engaged in both my science and ministry journeys, I was researching and reading on the origins of religion. I detail the account of this in the next chapter, Avocation: Origins of Religion.

■ **Synopsis of Translation Effort**

The translation effort is the inter-comparison and translation from Greek to English of the three primary Greek texts of the Gospels, summarized herein. The Classical Greek-English Lexicon[45] was primarily used as there was no Christian Church at that time. Other Biblical Greek-English and Hebrew-English lexicons and concordances were also used. I sought one English word for one Greek word according to grammar and usage. These were extensively annotated, showing all variations in the final writing.

This was accomplished using letter size paper in portrait orientation and 0.25 margins to created extensive tables of five rows and 7-8 columns (depending on longest Greek words) in a subset of the verses (2-5). After each subset the conjugated verb form was identified with the root form, and the translation for that set of verses was stated. Each chapter of each gospel was a single file.

The five rows were:

1. The syntax of the Greek word (word wrapped in cell).

2. Textus Receptus (Byzantine based Greek texts and basis for the King James Version)[46].

3. Nestle-Aland's 27th Edition of Novum Testamentum Graece[47] (based on the oldest manuscripts, typically Egyptian).

4. The Greek New Testament according to the Majority Text[48] (based on the frequency of words in the thousands of manuscript fragments found. This is the basis for the Eastern Orthodox churches Bible.).

5. The basic English translation (i.e., the pronoun gender, declension, or conjugation form was not expressed in the tables but in the verse when translated for reading).

Each column was for one Greek word from each text. If the same grammar form and the same word order, the words would be in the same column; however, if differences then extensive color coding and separate columns were used to highlight the differences. The details of this coding were specified in the file "Introduction to the Gospels of the Christian Scriptures."

Additionally, to keep track of usage between Gospels as the exact English translation was to be used throughout the four Gospels, I created my own cross-referenced tabular glossaries:

1. Greek - English having five columns:

   a. The language base form from which declensions and conjugations are derived.

   b. The grammar usage (noun, verb, preposition, etc.).

   c. A brief definition.

   d. English translation (base form).

   e. Where used by Gospel, chapter, and verse.

2. English - Greek having five columns:

   a. The language base form from which declensions and conjugations are derived.

   b. The corresponding Greek language base.

   c. The grammar usage (noun, verb, preposition, etc.).

   d. A brief definition.

   e. Where used by Gospel, chapter, and verse.

The final translation used symbols and color coding to express the differences in the verse. If the Gospel text required a different word definition according to syntax and meaning, then this was footnoted in the translated verse. Thus, the final documentation of the Gospels was extensively annotated with many types of coding to distinguish the grammar, syntax structure, word order in the versions, and the word usage, such as singular and plural since these are different forms in Greek but not necessarily in English. Most of the time in English the singular and plural meanings are determined from the context. These details were expressed in the "Introduction to the Gospels of the Christian Scriptures." This and only the finalized Gospels were posted on my website. The final translation was also copied to CDs in 2011.

Subsequently, James and 1 John were translated using the same format. These also had been posted on my website. None of these translations have been published otherwise.

As an example, I will quote my translation with its coding of Luke 18:13 and the comparison as found in the New International Version (NIV)[49]:

My Version: [13]And the toll-collector, having had stood at-a-distance, was **not** desiring, **not-even** to have wakened the eyes into the universe, but he was beating ⌐into¬ the chest of him saying, "The god, *be* conciliated [you] to me, the-one of-bad-character."

NIV version: [13]But the tax collector stood at a distance. He would not even look up to heaven, but beat his breast and said, 'God, have mercy on me, a sinner.'

Notes on the difference in word choice between translations may be nuances, but they are critical to the application to how one views his/her life:

- **Conciliated versus mercy**

  Conciliate connotes coming back into a relationship or reconciliation. However, mercy indicates compassion without necessarily coming back into a relationship or even being in a relationship. I can have mercy on a person with whom I am not in an intimate relationship, such as helping a homeless person, or my tendency to rescue people in need of help, sometimes to my detriment. My Christian understanding is that of an intimate relationship with God.

- **Of-bad-character versus sinner**

  The Greek is an adjective form of the word for failure or fault. Thus, the Greek is erroneous, erring, of-bad-character, but the English sinner connotes wickedness or evilness. These latter are more degrading than just admitting a failure or fault, which all humans do because of their being created imperfect. Unfortunately, I have not found the concept of imperfection in any Christian churches, only the idea that people are to be perfect with no agreement as to what perfect means.

Chapter 4

Avocation: Origins of Religion

Answering Fundamental Questions

In my training as a physical scientist, I observed in laboratory exercises what previous scientists had observed and from which they derived the laws governing much of what has been observed of how the earth system operates. It was not just accepting what was handed down but also thinking logically from basics and being open to new innovative views of how things work. Applying this approach, I will explain how I have arrived at answers to the questions under the Spiritual Aspect (Figure 2). Since believing that the ancients were equal in reasoning ability, they attempted to understand the earth environs in which they found themselves. My thought patterns and observations leading to the answers to the fundamental questions provide possible insight into ancients' reasoning. This reasoning established the many religious systems throughout human history. All these systems represent the truth to the believers in these religious systems. It is only in comparing religions that one may say this one is true, and all others are false.

Before I can provide answers to the questions under the Spiritual Aspect, I need to define the Creative Force or Living Spirit. Although I previously used the term Creative Force, I now prefer Living Spirit: the embodiment of universal energy and universal consciousness.

In my late teens and early twenties, during physical science studies, I observed that:

- The living and non-living entities in the universe have great complexity, such as humans being physiologically similar to large animals. Yet, the mental parts of humans are enormously more capable of creating and adapting to varying circumstances.

- Chemical interactions of both inorganic and organic molecules were highly selective. For example, a common household baking ingredient, cream of tartar (tartaric acid), exists in two isomeric forms, (+) or (-) optical rotation, caused by the interchange of two molecular groups on one atom. Living organisms have shown that they can digest the (+) of these but not the (-). This digestion was known as dissymmetry as early as 1840.[50]

- The smallest known distance for cosmic rays was on the order of 10^{-14} m[14].[51] Fifty years later, the smallest measurement having meaning is the Plank length 10^{-35} m; this is the limit of quantum mechanical system.[52]

- The nearest stars were 10.6 light-years or 1.1×10^{17} m from the earth.[53] Fifty years later, the most distant quasar to the earth is 13 billion light-years or 1.2×10^{26} m.[54]

From these observations, I concluded that the logical explanation is an unknown, unnamed, invisible entity, the Living Spirit. It was the creative source. Having realized that there is a Living

---

[14]One meter (m) is about one yard.

Spirit, how did I choose to characterize this entity? As in any investigation, I start with asking questions; albeit I will also supply the answers. They, being based on my understanding at that moment, are modifiable later as my understanding increases. My characterization is:

■ **Where did this Living Spirit originate?**

The Living Spirit has no gender as understood by humans in the earth plane. Also, the Living Spirit has no beginning and no end, i.e., it has always been and will always be. The ever-being of the Living Spirit is supported by:

● A long-observed history of plant and human life having been recorded in paleontological studies.

● Subatomic structure development indicating ever-smaller distances between particles (approaching minus infinity or no beginning), and astronomical system studies showing ever-greater distances occurring in space (approaching plus infinity or no end).

● The universe being minimally 13.8 billion years old or always has been relative to human life spans.[55]

■ **Does this Living Spirit have a physical form?**

Since it is invisible to the human eye, the Living Spirit's physical form is indeterminable. So, I chose to use the term "Living Spirit" to designate its physical form, always being everywhere present in the universe. Thus, the Living Spirit is omnipresent. Having the ability to make choices, I am an integral part of the Living Spirit, not a separate entity from it as expressed in western religious systems. One analogy that I use for the relationship with the Living Spirit is I am like a single cell in my body. This single cell is independent of each other cell, only existing by interacting with other cells to carry out its unique cell function by its position in the body. For example, a cell of the skin is like its neighbor, but positionally it does the same role at a different location. Just as the cells in the body interact and depend on others, I am interacting with everyone on earth in some fashion, with the Living Spirit providing and sustaining the mechanisms for all the functions within my humanness of body, mind, and spirit.

■ **Where does the Living Spirit's intelligence originate?**

From observation of the intricate nature of life forms, humans have only a little understanding of the mechanisms of physical life. The source of these complex life forms is the Living Spirit. For these forms, the Living Spirit is omniscience, i.e., always has all the intelligence needed to create and sustain everything in the universe according to some unknown operational processes. What is observed are the results of this Living Spirit's actions which have many dualities or polarities, such as seen - unseen, good - evil, being - non-being, is - is not, light - darkness, male - female forms of humans and large animal life, dry-wet periods, and hot-cold periods. As I look at my bodily functions, I see both beneficial chemical molecules to health being circulated within my body. Simultaneously, deleterious chemical molecules are also being circulated to the point where they can be excreted. If deleterious molecules stay, diseases or disabilities happen. By analogy, I see all dualities being totally within the Living Spirit. Without these dualities, there could be no free will for making choices for spiritual learning and experiencing life. How the Living Spirit handles those poor decisions is unknown, and what happens to their circulation within the Living Spirit can only be conjectured.

■ How can I describe how the Living Spirit acts?

From observation, I see that each human, barring physical and mental disabilities, can create by himself/herself many different forms of the same thing, which I observe that no other animal species does on its own accord. However, I do not really know how the Living Spirit acts. However, from observation, the Living Spirit has set in motion the laws and conditions whereby the universe exists. Humans, being created to make mistakes, are challenged to understand the laws and conditions of the universe for growth and experiencing life. In this understanding, they cannot see into the future of how their creations may cause harmful effects both by science and religion. As the years pass, other humans find their harmful effects and try to overcome these effects.

■ Does the Living Spirit communicate with its human creations, and if so, how?

From my experience, intuition (feeling), dreams, visions, and rarely audible voice are the primary communications, and when heeded, have resulted in positive solutions to the situations. However, these do not mitigate the use of literature, notably what has been termed sacred literature in various cultures and religious systems. This literature is written by humans to others, usually in past centuries. Some of this literature was later deemed sacred, which may or may not have applicability to what my actions are for my spiritual experience. The time and conditions have radically changed since the writing of the sacred literature; thus, relevance may be questioned. Also, the Living Spirit has, throughout all time, communicated with humans who are open to receiving this information through all forms of human endeavors, such as the sciences and arts, not just religion.

■ Does the Living Spirit require worship?

Worshipping and asking anything from the Living Spirit is impossible because I am part of the Living Spirit. I find dogmas and doctrines leading to rituals and particular places of worship hindering and stagnating the purpose for which my spirit is on earth. My most meaningful worship is a deep sense of loving gratitude in my inner being for life as I do my part. There is a sense of provision for what I am to experience, including what is termed negatives. For it is through these negatives that I also understand the positives. Coupled and not a separate action with this is practicing the universal law of "unconditional love, i.e., treat my neighbor as I want to be treated," using my limited abilities for the benefit of others while learning not to be harmful to own being.

■ Why does the Living Spirit allow suffering?

Because dualities exist, suffering must also exist as a means for experiencing what it is to suffer and what it is not to suffer. Some reasons for the existence of suffering are:

- From the adage "We learn from our mistakes," I make a choice that causes suffering which is beneficial to facilitate my experiencing other aspects of life.

- I fail to live unconditional love. By putting my desires above that of another, I may cause another to suffer in some manner. The converse is also true of others mistreating me.

- The spirit enters a physical body that is not considered perfect for its own experiences, as well as to teach love and be non-judgmental by both the deformed and fully functioning. For example, the story of Jesus healing the blind man who had this condition so that God could be glorified, and which taught the lesson that one was not to judge another based on one's physical condition.[56]

- Because duality implies stability-instability conditions, i.e., constant changes occurring reflected in the term entropy or everything goes to disorder. There are climatic and physical changes in the earth resulting in catastrophic suffering that is felt not only by those in the immediate vicinity but often others far away in unaffected areas as they are interrelated to those suffering.

Relationship to Aspects of Humans

Under the Spiritual Aspect (Figure 2), one's answers to the following fundamental questions shape the operation in the other aspects, in communicating, and in benefiting others. So, let us look at these questions in more detail.

- **How did the universe come into being that one is experiencing?**

  According to my Economic Aspect (Figure 2), the early societies had a few causative thinkers who were seekers of the first cause of the universe. This first cause was for the benefit of others in those societies. Based on their observation and understanding of how things happened, these thinkers offered explanations of the events around them. These explanations have come down to the present through translations and possible transliterations of written records, including archeological, anthropological, and other scientific studies. The renderings and studies are also colored by the worldviews or religious views of those transmitting the renderings and reporting the studies to the present-day readers. The origins of the universe are based on my 50+ years of readings:

  - Of the Roman Catholic Church and Orthodox Church history.

  - In comparisons between 18 recensions of the Judeo-Christian Scriptures in English, German, Hebrew, and Greek.

  - Of Biblical archeological reports concerning the same events from both liberal and conservative backgrounds.

  - In studying nuclear physics concerning atomic structure before quantum mechanics, which explained the atomic structure as understood today.

  - Comparative religion studies.

My observation is what we know about the origins of the universe in this early 21st century has been built iota-by-iota of learning on all that has progressed from the earliest times. There is also the possibility that they knew methods and processes that we do not know today because an event occurred that destroyed that knowledge, such as the ultimate destruction of the Alexandria, Egypt libraries in 391 CE.[57] Thus, I consider the earliest humans to have the same level of native intelligence and inquisitiveness for causes of events happening on the earth around them. As I have listened to children say how certain things occur, especially prior to our television and internet ages, their explanations will not be a reality as understood by adults. Thus, the earliest explanations by the earliest humans, when compared to 21st-century understanding, may be likened to a child's explanation.

The scientific or causative explanations by those making the observations millennia earlier are often termed mythology in the 21st century. From the Companion and Economic Aspects (Figure 2), a few offered these explanations, which others followed. Thus, a leadership developed which championed specific belief systems that have come down through the centuries, often with modifications and various versions. Those who became leaders indoctrinated others to be leaders and followers from which the aspects of governance for a society emerged. Those born into a given society would automatically be indoctrinated into the system and would follow it until a new leadership developed. This leadership questioned the foundation and brought about a novel approach with new thoughts built on the earlier system. The other possibility is for one to reject the existing system and begin a search for another explanation that formed a new system when promulgated.

One of the oldest writings on the quest to know the origins of the universe is the "Creation Hymn," or the "Nasadiya Sukta" of the Rigveda, considered to have been written between 6000 BCE and 3000 BCE.[58] This hymn speaks of questions of the seeker of the unknown and where did the universe originate. It is the answers to these questions that have given rise to the many truths in the various human societies. It is also the quests that still go on today, including my own, in science and the challenges to current religious systems. There are several translations; the following is by Prof. Raimundo Panikkar.[59]

"At first was neither Being nor Nonbeing.
There was not air nor yet sky beyond.
What was wrapping? Where? In whose protection?
Was Water there, unfathomable deep?

There was no death then, nor yet deathlessness;
of night or day there was not any sign.
The One breathed without breath by its own impulse.
Other than that was nothing at all.

Darkness was there, all wrapped around by darkness,
and all was Water indiscriminate, Then

that which was hidden by Void, that One, emerging,
stirring, through power of Ardor, came to be.

In the beginning Love arose,
which was primal germ cell of mind.
The Seers, searching in their hearts with wisdom,
discovered the connection of Being in Nonbeing.

A crosswise line cut Being from Nonbeing.
What was described above it, what below?
Bearers of seed there were and mighty forces,
thrust from below and forward move above.

Who really knows? Who can presume to tell it?
Whence was it born? Whence issued this creation?
Even the Gods came after its emergence.
Then who can tell from whence it came to be?

That out of which creation has arisen,
whether it held it firm or it did not,
He who surveys it in the highest heaven,
He surely knows - or maybe He does not!"

Attempting to describe how the Living Spirit created the universe is only conjectures or imaginations stated as reality. The many creation myths[15] are from these conjectures or imaginations in the various religious systems discovered among the many different peoples having existed and existing today. These myths are truth to those cultures as based on the understanding of nature at their times. Are these myths based on something that went before, or was there a quantum leap, as all learning is based on what has gone before because my observation is that one learns iota-by-iota? Quantum leaps are based on what has gone before, but a new challenge had arisen that could no longer be explained by known theories. Thus, a new theory is developed, like quantum mechanics refining classical mechanics for the atomic level in substances. The answer to the question of the origins of the universe cannot be known without further paleontological and archeological evidence.

Since the creation of the universe in the myths have many similarities going back at least 4000 years and maybe even longer without worldwide travel being evident, the question arises, "Has the Living Spirit endowed all these groups with the same message and only they have explained it differently?" I do not know the answer; however, it is worth pondering as other similarities also occur across religious systems across the continents.

- ■ **What do some causative thinkers say is the starting point for the creation of the observed universe in various cultures around the earth?**

---

[15]Comparative religion's technical term for society's truths, and not the common connotation of lies by a religious systems' arrogance that their truths are right, and all others are wrong.

- Chaos (considered to be total disorder) which was a great vast sea in which all elements were intermingled together:
  - ◆ Without form and in darkness; Greek matriarchal tradition.[60]
  - ◆ The sea is oily and no mention of darkness; Japanese tradition.[61]
- Geia, the earth, and a great sea of Chaos; Greek patriarchal tradition.[62]
- Ormazd, the omniscient, was separated by a vast abyss of the cosmos from Ahriman, the source of all suffering, sin, and death; Zoroastrian tradition.[63]
- There is only Creator existing:
  - ◆ Hebrews have God Who made heaven and earth, which was a formless void with darkness over the deep and a wind sweeping over the water.[64]
  - ◆ The Bantu Fans of Africa have a tradition saying, "In the beginning, there was nothing but Nzame."[65]
  - ◆ The Northwest American Indian Tribe Chelan has only a Creator existing who makes the world.[66]
  - ◆ The Tahitian tradition has Taaroa existing alone and who changes himself into the universe.[67]
  - ◆ The Hindu Sikh tradition has the Limitless Divine Ordinance as forming the gods and universe.[68]
  - ◆ The Eastern Canadian Mik'Maq Indian tradition has Gisoolg who is the one who made everything.[69]
- There was no heaven above nor an earth beneath, only a vast bottomless deep shrouded in an atmosphere of mist, The Elder Edda, Icelandic tradition.[70]
- The heavens and earth were still one, and all was chaos with Pan-Gu inside, non-dog Pan-Gu Chinese tradition.[71]
- There are two creating gods acting together:
  - ◆ The Mexican Maya Indians have Tepeu and Gucumatz who sat together and thought, and whatever they thought came into being.[72]
  - ◆ The Ekoi of southern Nigeria who has two gods, one in the sky and one on the earth, acting together in creating life on earth.[73]
- There was the sky, and the world (earth) was a watery, formless Chaos that was neither sea nor land, but a marshy waste, West African Yoruba tradition.[74]
- The Watery Abyss, Egyptian tradition.[75]
- Nothing but darkness and water which sloshed around, causing spray which congealed to form the sky, American Yuma Indian tradition.[76]
- There was no earth, nor sea, nor sky:

- ♦ Only the emptiness of Ginnungagap, waiting to be filled, Scandinavian tradition.[77]

- ♦ Only darkness was everywhere, American Indian Apache tradition.[78]

- Traditions without mention of a universe creation but start with an existing sky and earth:

  - ♦ The five powerful American Indian Tribes in the state that is now New York.[79]

  - ♦ The American Indian Hopi have a sky god Tawa and earth goddess, Spider Woman, to whom all the mysteries of their respective realms belong.[80]

- Coalesced matter of unspecified origin exploded in a gigantic bang according to the physics Big Bang Theory, thereby creating the universe.[81]

- No interest in the origins of the universe.[82]

- An infinite universe has always been in existence.[83]

This list is not exhaustive and shows how widely varying are the truths of the universe's origins from ancient times to modern times, i.e., the last three listed. Some of the truths exist in different versions within a tradition. What is noted are similarities, although coming from widely distant cultures around the earth and considerably distinct from neighboring cultures. There is no adequate way to date when these cultures came into being. These traditions can only be declared false when based on evidence that is not prejudiced by one's beliefs. What is acceptable evidence? Verifiable facts in dictating these conjectures? I have not found facts, only further conjecture that is biased by the writer's worldview for what is the truth of creation.

■ **What is the origin of life in this universe and thus also one's life?**

My physical life is a result of a long procession of births by parents going far back into history. Just like the little child that asks his parents where did he come from, so I also ask myself, where did my form of life originate? My answer is that the Living Spirit had to form this most intricate entity with its three faculties and six aspects (Figure 2) in some manner that I cannot explain.

This origin of life is not only my question but has been the question of humans for millennia, and the answer is a wide variety of explanations. Some of these are:

- Formed from the earth under different processes:

  - ♦ In Judaism, Yahweh Elohim forms man from the dust of the earth and breathes life into man to become a living being.[84]

  - ♦ In Sumerian, Enki creates man from dust and water and in a second version from the blood and flesh of a slain god mixed with earth. The spirit of the god becomes the spirit in humans.[85]

- ◆ The West African Yoruba have a lower god Orisha Nla for the humans from earth, but the supreme Being Orolrun gives the life.[86]

- ◆ In Madagascar, the Creator brings into being the first humans by breathing life into the clay dolls his daughter, Mother Earth, was making.[87]

- ◆ The southern California Digueno Indians have Tu-chai-pai creating the first Indians from mud (water and earth).[88]

- ◆ The Hungarian tradition has seeds from the bottom of the Eternal Sea brought to the surface which become humans.[89]

- Brought forth from within the Creator God:

  - ◆ The Central African Bantu tribe Boshongo has Bumba, the Creator giving form to man from within himself.[90]

  - ◆ Hindu have Brahman taking a temporary body of Brahma and splitting into male and female counterparts.[91]

  - ◆ The Egyptian tradition has humans created from the tears of the god Ra.[92]

- Brought forth from plant life:

  - ◆ Norse tradition has Odin forming man from the ash tree and the woman from the elm tree.[93]

  - ◆ The North American Plains Sioux Indians have humans coming from the roots of stumps of two trees: an older tree and a younger tree beside it.[94]

- Brought forth by animal life:

  - ◆ South Dakota Arikara Indians have spiders producing all other life forms, including humans.[95]

- Brought forth from celestial objects:

  - ◆ The central North American Pawnee Indians have humans coming from the union of Daughter-of-Evening-and-Morning-Star and the Son-of-Sun-and-Moon.[96]

- No mention of how human life was formed:

  - ◆ The Japanese Creation myth Kojiki.[97]

  - ◆ Buddhism (life is a continuum of cycles of birth and death).[98]

  - ◆ Modern biological science study of the evolution of life starting with Darwin's "Origin of the Species."[99]

- Life was created experimentally by beings from another planet.[100]

All explanations on how the first humans came into being show man's interest in first causes and the fascination of how humans evolved into the earth system. The last thought is 21st century showing that humanity continues to explore new ideas on how humans came into being. As these are further studied, one finds that these beliefs in human creation have influences in every aspect of these people's lives: companion (social) structure, economic structure, political structure, and spiritual expressions.

■ **What is the source of one's consciousness, disposition, talents, etc.?**

The process of forming a life starts when the sperm and egg unite. Since sperm are observed with activity in the ejaculate so that they may move to unite with an egg, the energy to do this must come from the universal energy and may also be a form of consciousness as well. Observations of infants show that each has consciousness and dispositions when birthed. During fetal development, the mother feels the fetus kicking, and heartbeats are detected. Thus, the universe must provide this at conception when the portion of the Living Spirit's consciousness and energy start the life-forming process.

From the observations of my two daughters at birth and the early days of their lives, the girls were different in some manners and similar in others. As they grew, these differences became unique as they became their own individuals. Their abilities and dispositions appeared not to come from their parents. This difference in abilities and dispositions was also evident in my brothers, who all differed in temperament, abilities, and motivations towards life.

From my study of the Judeo-Christian Scriptures, they say that God created everything.[101] Thus, this means that from observation: He created everything to be imperfect and constantly changing, giving all the variations in earth's environment and people's consciousness, disposition, talents, etc. All these observed variations were created so that one may experience life as he/she journeys through life as human beings rather than robots.

God's creative work is further extended to the creation of all healthful and unhealthful conditions in living life on planet earth. Thus, for example, the bacteria and viruses that cause diseases are also his handy work. These same Scriptures say He is merciful. Therefore, in His mercy, He must have gifted selected individuals with understanding iota parts to His work of how His creation works. Those with these understandings interact with others to explain and make remedies to these diseases for the benefit of all peoples. Too often, I see church teachings saying not to rely on health sciences, yet in today's world, everything that we enjoy has been developed by other scientists. So why only the rejection of health sciences and only relying on God to correct the situation? I see the misconception of God's mercy being supplied through others as not matching the concept of mercy in a person's mind and maybe as instructed by a religious leader.

As a scientist myself, I see who I am as an iota part of His work to benefit others. This idea has been true for all people living in past times regardless of religious thought throughout history. The problem that I have observed in my Christian church affiliations is their distortion of this merciful part of God being extended to this thinking because of the picking and choosing of selected verses for their views rather than seeing an integrated whole. This selection process has resulted in the teachings of man under the guise of the teachings of God and Jesus Christ. These teaching are an anthropomorphized God rather than a humanly unknowable creative entity. All gods are creations of man's attempt to explain how the universe works that we humans find ourselves experiencing.

■ What is one's purpose in life?

From the Economic Aspect, one's purpose in life is to use their talents and abilities for first maintaining their physical life and secondly to benefit others. Since life is a journey each day into the unknown, even if we think that we are walking on a known path, unforeseen obstacles will occur. Thus, the idea that each moment occurring next is an unknown. These bring challenges, enabling new experiences in all aspects of life. Therefore, each of us needs the talents and abilities of others, whether directly interacting with them daily or acting in the Political Aspect (Figure 2) affecting what we are doing. Coupled with these are one's own Spiritual Aspect's concepts and living of those concepts. These are all important for living a meaningful and purposeful life.

Having journeyed in western religious thought from my upbringing to eastern religious thought, I think the purpose of life is to change our spiritual consciousness over many reincarnations. One of the spiritualities is to become more compassionate and empathic with our sojourners in this plane, earth. In this process, we help others make changes in their own consciousness during their journey. One of these incarnations was my late partner and I feeling that we were significant others in past lives. In this life I was able to assist him in having a meaningful life. We journeyed through his final years expressing love by walking along aside each other. This was not lost on his friends for some of them offered and are taking care of me.

For myself, this meant using my knowledge of the physical sciences for improving processes and systems for better products. However, from my lack of childhood playmates because of the isolation that my parents created, I went overboard in giving myself, such that I did not have balance in my life. This imbalance led to workaholism interrelated with alcoholism. Based on my work with counselors and therapists, my workaholism and alcoholism were not the usually associated conditions. Thus, my recovery work has not been in any way traditional, partly because of the religious nature of these programs as generally expressed. Within these recovery programs, I slowly came to grips with the issues of my suppressed emotions. Thus, my life experiences help others in their recovery. It is also one reason for writing this book.

■ Is one's interaction with others a function of religious systems?

This question and the one following have laid dormant since the start of this essay several years ago, just like many a seed does before it finally has the energy to spring forth. Since religious systems need a group of people, the earliest group of people defined how they would act as a cohesive group to maintain life and its continuance through reproduction and daily living. In order to give a sense of greater authenticity, these innovations of what is and is not acceptable behavior were incorporated in the social fabric of their lives. Then, these observances were transmitted, first orally, to a special leader preserving them as sacred texts for the group. Later when writing was devised, they were recorded. At some point in time, these formulations having originated in human thought became stated as from the group's god system although this system also originated in human thought for the group's cohesion.

Since spirituality can be thought of as

Table 1. The Theism-Atheism Polarity	
Theism	**Atheism**
Belief in one or many gods existing	Lack of belief in any god existing
Systems: monotheism or pantheism	Not a system nor a philosophy or an ideology, but it can be part of a philosophy, ideology, or worldview
Worship of god(s) through rituals, dogmas, etc.	No worship since god does not exist
Moral code based on transcendental and supernatural beliefs	Moral code based on treatment of others as one wants to be treated.
Worldviews based upon these beliefs, and around which people organize their lives	Not a worldview and does not promote any one worldview.

having the polarity extremes of theism and atheism, this is likened to our coins which have a head on one side and something else on the other side such that we speak of heads and tails of coins, yet they are connected whole. What is expressed in Table 1 is simplistic as the literature has many different connotations for both theism and atheism, especially since atheism has become more acceptable to discuss. Also, many people attribute spirituality only to theistic systems; however, spirituality, as expressed here, is independent of theistic systems.

When I left the monastic life the second time, I for a while considered only a Creative Force for giving meaning to the formation of the universe and my part in it. With my marriages, I participated in their religious system, only to walk away after the divorces. Currently, after walking through many other Christian religious systems as well as exploring Zen Buddhism, I moved back to the atheism end of the theism-atheism polarity of being an integral part of the universal energy and universal consciousness. The culminating change occurred when completing the inter-comparison of three Greek texts of the Christian Bible using Classical Greek for one English word for one Greek word. At this point, I concluded that Biblical literature is fiction and not believable as a way of life for me. I currently practice no rituals or other aspects of what is considered part of a religious system (see Spirituality versus Religion).

■ **Why is there suffering and mistreatment of people by others?**

From my observation of the nature of all aspects in this plane termed earth, suffering (the negative pole) is one end of an extreme, with the other end being elation (the positive pole). Growth needs these poles. Both suffering and elation have various degrees of intensity at different times. The time in each depends on the circumstances associated with the condition. Life is one continuous cycling between these two extremes, and the times in each are necessary parts for all forms of human experience. Some suffering is man-made (such as murder, wars, or depredation through control of others), while others are the result of environmental changes (such as famines, floods, or earthquakes). Similarly, the same goes for elation. Since humans, as well as higher animals, all show emotions, the various types of emotions are within this polarity.

Mistreatment of others is related directly to how much one wants to control others, especially those with opposing views. This mistreatment is dramatically evident in the world's political and religious systems as affecting all forms of life and the environment.

Just as I experience pain in my physical body when there are issues with it not functioning well, so I experience emotional pain when my needs in the psychological aspect of my life are not met. However, there are also those changes in the body where no pain is felt, but corrective actions are needed, such as my having corrective lenses prescribed for better eyesight.

Because I was not to be myself, I experienced much bullying as a child, which was coupled with my parents not providing me with playmates my own age throughout my childhood. This lack of playmates has affected all my relations in adult life as I have had to learn socialization and heal from those wounds. As I healed from these wounds, I caused suffering in others through separations, such as divorces and the breakup of intimate relationships. Learning to say "no" to another's request may also cause that person to suffer because they did not get what they wanted. Saying "no" was an important part of my recovery work from workaholism and alcoholism. Sometimes having "no" said to us is for our benefit, such as medical restraints, or in what is termed "tough love" for emotional growth.

In my recovery work, I have seen the harm and suffering done by those who insist on addicts needing to do their recovery work like others have done theirs, especially when done with a strong religious view of only being successful with a belief in God or Jesus.

■ Where does one's spirit go when one dies, as observation shows all die?

Since death is end of the life-death cycle and an inevitable fact, what happens after death is a perennial question. No answers are comprehensively satisfactory as no one has come back to tell those living what has happened. The closest understanding may come from the reports of near-death experiences[102] and from mystics who have reached higher consciousness.[103] My observation is that there is an entity Living Spirit that causes the physical and mental functions to operate in the way that they do. At death, I have a body that ceases to function, so the chemical makeup is not functioning independently but must have another cause, i.e., the iota of the Living Spirit. Where it goes, I do not know and can only conjecture that I return to be united in another way with the Living Spirit.

In 2017, my own out-of-body experience when taking a break from my computer work was one of extreme joy and happiness. I have not had such joy and happiness at any previous time in my life. My consciousness left the body briefly while still attached and was going forth to explore the universe. There was a sense of oneness with the universe and not a separate entity.

Humans have developed various conjectures as to what the spirit experiences in the afterlife upon the death of the physical body. Some systems speak of a fourth entity, the soul, which comprises the mental and emotional aspects or consciousness from physical life that goes with the spirit and lives with it in the spirit realms. The after-physical-life places are described as highly dependent on how one has lived this physical life on earth. Some of these are:

- Western North American Western Plains Arapaho Indiana have a place of bliss for all without any judgment; those termed good and bad all share the same place.[104]

- A place of eternal bliss (heaven) or eternal torment (hell) depending on how one lived life:

  - Zoroastrian tradition teaches that souls go to either heaven or hell after a final judgment dependent on the balance of good and bad deeds in the life one led. There was a separate place for those that had equally good and bad deeds.[105]

  - Eternally in heaven, if you accepted Christ as your Savior or eternally in hell if you rejected him at the final judgment.[106]

- The soul lives on and is reincarnated again on earth in animals.[107]

- No life after death:

  - Many atheists believe there is only awareness in this life that ceases on death.[108]

  - The Sadducees at the time of Jesus did not believe in life after death or judgment or resurrection.[109]

- There is no soul, only Eholim (not the God of Hebrew Scriptures, but beings who are more advanced intellectually than humans) whose scientific advances will enable a few to have eternal life.[110]

- The soul and spirit are ever learning and living when not in physical manifestation on earth but also in the soul and spiritual realms in preparation for the next human incarnations on earth.[111,112]

Spirituality versus Religion

Just as in the duality theism-atheism, there is no one term describing Spirituality. Instead, it is experiencing life in union with the Living Spirit of the universe characterized by:

- Having one's mindset on what the Living Spirit desires as understood by one.

- Realizing one's spirit is alive through the Living Spirit in one.

- Experiencing life in the physical body through the Living Spirit being in union with one.

The term spirituality also refers to living by the spirit as distinguished from religious systems. This spirituality connotes a deep inner connectedness within one of the awareness of the spiritual nature of one's life and between two people through mutual actions, raising their spirits to conjoin each other with or without a spiritual entity being present. What is expressed in Table 2 is from my artistic presentation in an art gallery in 2007[16]. This pictorial representation of the concepts forming the basis for this book is shown in the Appendix. It is simplistic, as the literature has various ways of explaining the relationship between spirituality and religion.

Religious Systems

In my studies, I have noted that authors' views on a subject are influenced by their worldview perspective. For example, in the duality of western-eastern

Table 2. Contrasting Spirituality and Religiosity	
Spirituality	**Religiosity**
Humanity is in an intimate experiential relationship with the Spirit of the Universe.	Created by Humanity to explain: • How the universe and people came into existence. • The suffering and catastrophic earth events. • Humanity's purpose for a society. • Acceptable behaviors in a designated society.
The intimate experiential relationship brings: • Worthiness: Humanity is created imperfect for learning to live in harmony and respecting the entire universe. • Wholeness: The innate longing (sometimes referred to as the void within) is fulfilled, resulting in inner peace and serenity.	Experience expressed in duality extremes: • Above: heaven, perfect, sacred. • Below: earth, flawed, profane. Gives rise to: • Addictions which fail to satisfy the void within. • Arrogance of one's belief system as true, all others false. • Strife of all kinds for the control of others and resources by the more powerful.
Spirit's unconditional love flows to all creation: • Flows out of Spirit through humanity given wholly to the Spirit. • Enables loving others as oneself. • Sees all others as equals regardless of talents and abilities; each is no better or the worse than another.	Spirit of the Universe: • Resides in the heaven. • Detached from earthly events. • Sacred or holy qualities. • Given many different names. Humanity: • Resides on the earth. • Detached from heavenly events. • Profane or unworthy qualities. • Dualistic characteristics.
Oneness: • Humanity in the Spirit of the Universe and the Spirit of the Universe in humanity. • Earth is a spot in the unbounded universe.	There is a barrier to the holy: • Spirit's system provides for life sustainability. • Human rituals and works to appease the Spirit.
Relationship Development: • Brings about thankfulness in all circumstances both the blessings and the trials. • Walks a path of sifting and challenging experiences. • Grows exposing hindrances which become dim and are shed. • Is taken with one when the physical body is shed.	Transmission to future generations: • Developed based on forerunners through oral traditions into writings which are defined later as sacred whether considered Spirit revealed or not.

[16]This work was created for an art gallery friend asking for original works on spirituality for an exhibition. The work was approximately a 6'x9' presentation titled "What Is Your Journey in the Spirit of the Universe?" had a central picture of myself standing on the shore of Lake Michigan, Figure 2 was imposed on top of me. There were six individual pictures associated with facets of life for each of the base triangle aspects. The graphics for the apex of the pyramid was a picture of the "Rodin's Thinker" and a large Question Mark. The blocks in Table 2 were 8.5"x11.0" graphics on the right and left sides under the table headings created in wire inserted in line ovals pointing towards the apex. Kelly Courtney, an artist friend, assisted in the process. A four-page handout was available showing the key pictures and a one-page statement of my journey. The work was taken down when the art gallery moved and not rehung. The work has been updated for use herein.

religions, western writers having a Judeo-Christian worldview relate eastern religious systems quite differently than eastern authors. This expression difference requires sifting for the actual meaning in a religious system. In addition, the complexity and the interrelatedness amongst the aspects render difficulties in being succinct. Thus, what follows will not be in-depth but will be my attempt at saliency by treating all systems as being equally true.

Most religious systems that I have studied assign the causative understanding of physical phenomena to a deity system more powerful than humans and controlling these phenomena. These systems are often anthropomorphic in ascribing human characteristics to deities or animals or plants, which are the actors in creating the universe. Also, these systems are either monotheistic or polytheistic, with the gods and goddesses having a societal structure, with one god or goddess being the chief and the creator or assigning creation activities to a lesser god.

To communicate about the gods and goddesses, they are given names and may be associated with certain physical phenomena. However, in the languages (English, Latin, German, Hebrew, and Greek) that I have some familiarity, there is no word that can describe The Living Spirit, who has no gender. Just as my Living Spirit is a human concept, so are all other gods. Since gods are more considered the origin of the universe and life, no one god of any religious system can be better, powerful, or any other characteristic than any other god. Thus, stating my god is the true one is arrogance on the part of that religion for control of others. Because the language formation is based on the observation of life forms existing in two genders for procreation, the masculine gender is usually ascribed to the chief god in a system. The chief god is similar and known in some other religious systems as:

- Kṛṣṇa (Krishna) in Hindu[113]

- יַהְוֶה/אֱלֹהֵי (Yahweh/Elohim) in Judaism[114]

- Word was God in Christianity[115]

- Allah of Islam[116]

- Ormazd[117] or Ahura Mazda[118] of Zoroastrianism

- Olorun of West Africa Yoruba[119]

- Tirawa Atius of the central North American Pawnee Indians[120]

- Nesaru of the South Dakotan Arikara Indians[121]

- Kokomaht of the southwest American Yuma Indians[122]

- Nzame of the West Africa Bantu Fans[123]

- Taaroa of Tahiti[124]

- Gisoolg of the eastern Canadian Mik'Maq Indians[125]

In all cases, these names are either transliterations or translations from another language into English by writers who had to learn that language first. Different writers may use other names for these same creators, such as above: Ormazd by J. F. Bierlein and Ahura Mazda by Joseph Campbell for the chief God of the Zoroastrians.

These chief gods are thought to reside or arise in various locations in the universe. Some examples are:

- Heaven:
  - יַהְוֶה/אֱלֹהִים (Yahweh/Elohim) in Judaism[126]
  - Izanagi and Izanami in Japan[127]
- Sky:
  - Olorun of West Africa Yoruba[128]
  - Nesaru of the South Dakotan Arikara Indians[129]
- Water:
  - Great Ra in Egypt[130]
  - Eurynome, the Great Goddess of all things, in Greece[131]
- Underneath the earth:
  - Ungambikula of the Australian Aboriginal[132]
- Underneath the water:
  - Kokomaht of the southwest American Yuma Indians[133]

A few of the Creators have a polar antagonist, i.e., a duality exists of good and evil. Some examples are:

- Zoroastrianism has Ormazd, the Wise Lord and source of all that is good, and Ahriman, the source of all suffering, sin, and death.[134]

- The North American Algonquin Indian linguistic has Glooskap, the good, wise, and creative; and Malsum, the evil, selfish, and destructive.[135]

- The southwest American Yuma Indians have Kokomaht, the maker of all things good, and Bakotahl, the maker of all things evil.[136]

- Throughout the Judeo-Christian Scriptures, God is portrayed as providing all good things and Satan as the deceiver inciting evil deeds.[137]

Extending my observations to society in general, every society has a system that describes the society's truths of the:

- Reconciliation of waking consciousness to the tremendous and fascinating mystery of the universe.

- Total interpretative image in the waking consciousness of the powers sustaining the source in the universe.

- Enforcement of the moral order resulting from the interpretative image.

Another way to understand the mystery of the universe is:

- Humans desire to explain the world around them by individually asking themselves:

- Who am I?

- Where did the first man and woman come from, i.e., where am I from?

- Why am I here on earth?

- Where will I end up after death?

■ Humans realize from observing the universe that there is a force or source greater than humankind. Some religious systems' expressions are:

- This source creates the universe and humans in its image.

- Humans are for its service.

- Humans are rebellious against this source.

- The source sends a Savior.

- The Savior is from the source in the form of a man born either of a goddess or a human virgin woman.

- The Savior dies, i.e., shedding blood as a sacrifice, and resurrects for man's salvation.

■ Humans establish a religious system as the means to explain this source and nature:

- No culture has been observed not to have some form of belief system.

- The earliest systems tend to be polytheistic and later evolving into monotheistic systems.

- The same themes often appear in religious systems around the world, indicating a potential universal source.

- The religious system controls through its intertwinement with the political system as the masses, for most do not want to be excluded.

- Those who challenge the system are to be ostracized, exiled, or put to death.

■ The religious systems change in accordance with the natural world functioning becoming better understood:

- Religious systems may divide activities into sacred and profane, seeing them as contrasts instead of an integrated whole:

- Variation is observed in everything, meaning that there are opposing extremes in the contrasts.

- Religious systems often try to make absolutes only to find that there are variations that produce gray areas to the absolutes.

- From the sacred and profane comes what is acceptable and unacceptable behavior in a religious system.

- Religious systems are intertwined with the social and political life of a group.

- One enters the religious system by initiation or some ritual, such as infant baptism in some Christian denominations. Everyone else is excluded, needing to be converted into the system. Some being deemed abhorrent are not allowed into the group and may be deserving of death.

- Religious systems evolve as man understands more and more about the seen-unseen duality in the universe.

Thus, a Religion or Religious System may be defined as: a unified function of man-made beliefs, rituals, and practices relative to the origins of the universe and life in the universe and the humans' relationships in the universe. The unified function gives answers to the questions posed in the Spiritual Aspect and governs what one does in the other three aspects. The beliefs, rituals, and practices are primarily related through stories and some tenets and subsequently esteemed as sacred things, i.e., things set apart and forbidden from profane things, the three aspects forming the base of the triangular pyramid base (Figure 2). The beliefs, rituals, and practices unite all those who adhere to them into a single moral community and become controlling. Differences are not tolerated, resulting in coercion, exile, or death. Religious systems do evolve very slowly with much resistance because of these latter differences. Even if a religious system says that its sacred texts are god-written, it is man who interprets what a god wrote through human intermediaries.

The common perception that religion implies a Creator, particularly of Christian belief origin, is inconsistent with this definition. Denial of the existence of a god, as in atheism or Buddhism, is one of the two possible answers to the first question under the Spiritual Aspect and thus does not preclude them from being classified as religions.

Sacred Writings

- **Origins**

  As I read the lives of the significant religious system founders, I am not left with a sense of these people being on a search for the Creator or having a personal relationship with the Creator. However, I believe that these people sought a personal relationship with a Creator from my own personal journey. In this relationship, they experienced two worlds, the physical sensory of everyday life and its complementary, the spiritual world. The physical sensory world is characterized by limits, individuality, and time moving forward. In contrast, the spiritual world is characterized by relationships, everything is, and time does not exist, so that past, present, and future are one. Thus, sacred writings explain and show in physical sensory terms what the founders glimpsed in experiencing the spiritual world and how they related to physical life.

  Rather than search by themselves, most people tend to follow anyone who remotely suggests that they have a way to a relationship with their version of a Creator to satisfy the inner longing for that fulfillment. Thus, all the founders of world religions have found themselves with disciples or adherents. This discipleship then led to subsequent leaders often defining narrowly what is acceptable for behavior in society and the exclusion of anyone who would question or explore other avenues of relating spiritually to the Living Spirit.

It is generally accepted that the founders of religious systems taught orally and did not leave any writings. The religious systems that have survived have writings by disciples, often over thousands of years and then later defined as sacred. From these writings, a system of beliefs and rituals has been developed for the people of the society to follow.

The Judeo-Christian Scriptures were written over many centuries by many different writers from different cultures and languages. Thus, their history is borrowed from other sacred writings except that the writers mixed their own experiences of their version of a Creator directly speaking certain messages. However, the early accounts of the origins of the physical sensory world and the early history in the Judeo-Christian Scriptures have many parallels in cultures all around the world that cannot be explained by travel from one area of origin. My sense is that the Creator has instructed every people how that they should live. I also get this sense from the writings in the Hebrew Scriptures of the Minor Prophets' proclamations concerning Israel's city-states.

■ **Scriptural Inspiration**

At some point in time after the writings, the adherents defined them as sacred and authoritative for guiding one's life and the control of society. The sacred writings may even be said to be given directly by the Creator or God or divine entity. Many sects in Christianity consider the Judeo-Christian Scriptures the literal word of God. However, these sects are not alone in this concept; the Hindu religious system has writings called sruti that are considered divinely inspired and the very word of God. The sruti are the Vedas and some of the Upanishads, regarded as divinely revealed.[138]

The Judeo-Christian Scriptures comprise two parts: the Hebrew Scriptures and the Christian Scriptures. The divine inspiration of the Hebrew Scriptures appears to be founded by some Greek interpreters circa 300 BCE. Yet, other Greek interpreters during this time saw the Hebrew Scriptures as authored by humans with selected intervention by the Creator, who is most often called God. Both views continue with application to the Christian Scriptures as well.[139]

■ **Translational Issues**

The challenge to translators is to study and understand the development and changes in the ancient codes or symbols, which are termed languages, and then convert the original languages into understandable modern languages, such as English. These ancient writings provide challenges as each has its own syntax, word meanings, and writing styles of authors from different time periods and cultures. Because scholars have disagreements as to the meanings of these codes and symbols with all their possible nuances as well as newer understandings over time, there are many versions of the writings; for example, there are over 100 English versions of the Judeo-Christian Scriptures. You may find additional insights into word meanings and a passage's context in reading more than one version.

I experienced these in my own translations of the Gospels, James, and I John when inter-comparing the Greek texts:

- Textus Receptus[140] (Byzantine based Greek texts and basis for the King James Version)

- The Nestle-Aland Text[141] (based on Egyptian documents)

- The Majority Text[142] (based on all known ancient documents)

In my work[143], I used Classical Greek lexicons as Church Greek would not have existed at the currently accepted time of the writings. I wanted to have one English word for one Greek word; thus, my work is coded showing all the differences with annotations, as necessary. I found that there are words identified as strictly Christian, indicating editing and/or additions to the documents by later transcribers.

■ **Hermeneutics or Principles of Interpretation**

Because the Scriptures of religious systems explain and show in human terms how to live the spiritual life, they must be spiritually discerned through guidance by the Living Spirit for application to one's life. This spiritual discernment is critical since it is evident from the writings that these writers had experiences in the spiritual world and a personal relationship with the Living Spirit.

As you read or study the Scriptures of any religion, you automatically interpret the Scriptures according to your understanding and experiences in life. Interpreting the Scriptures requires you to understand:

- The history of the times of the authors.

- What it says through its various literary forms.

- How you may apply it for your spiritual growth.

For example, the literalism of the Bible became more pronounced with the Enlightenment in the 17th and 18th centuries CE, especially when science started to explain how the physical world functioned. The explanations were at odds with certain Judeo-Christian Scriptures because they didn't align with current interpretations. Biblical literalism is considered being a preoccupation with literal truth as a product of the scientific revolution.[144] These events also were eroding the power of the religious establishment to control the minds of the people. Thus, to assert the authority of the Judeo-Christian Scriptures, the religious leaders espoused literalism with at least two interpretations: one word for word and another allowing for literary forms. In these interpretations, the use of allegory, dogmatic, or rational methods is considered erroneous. All methods of interpretation may miss the deeper spiritual meaning embedded within the writings expressing the authors' deep personal relationship with the Living Spirit and authors' at-oneness with the universe as experienced by mystics.

Consider a Non-Religious Origin of the Universe and Religion

Throughout this writing, I have used the terms; Creator, Creative Force, Living Spirit for an entity that is not the god(s) of the religious systems. My terms are an attempt to define within my native English language that has no term adequately describing an entity in the unseen world that has not been anthropomorphized in terms of human genders and behaviors. Repeating my key aspects from my thoughts from Fundamental Questions: Defining the Living Spirit rephrased:

- **Where did this Living Spirit originate?**

  It has no gender as understood by humans in the earth plane. Also, it has no beginning and no end, i.e., it has always been and will always be.

- **Does this Living Spirit have a physical form?**

  Since it is invisible to the human eye, its physical form cannot be determined; therefore, it is omnipresent. Having the ability to make choices, one is an integral part of the Living Spirit, not a separate entity as postulated by major western religious systems.

- **Where does the Living Spirit's intelligence originate?**

  From observation of the intricate nature of physical life forms of which humans have only a small understanding of the mechanisms involved, the Living Spirit is omniscient, i.e., always has all the intelligence needed to create and sustain the universe according to some unknown processes of operation. What is observed are the results of this Living Spirit's actions, which have many dualities, and without these dualities, there could be no free will for making choices for spiritual learning. How the Living Spirit handles those when poor choices are made is unknown, and what happens to their circulation within the Living Spirit can only be conjectured.

- **How can I describe how the Living Spirit acts?**

  From observation, each human, barring physical and mental disabilities, can make by him/herself many different forms of the same thing, which is not observed in other animal species. However, how the Living Spirit performs any of the acts attributed to it is unknown. Human beings' creative abilities are residing in the Living Spirit.

- **Does the Living Spirit communicate with its human creations, and if so, how?**

  Intuition (feeling), dreams, visions, and rarely audible voice are the primary communications and, when heeded, have resulted in positive solutions to situations. These do not mitigate the use of literature, particularly what has been termed sacred literature in various cultures and religious systems.

- **Does the Living Spirit require worship?**

  Worshiping and asking anything from the Living Spirit is impossible. The most meaningful sense of wholeness in the Living Spirit is a deep sense of loving gratitude in one's inner being for life by doing one's part.

- **Why does the Living Spirit allow suffering?**

  Because dualities exist, suffering must also exist as a means for experiencing what it is to suffer and what it is not to suffer.

Now I explore this further in the final chapter with additional thoughts. Since I am a thinking entity, I have a thought for an idea that I would like to explore, act upon, or put into effect. This expression is termed "awareness." I then make a choice of whether to do, not do, or delay. This choice expression is termed "acceptance." If I choose to do, then this is termed "action." At this point then, I experience my thought through action.

Since I see myself as part of the Living Spirit who has endowed me with these characteristics, I give the Living Spirit these same qualities; otherwise, I would not have them since the Living Spirit has to be the source of all I am as being part of it. These expressions of the Living Spirit also explain the source of my consciousness, basic disposition, talents, and abilities that I was endowed with at the time of birth. I do not see these as having come from my parents. I see all other living creatures have the same source but a different expression of the Living Spirit. I would say the Living Spirit is experiencing itself through all aspects of creation.

If reincarnation happens, then we would need to forget the previous life, as the conditions now would be different from before, and our oneness with the Living Spirit. My late partner and I felt that we had been partners in a previous life. A previous life was vividly recorded in an article describing a young boy experiencing nightmares. His nightmares recount his previous life as a World War II fighter and being authenticated with the family survivors of this pilot.[145] Thus, the Living Spirit generally forgets part of itself in the expression it gives individually in its creation. However, it allows some, being new persons, to relive details of who they were before so that others may see each life as a continuous cycle of life and death at different times in the earth plane. Accounts like these confirm that one's consciousness is innate in the body and leaves the body at death.

If everything and conditions are an expression of the Living Spirit, then it experiences itself through all the actions of everything in the universe that it created, sustains in its current condition, and knows what the ending will be. All is without past, present, and future in the Living Spirit, as many mystics have experienced in transpsychic reality[17].[146] Thus, the various forms of religion all exist within the atheism-theism polarity. This everything and conditions expressed by the Living Spirit explain why there are many similarities among religious systems, the ones seeing humans separate from their god and those seeing humans as one with their god. Also, there is no perfection, only imperfection coinciding with polarity for experiencing life.

Conclusions Drawn from These Four Chapters

As humans find themselves in this plane termed earth, they seek answers to fundamental questions to understand the unseen world and their relationship to it and the seen world. From observations, they see themselves as having intellect and the ability to reason. The ability to reason is short-term as no real long-term future can be seen for how life will unfold, or what proposed actions will do, or thoughts as the variability is much larger than conceivable. For example, many deleterious effects that were not conceivable when products were introduced come to light years later. Likewise, religious systems fail to see the deleterious impact on people's psychological makeup with their proclamations of what life is.

In interactions with others, people find a wide range of thoughts that can be characterized as a series of polarities, with many variations between the two poles. One of the difficulties this presents is control, leading to suffering for others, not in the same area between the poles. Science

---

[17] Transpsychic reality is the highest form of consciousness as understood by mystics.

has developed significant destruction forces for control of others. Religion also plays a significant role in how societies operate and interact with other cultures, resulting in suffering and destruction. It appears that this is necessary for one to form his own worldview and interact with others. Thus, from my perspective, the purpose of life is to change one's consciousness over many reincarnations living in this plane in different bodies and cultures, thereby helping others likewise.

This chapter concludes 50+ years of my lived experimental journey for understanding the dichotomy between science and religion. I do not see these as mutually exclusive aspects of the seen-unseen polarity. They are the necessary parts of a larger unseen entity, my Living Spirit. What I do see is unacceptance of each other being interrelated in a larger worldview. Since the lived experimental journey is continuing as I write this book, I now explore the last few years of research of what a few others have said in the next and final chapter.

Chapter 5

Recent Concepts

Confirming Thoughts from Others

Since this chapter is completing the endeavor by looking at a few more recent researched works of the many out there, it contains many quotes (from a sentence to multiple paragraphs), some of which will have references within the quote, such as Wikipedia internet articles. These within references will be distinguished as footnotes using bracketed [ ] superscripted numbers indicating many more works that were not explored.[18]

Internet references are cited with the date of access as they are continually being reviewed and updated. Some may be no longer available or having been revised such that the referenced material is no longer in the current Internet article but was when accessed. This also applies to Internet references in previous chapters.

From the view that each person ever having lived was an iota expression of the Living Spirit at that time in history and in that culture, all quotes were not edited to conform to modern American English to respect that person and culture, whether deceased or living.

Because I mentioned the need to understand something about authors in Chapter 1, Communication, thus, when a quote is cited: the author's lifetime dates, if available, and their field of expertise when first referenced. The author(s) information will be inserted in bracketed italics. [ ]

Where I have inserted material for clarification, it is in { } unless I state changes are being made in the quoted material.

From my observations and study, there are two forms of events: historical and reproducible. Historical are those events, conditions, etc., which cannot be reproduced. For example, there is no way to reproduce myself or fossil finds. Reproducible events are those which can be reproduced, such as in a laboratory which we call science, yet most of these are following behaviors of something that cannot be reproduced, such as the creation of an electron. For example, I may think of bringing together chlorine and sodium atoms and making salt under the right conditions, yet I am only following the behavior of these atoms. Thus, one of the most challenging aspects of understanding a topic is the nuances of the terms one is using and reading.

The unseen world is part of us. One aspect of this is our consciousness, through which we have awareness of our own existence, sensations, thoughts, surroundings, etc. It is also thought of as the mind and to reside in the brain. Yet mystics and paranormal actions, such as out-of-body experiences, see this as an entity that separates from the body. It is thought to leave a body at death and returns in a new body when a person remembers an event or article from a previous life, or

---

[18]These footnote references will be reformatted for consistency and are updated for missing information for more completeness in this work. I have not attempted to read these many references nor have corrected formatting.

one has the sensation that someone died when they were not present with the person. Also, this identifies one as part of the unknown, undefined creator in various cultures and philosophies.

My experiences of interactions with the unseen:

- Prior to my going to study for the priesthood at 14, I played saying mass. During one of those times, I sensed an unseen entity entering my body, causing no physical or mental changes in me.

- I was not at my partner's bedside when he passed, yet I knew he had passed as he said to me, "Was I upset that it took so long?" I answered, "I was not going there."

- I had an out-of-body experience, most notably a sense of extreme happiness and joy as I went to explore the universe.

- I sensed my deceased adult family members visiting me while in a rehabilitation facility after my femur break from a fall. My mother and brothers were next to my bedside with dad in the line but aside and some distance back. Also, my deceased infant sister was not present.

- Being a reserved unemotional person suffering from childhood emotional neglect, as I was reading *Physics and Beyond Encounters and Conversations*[147] by Werner Heisenberg [*1901-1976, German theoretical physicist*[148]] concerning the development of quantum physics in 1920-30s in Germany, there was a sense of being part of that development. During the reading as I finished the third chapter, I started crying like I never cried. No other reading has brought such an emotional outlet[19]. If the iota of my consciousness was alive during that time[149], then, I had to have died to be reincarnated in 1940 for this lifetime. Was this previous possible life why I enjoyed that nuclear portion of my physics studies more than the others? In addition, was my strong aversion to being in the military related to this previous lifetime also?

- Since early childhood night dreams often tell a little of a previous lifetime, I wonder if during my early childhood, the night visions of burning buildings is related to my past lifetime by being burnt to death. At a school movie outing in which a child was going into a home that was implied to be burning, I bolted from the theater and sat in the lobby. There have been many other instances of violence in movies in which I absolutely must leave the area. Were all these instances related to a previous life or lives?

How we come to an understanding of what follows involves our usage of language forms, such as syntax, nuances, and semantics in the languages involved in the relating experiences and reporting the conduction and results of the studies. Keep in mind that the originator of oral or written communication interprets his/her thoughts in words that cannot convey all the nuances that are engendered in the thoughts. And secondly, the hearer or reader then further interprets what he/she hears or reads based on what the words mean in his/her own experiences in life. This

---

[19]Having inquisitive to find something in these chapters, I read them again months later, experiencing the same emotional outlet but not as strong. However, I could not find anything that should trigger this outlet. Thus, it must be buried in my subconscious from a past life during that time period.

communication will be true if both have similar shared experiences. However, within this culture, if one does not have similar shared experiences, one will not communicate with another unless they are willing to listen to find a related terminology.

Let us explore what a few others have said and relate them to my life's journey. Although I used computers at work and wrote technical booklets on Statistics, published in 1993, I was very reluctant to have one at home because of my workaholism, being a human doing starting in my teens and possibly earlier. This reluctance resulted from my philosophy that my talents and abilities were to be used for others which led to shortchanging what I really needed. I finally bought a computer in 1998 for home use. With the advent of the Internet, there has been an explosion of information available concerning ideas in every field of study that was not previously available, so I am using this tool in this portion of the paper.

Definition of Human Being

The following lists some key aspects that define others and me as humans derived from the Wikipedia article concerning Human:[150]

- "Humans are a terrestrial animal characterized by their erect posture and bipedal locomotion; high manual dexterity and heavy tool use as compared to other animals; open-ended and complex language use as compared to other animal communications; larger, more complex brains than other animals; and highly advanced and organized societies.[20][21]

- Because of the evolutionary process, a larger brain with a well-developed neocortex, prefrontal cortex and temporal lobes has enabled advanced abstract reasoning, language, problem solving, sociality, and culture through social learning. Humans use tools more frequently and effectively than any other animal; and are the only extant species to build fires, cook food, clothe themselves, and create and use numerous other technologies and arts.

- Humans uniquely use systems of symbolic communication as language and art to express themselves and exchange ideas. They organize themselves into purposeful groups. Humans create complex social structures composed of many cooperating and competing groups, from families and kinship networks to political states. Social interactions between humans have established an extremely wide variety of values[22], social norms, and rituals, which together undergird human society. Curiosity and the human desire to understand and influence the environment and to explain and

---

[20]Goodman M,; Tagle D,; Fitch D,; Bailey W,; Czelusniak J,; Koop B,; Benson P,; Slightom J (1990). "Primate evolution at the DNA level and a classification of hominoids". *J Mol Evol*. 30 (3): 260–66. Bibcode:1990JMolE..30..260G. Cham, Switzerland: Springer Nature Switzerland AG Gewerbestr. doi:10.1007/BF02099995. PMID 2109087.

[21]"Hominidae Classification". *Animal Diversity Web @ UMich*. Archived from the original on 5 October 2006. Ann Arbor: MI, University of Michigan—Animal Diversity Web, in the Literature, Science, and the Arts, Museum of Zoology, [Retrieved 25 September 2006].

[22]Marshall T. and Poe A. (2011). *History of Communications: Media and Society from the Evolution of Speech to the Internet*. Cambridge, IL: Cambridge University Press. ISBN 9780521179447

manipulate phenomena (or events) have motivated humanity's development of science, philosophy, mythology, religion, anthropology, and numerous other fields of knowledge.

■ The human brain perceives the external world through the senses, and each individual human is influenced greatly by his or her experiences, leading to subjective views of existence and the passage of time. Humans are variously said to possess consciousness, self-awareness, and a mind, which correspond roughly to the mental processes of thought. These are said to possess qualities such as self-awareness, sentience, sapience, and the ability to perceive the relationship between oneself and one's environment. The extent to which the mind constructs or experiences the outer world is a matter of debate, as are the definitions and validity of many of these terms."

The above is the understanding of many that have gone before me as well as contemporary with me. This understanding of a human being is true of every aspect of life as I only know and understand an iota of all that can be known and understood. Even though each person is considerably similar biologically except in reproduction functions, there are considerable variations in the chemical makeup and behavior of these chemicals in the bodily functions. In addition, I think there is a great deal more variation in the mental aspects alluded to in the above.

There is one aspect that appears to be missing in the above, and that is inquisitiveness. It is seen particularly early in children as they explore the world that they find around them. We, the caregivers, need to provide guidance so they do not to harm themselves while at the same time encouraging the activity. This inquisitiveness underlies all the rest of one's life as he/she goes about experiencing life's journey. In such mundane actions as buying groceries, we look at fruits to see if they are ripe or damaged; or which size do we buy. Our careers are centered on our interests in a topic, and our inquisitiveness leads to developing the topic further. My own work in writing this is centered on my inquisitiveness of this topic. To a lesser degree, I see inquisitiveness in animals, especially dogs wanting to meet other dogs or people when people are walking their dogs.

The question then becomes, "Where do these mental variations come from and where are they centered in humans?"

The Role of Consciousness

The mental aspects and the life force have been attributed mainly to spirit, soul, mind, and consciousness. Other terms may be used depending on one's background. Humans have been confronted with life and death from the early existence of human forms. This life-death reality has given rise to many different theories of which all are or may be partially true, for this is one of the historical aspects that cannot be duplicated and gives rise to all the philosophies and religions of the world. Even modern science is grappling with these facts of life. To get a sense of the issues, let us look at the definitions of these terms from the same source; the introductory paragraphs from Wikipedia are quoted:

■ **Spirit**[151]

"In folk belief, spirit is the vital principle or animating force within all living things. As far back as 1628 and 1633 respectively, both William Harvey and René Descartes speculated that somewhere within the body, in a special locality, there was a 'vital spirit' or 'vital force', which animated the whole bodily frame, such as the engine in a factory moves the machinery in it.[23] Spirit has frequently been conceived of as a supernatural being, or non-physical entity, for example, a demon, ghost, fairy, or angel.[24]

Historically, spirit has been used to refer to a "subtle" as opposed to "gross" material substance, as put forth in the notable last paragraph of Sir Isaac Newton's Principia Mathematica.[25] In English Bibles, "the Spirit" (with a capital "S"), specifically denotes the Holy Spirit.

The concepts of spirit and soul often overlap, and both are believed to survive bodily death in some religions,[26] and "spirit" can also have the sense of ghost, i.e., a manifestation of the spirit of a deceased person. Spirit is also often used to refer to the consciousness or personality."

- **Soul**[152]

"The soul, in many religious, philosophical, and mythological traditions, is the incorporeal essence of a living being.[27] Soul or psyche (Ancient Greek: ψυχή *psykhḗ*, of ψύχειν *psýkhein*, "to breathe") comprises the mental abilities of a living being: reason, character, feeling, consciousness, memory, perception, thinking, etc. Depending on the philosophical system, a soul can either be mortal or immortal.[28]

Greek philosophers, such as Socrates, Plato, and Aristotle, understood that the soul (ψυχή *psūchê*) must have a logical faculty, the exercise of which was the most divine of human actions. At his defense trial, Socrates even summarized his teaching as nothing other than an exhortation for his fellow Athenians to excel in matters of the psyche since all bodily goods are dependent on such excellence (Apology 30a–b).

In Judeo-Christianity, only human beings have immortal souls (although immortality is disputed within Judaism and the concept of immortality may have been influenced by Plato).[29] For example, the Catholic theologian Thomas Aquinas attributed "soul"

---

[23]Michels, John (January 18, 1884). *Science: Volume 3. Highwire Press, JSTOR:* Washington, DC: *American Association for the Advancement of Science.* p. 75. [Retrieved 10 October 2019].

[24]François 2009, p.187-197 Referred from: François, Alexandre (2008), *"Semantic Maps and the Typology of Colexification: Intertwining Polysemous Networks across Languages"*, in Vanhove, Martine (ed.), *From Polysemy to Semantic Change: Towards a Typology of Lexical Semantic Associations,* Studies in Language Companion Series, 106, Amsterdam, Netherlands: John Benjamins Publishing Co. pp. 163–215.

[25]Burtt, Edwin A. (2003). *Metaphysical Foundations of Modern Physical Science.* Mineola, New York: Dover Publications, Inc. p. 275.

[26]"spirit 2.a.: The soul of a person, as commended to God, or passing out of the body, in the moment of death." *Oxford English Dictionary (OED).* Oxford, UK: Oxford University Press.

[27]"soul". *Encyclopædia Britannica. 2010. Encyclopædia Britannica 2006 CD.* New York, NY: Charles Scribner's Sons. [Retrieved 13 July 2010].

[28]"soul (noun)". *Oxford English Dictionary (OED) online edition. Oxford English Dictionary (OED).* Oxford, UK: Oxford University Press. [Retrieved 1 December 2016].

[29]"Immortality of the Soul". *www.jewishencyclopedia.com. Archived from the original on 20 December 2016.* [Online of the original 1906 published by Funk & Wagnalls New York, NY] [Retrieved 14 December 2016].

(*anima*) to all organisms but argued that only human souls are immortal.[30] Other religions (most notably Hinduism and Jainism) hold that all living things from the smallest bacterium to the largest of mammals are the souls themselves (*Atman, jiva*) and have their physical representative (the body) in the world. The actual self is the soul, while the body is only a mechanism to experience the karma of that life. Thus, if we see a tiger then there is a self-conscious identity residing in it (the soul), and a physical representative (the whole body of the tiger, which is observable) in the world. Some teach that even non-biological entities (such as rivers and mountains) possess souls. This belief is called animism.[31]

The current consensus of modern science is that there is no evidence to support the existence of the soul when traditionally defined as the spiritual breath of the body. In metaphysics, the concept of "Soul" may be equated with that of "Mind" in order to refer to the consciousness and intellect of the individual."

- **Mind**[153]

"The mind is the set of cognitive faculties including consciousness, imagination, perception, thinking, judgement, language and memory, which is housed in the brain (sometimes including the central nervous system). It is usually defined as the faculty of an entity's thoughts and consciousness.[32] It holds the power of imagination, recognition, and appreciation, and is responsible for processing feelings and emotions, resulting in attitudes and actions.

There is a lengthy tradition in philosophy, religion, psychology, and cognitive science about what constitutes a mind and what are its distinguishing properties.

One open question regarding the nature of the mind is the mind–body problem, which investigates the relation of the mind to the physical brain and nervous system.[33] Other viewpoints included dualism and idealism, which considered the mind somehow non-physical.[34] Modern views often center around physicalism and functionalism, which hold that the mind is roughly identical with the brain or reducible to physical phenomena such as neuronal activity,[35] though dualism and idealism continue to have many supporters. Another question concerns which types of beings are capable of having minds (New Scientist 8 September 2018 p10). For example, whether mind is exclusive to humans, possessed also by some or all animals, by all living things,

---

[30]Eardley, Peter and Still, Carl (2010). *Aquinas: A Guide for the Perplexed.* London, UK: Continuum. pp. 34–35.

[31]"soul". *The Columbia Encyclopedia*, (6th ed. 2001–07). New York, NY: Columbia University Press. [Retrieved 12 November 2008].

[32]"mind – definition of mind in English | Oxford Dictionaries". *Oxford Dictionaries | English.* Oxford, UK: Oxford University Press. [Retrieved 8 May 2017].

[33]Clark, Andy (2014). *Mindware: An Introduction to the Philosophy of Cognitive Science.* Oxford, UK: Oxford University Press. pp. 14, 254–256. ISBN 978-0-19-982815-9.

[34]*ibid.*

[35]Smart, J.J.C. "The Mind/Brain Identity Theory". *The Stanford Encyclopedia of Philosophy (Fall 2011 Edition),* Edward N. Zalta (ed.). Palo Alto, CA: Metaphysics Research Lab, Stanford University.

whether it is a strictly definable characteristic at all, or whether mind can also be a property of some types of human-made machines.

Whatever its nature, it is generally agreed that mind is that which enables a being to have subjective awareness and intentionality towards their environment, to perceive and respond to stimuli with some kind of agency, and to have consciousness, including thinking and feeling.

The concept of mind is understood in many different ways by many different cultural and religious traditions. Some see mind as a property exclusive to humans whereas others ascribe properties of mind to non-living entities (e.g., panpsychism and animism), to animals and to deities. Some of the earliest recorded speculations linked mind (sometimes described as identical with soul or spirit) to theories concerning both life after death, and cosmological and natural order, for example in the doctrines of Zoroaster, the Buddha, Plato, Aristotle, and other ancient Greek, Indian and, later, Islamic and medieval European philosophers.

Important philosophers of mind include Plato, Patanjali, Descartes, Leibniz, Locke, Berkeley, Hume, Kant, Hegel, Schopenhauer, Searle, Dennett, Fodor, Nagel, and Chalmers.[36] Psychologists such as Freud and James, and computer scientists such as Turing and Putnam developed influential theories about the nature of the mind. The possibility of nonbiological minds is explored in the field of artificial intelligence, which works closely in relation with cybernetics and information theory to understand the ways in which information processing by nonbiological machines is comparable or different to mental phenomena in the human mind.[37]

The mind is also portrayed as the stream of consciousness where sense impressions and mental phenomena are constantly changing.[38][39]"

- ### Consciousness[154]

"Consciousness at its simplest refers to "sentience or awareness of internal or external existence".[40] Despite centuries of analyses, definitions, explanations and debates by philosophers and scientists, consciousness remains puzzling and controversial,[41]

---

[36]Leiter, Brian (January 20, 2016). "20 "Most Important" Philosophers of Mind since WWII". *Leiter Reports: A Philosophy Blog.* https://leiterreports.typepad.com/blog/. Chicago, IL: University of Chicago. [Retrieved on 25 March 2015]

[37]Klopf, Harry (June 1975). "A Comparison of Natural and Artificial Intelligence". *ACM SIGART Bulletin (52): 11–13.* New York, NY: Association for Computing Machinery. doi:10.1145/1045236.1045237.

[38]Karunamuni, N. and Weerasekera, R. (Jun 2017). "Theoretical Foundations to Guide Mindfulness Meditation: A Path to Wisdom". *Current Psychology (Submitted manuscript).* 38 (3): 627–646. New York, NY: Springer New York, LLC. doi:10.1007/s12144-017-9631-7.

[39]Karunamuni, N.D. (May 2015). "The Five-Aggregate Model of the Mind". *SAGE Open.* 5 (2): 215824401558386. Los Angeles, CA: SAGE Publications Inc. doi:10.1177/2158244015583860.

[40]"consciousness". *Merriam-Webster Dictionary.* Springfield, MA: G. & C. Merriam Co. [Retrieved June 4, 2012].

[41]Robert van Gulick (2004). "Consciousness". *Stanford Encyclopedia of Philosophy.* Palo Alto, CA: Metaphysics Research Lab, Stanford University.

being "at once the most familiar and most mysterious aspect of our lives".[42] Perhaps the only widely agreed notion about the topic is the intuition that it exists.[43] Opinions differ about what exactly needs to be studied and explained as consciousness. Sometimes it is synonymous with 'the mind', other times just an aspect of mind. In the past it was one's "inner life", the world of introspection, of private thought, imagination, and volition.[44] Today, with modern research into the brain it often includes any kind of experience, cognition, feeling or perception. It may be 'awareness', or 'awareness of awareness', or self-awareness.[45] There might be different levels or "orders" of consciousness,[46] or different kinds of consciousness, or just one kind with different features.[47] Other questions include whether only humans are conscious or all animals or even the whole universe. The disparate range of research, notions and speculations raises doubts whether the right questions are being asked.[48]

Examples of the range of descriptions, definitions or explanations are: simple wakefulness, one's sense of selfhood or soul explored by "looking within", or "nothing at all"; being a metaphorical "stream" of contents, or being a mental state, mental event or mental process of the brain; having phanera[49] or qualia[50] and subjectivity; being the 'something that it is like' to 'have' or 'be' it; being the "inner theatre" or the executive control system of the mind.[51]"

These thoughts about consciousness depends on the semantics and worldviews associated with the term 'consciousness'. Let us look further at some of these worldviews using the introductory definitions from the online Stanford Encyclopedia of Philosophy:

---

[42]Schneider, Susan and Velmans, Max (2008). "Introduction". *The Blackwell Companion to Consciousness*. Hoboken, NJ: Wiley. ISBN 978-0-470-75145-9.

[43]John Searle (2005). "Consciousness". *In Honderich T (ed.). The Oxford Companion to Philosophy*. Oxford, UK: Oxford University Press. ISBN 978-0-19-926479-7.

[44]Jaynes, Julian (2000) [1976]. *The Origin of Consciousness in the Breakdown of the Bicameral Mind (PDF)*. Boston, MA: Houghton Mifflin. ISBN 0-618-05707-2.

[45]Rochat, Philippe (2003). "Five Levels of Self-Awareness as They Unfold Early in Life" (PDF). *Consciousness and Cognition*. 12 (4): 717–731. Amsterdam, Netherlands: Elsevier Book Publishing. doi:10.1016/s1053-8100(03)00081-3.

[46]Carruthers, Peter (15 Aug 2011). "Higher-Order Theories of Consciousness". *Stanford Encyclopedia of Philosophy*. Palo Alto, CA: Metaphysics Research Lab, Stanford University. [Retrieved 31 August 2014].

[47]Antony. Michael V. (2001). "Is Consciousness Ambiguous?". *Journal of Consciousness Studies*. 8: 19–44. Exeter, UK: Imprint Academic.

[48]Hacker, P.M.S. (2012). "The Sad and Sorry History of Consciousness: Being, among Other Things, a Challenge to the "Consciousness-Studies Community"" (pdf). *Royal Institute of Philosophy Supplements*, Volume 70, July 2012, London, UK: Royal Institute of Philosophy. pp. 149-168. Published online by Cambridge, UK: Cambridge University Press. doi: https://doi.org/10.1017/S1358246112000082. [Retrieved 12 April 2012].

[49]Plural of phaneron, a philosophical term meaning, "That which is perceived by the mind, regardless of whether it corresponds to reality." Author's footnote insertion from Wiktionary to define the term. [Accessed 27 January 2022]

[50]Plural of quale, a philosophical term meaning, "An instance of subjective, conscious experience." Author's insertion from Wiktionary to define the term. [Accessed 27 January 2022]

[51] Farthing, G. (1992). *The Psychology of Consciousness*. Englewood Cliffs, NJ: Prentice-Hall. ISBN 978-0-13-728668-3.

- **Physicalism**[155]

"Physicalism is, in slogan form, the thesis that everything is physical. The thesis is usually intended as a metaphysical thesis, parallel to the thesis attributed to the ancient Greek philosopher Thales, that everything is water, or the idealism of the 18th Century philosopher Berkeley, that everything is mental. The general idea is that the nature of the actual world (i.e. the universe and everything in it) conforms to a certain condition, the condition of being physical. Of course, physicalists don't deny that the world might contain many items that at first glance don't seem physical — items of a biological, or psychological, or moral, or social, or mathematical nature. But they insist nevertheless that at the end of the day such items are physical, or at least bear an important relation to the physical."

- **Panpsychism**[156]

"Panpsychism is the view that mentality is fundamental and ubiquitous in the natural world. The view has a long and venerable history in philosophical traditions of both East and West and has recently enjoyed a revival in analytic philosophy. For its proponents, panpsychism offers an attractive middle way between physicalism on the one hand and dualism on the other. The worry with dualism—the view that mind and matter are fundamentally different kinds of thing—is that it leaves us with a radically disunified picture of nature, and the deep difficulty of understanding how mind and brain interact. And whilst physicalism offers a simple and unified vision of the world, this is arguably at the cost of being unable to give a satisfactory account of the emergence of human and animal consciousness. Panpsychism, strange as it may sound on first hearing, promises a satisfying account of the human mind within a unified conception of nature."

- **Dualism**[157]

"This entry concerns dualism in the philosophy of mind. The term 'dualism' has a variety of uses in the history of thought. In general, the idea is that, for some particular domain, there are two fundamental kinds or categories of things or principles. In theology, for example a 'dualist' is someone who believes that Good and Evil—or God and the Devil—are independent and more or less equal forces in the world. Dualism contrasts with monism, which is the theory that there is only one fundamental kind, category of thing or principle; and, rather less commonly, with pluralism, which is the view that there are many kinds or categories. In the philosophy of mind, dualism is the theory that the mental and the physical—or mind and body or mind and brain—are, in some sense, radically different kinds of thing. Because common sense tells us that there are physical bodies, and because there is intellectual pressure towards producing a unified view of the world, one could say that materialist monism is the 'default option'. Discussion about dualism, therefore, tends to start from the assumption of the reality of the physical world, and then to consider arguments for why the mind cannot be treated as simply part of that world."

- **Idealism**[158]

    "This entry discusses philosophical idealism as a movement chiefly in the eighteenth and nineteenth centuries, although anticipated by certain aspects of seventeenth century philosophy and continuing into the twentieth century. It revises the standard distinction between epistemological idealism, the view that the contents of human knowledge are ineluctably determined by the structure of human thought, and ontological idealism, the view that epistemological idealism delivers truth because reality itself is a form of thought and human thought participates in it, in favor of a distinction earlier suggested by A.C. Ewing, between epistemological and metaphysical arguments for idealism as itself a metaphysical position. After discussing precursors, the entry focuses on the eighteenth-century versions of idealism due to Berkeley, Hume, and Kant, the nineteenth-century movements of German idealism and subsequently British and American idealism, and then concludes with an examination of the attack upon idealism by Moore and Russell and the late defense of idealism by Brand Blanshard."

Bernardo Kastrup [*?-present, a Dutch philosopher (ontology, philosophy of mind) and computer engineer*[159]] in his book, *The Idea of the World*[160], a compilation of peer-reviewed articles that he wrote for various journals, discusses these from the interactions of the various philosophies and sciences and concludes that idealism is the fundamental ontological form for universal consciousness.

This statement confirms my development of universal consciousness in the first four chapters upon reading this book. Bernardo Kastrup has shown the mechanism for this view. We agree that each of us is a part of this universal consciousness and is an expression of a small part giving rise to the wide variations of thoughts and actions seen in people of the world, i.e., all the agreements and disagreements between people concerning life situations.

Although there is much scientific research regarding consciousness, it appears to me that they are denying their own thought processes in trying to categorize it in the mechanistic terms of western philosophy. In eastern philosophy, consciousness may be equated with the divine or western concept of the creator god.

My term Living Spirit comprises all these as there must be a universal energy that gives animation and a universal consciousness that gives meaning and the ability for reasoning and thinking. All the variations in thought and expression above do not appear to be happenstance. Instead, it appears as each expression is one small part of something greater. The variations appear to be necessary to give meaning to each person's life journey. Their expression is why they have come into this plane at their time. Western philosophical, scientific, and religious thought built on the mechanistic theory of the universe denies this concept. Yet, where do the reasoning and thinking originate for formulating the theories?

Homo Habilis ~2.3-1.4x10⁶ years ago	Homo Erectus ~1.8-0.3x10⁶ years ago	Archaic Homo Sapiens (Neandertals) ~0.23-0.04x10⁶ years ago	Early Homo Sapiens ~0.1-0.04x10⁶ years ago	Modern Homo Sapiens Starting ~0.04x10⁶ years ago
Increased Intelligence	Self-Awareness	Awareness of others' thoughts (theory of mind)	Introspection	Ability to Time travel (autobiographical memory)

Figure 5. The development of brain functions over time

Development of Today's Human Beings

Fuller Torrey [*1937-present, American psychiatrist and schizophrenia researcher*[161]], in *Evolving Brains Emerging Gods*[162], traces the development of the functioning of the brain over time, see Figure 5. Although he does not mention consciousness as part of human beings, the topics in the progression are the omnipresent universal consciousness being expressed at these stages of human development.[163,164] Another aspect of this development is the increasing size and complexity of the brain found in the specimens during this history, with Modern Homo Sapiens having the largest.

Theory of mind *is noted in Figure 5 at the stage of awareness of others. Based on the above definition of 'mind,'* The Wikipedia definition "Theory of Mind is the ability to attribute mental states — beliefs, intents, desires, emotions, knowledge, etc. — to oneself, and to others, and to understand that others have beliefs, desires, intentions, and perspectives that are different from one's own. Theory of mind is crucial for everyday human social interactions and is used when analyzing, judging, and inferring others' behaviors."[165]

With the development of the brain to handle more complex actions, there are some questions that come from these developments:

Where does this consciousness, ability to think, create, and all other actions come from, including the universe itself?

> From my religious upbringing as a Roman Catholic, I was taught that I was created in the image of God as a separate entity from Him, in this case, a religious God to be served. I have rejected this view of God, for I realize that I am part of universal energy and universal consciousness. My life is a small intimate expression of a universal infinite intelligence. This statement is more in line with Eastern Religions stressing oneness with the universe.
>
> Bernard Haisch [*?-present, a German-born American astrophysicist*[166]], in *The God Theory*[167], a book that resonated within me like no other book ever has but without the bursting forth emotions that burst forth during the reading of *Physics and Beyond Encounters and Conversations*.
>
> *The God Theory* concepts reinforce how my expression of the universal consciousness operates. Haisch states, "An infinite intelligence exists that acts in doing, rather than

just being. Its manifestations are none other than all of us and all the things we perceive around us. By doing, the infinite intelligence experiences itself, and thus knows our thoughts which are part and parcel of this infinite consciousness."[168] The term 'God' as used by Haisch is not to be confused with the God or god(s) expressed in any religious system. Haisch's term 'God' is the same as my Living Spirit; thus, I will replace Haisch's term God with Living Spirit to avoid confusion with the God term. Capitalized God too often connotes the Christian God, and I am attempting to avoid that connotation in the reader. The following are quotes from his book:

- **What does Haisch say about the implications of this Living Spirit?**

    ♦ "The Living Spirit cannot require anything from us for his own happiness.

    ♦ The Living Spirit cannot dislike, and certainly cannot hate, anything we do or are.

    ♦ The Living Spirit will never punish us because it would ultimately amount to self-punishment.

    ♦ There is no literal heaven or hell.

    ♦ These corollaries of the God Theory do not, however, relieve us of duty, responsibility, or ethical behavior. Quite the contrary. In fact, if you follow the God Theory to its logical conclusion, the golden rule in which we were all schooled—do unto others as you would have them do unto you[52]—becomes far more than a pious maxim."[169]

- **Further corollaries from these implications are:**

    ♦ "The purpose of life is experiences; Living Spirit wishes to experience life through you.

    ♦ Living Spirit desires your partnership, not your servility. Therefore, if you choose to praise and worship him it should be out of love not fear, and is for your own benefit, not his.

    ♦ The consequence of your negative actions is negative things happen to you, though not necessarily immediately; in this sense you create your own hell.

    ♦ Ultimately, your individual consciousness will be fully reunited with the infinite consciousness of Living Spirit; this can be characterized as heaven (or Hindu *Samadhi*).

    ♦ The point of a created universe is to experience it. Life is the Living Spirit made manifest.

---

[52]My note: "Humans have subverted this by considering others not worthy of love but scorn, i.e., be like us as we define it or be considered sinners and not worthy of our love, including some cases, worthy of death."

◆ It is in your own best interest to live life worthy of the creating intelligence, because that is the path to spiritual evolution and ultimate satisfaction.

◆ Your consciousness can be transformed, but it can never die. Your body and mind are merely tools for experiencing physical existence.

◆ The pursuit of experience through physical life is how the infinite mind actualizes its full potential."[170]

● **How does the Living Spirit create?**

◆ "Thought is the first level of creation…According to esoteric tradition, this thought became actualized into a metaphysical state…which in turn gave birth to the physical universe as we know it…Tradition is quite clear about an unseen realm that is called metaphysical, supernatural, or spiritual."[171]

◆ "Creation of the real (the manifest) involves subtraction from the infinite potential…The process of intelligent subtraction can also be interpreted as creation of polarity…simply a dualistic, this-versus-that relationship…Creation comes about when the Godhead {Living Spirit} selectively limits itself…it is intelligent and selective subtraction…We are nothing less than part of the Living Spirit, quite literally."[172]

◆ "But for Living Spirit to experience the game of creation, these beings need to think they are not Living Spirit. In other words, the Living Spirit, in the form of created beings, must forget its own infinity to accomplish its divine purpose of experiencing infinite potential actualized. Who are these created beings; everyone and everything else that is—seen and unseen."[173]

◆ The Living Spirit gives humans free will which is a small ability of the Living Spirit to act like it did in the creation process so that they can experience life through thinking, and acting on what they think, whether it is good or evil within the variations of the good-evil polarity or duality.[174]

● **Now let us look at some other sources:**

◆ Haisch states that according to esoteric traditions:

  ❑ "A desire arises in the unmanifest Living Spirit to experience itself from the point of view of "not Living Spirit".

  ❑ Living Spirit is infinite potential. But potential—infinite or not—is not the same as experience.

  ❑ The unmanifest and trans-infinite Living Spirit—greater than all and less than nothing—thus transforms into Living Spirit, the Creator; Living Spirit made manifest.

- ◻ Being becomes doing; the Living Spirit becomes relative. Out of the absolute, a realm of the relative is created.

- ◻ The realm of the relative is a realm of polarity {or duality}...Without polarity experience is impossible."[175]

♦ Kabbalists (followers of the ancient Jewish mystical tradition of Kabbalah) as stated in *The God Theory*:

- ◻ "It is possible to think of God {*Here I have retained the Jewish concept of God being implied; however, it reads closer to the Living Spirit than the generally held Jewish God concept.*} either as God himself with reference to his own nature alone or as God in His relation to His creation.

- ◻ No religious knowledge of God, even the most exalted kind, can be gained except through contemplation of the relationship of God to creation.

- ◻ God in Himself, the absolute Essence, lies beyond any speculative or even ecstatic comprehension.

- ◻ God in Himself, the absolute Essence, is absolute perfection without any distinction or differentiation. This nature is beyond comprehension by any created being.

- ◻ Mind is not "in" the realm of the Absolute, but it is the realm of the Absolute.

- ◻ The decision to emerge from concealment into manifestation and creation is not in any sense a process which is necessary consequence of the essence of the Absolute; it is a free decision which remains a constant and impenetrable mystery."[176]

♦ Neale Donald Walsh [*1943-present, started writing after traumatic experiences without a documented college education but open-mined to reading comparative theology[177]*] writes in *Conversations with God*[53] [*The italics are in the source.*]:

- ◻ "In the beginning, that which *Is* is all there was, and there was nothing else. Yet All-That-Is could not know itself—because All-That-Is is all there was, and there was *nothing else*. And so, All-That-Is ...was *not*. For in the absence of something else, All-That-Is, is *not*.

  This is the great Is/Not Is to which mystics have referred from the beginning of time.

---

[53]This is the same as Living Spirit used herein, not the anthropomorphized God of Christian religion.

Now All-That-Is *knew* it was all there was—but this was not enough, for it could only know its utter magnificence *conceptually*, not *experientially*. Yet the *experience* of itself is that for which it longed, for it wanted to know what it felt like to be so magnificent. Still, this was impossible because the very term "magnificent" is a relative term. All-That-Is could not know what it *felt* like to be magnificent unless *that which is not* showed up. In the absence of *that which is not*, that which IS, is *not*."[178]

◘ "The one thing All-That-Is knew is that there was *nothing* else, And so It could, and would, never know Itself from a reference point outside Itself. Such a point did not exist. Only one reference point existed,! and that was a single place within. The "Is-Not Is."; The Am-NotAm...

And so All-That-Is divided Itself—becoming, in one glorious moment, that which is *this* and that which is *that*. For the first time *this* and *that* existed, quite apart from each other. And still both existed simultaneously. As did all that was *neither*...

It is the nothing which holds the everything. It is the non-space which holds the space. It is the all which holds the parts...

From the No-Thing thus sprang the Everything—a spiritual event entirely consistent, incidentally, with what your scientists call the Big Bang theory."[179]

◘ "In rendering the universe as a *divided version of itself*, God[54] produced, from pure energy, all that now exists—both the seen and the unseen.

In other words, not only was the physical universe thus created, *but the metaphysical universe as well.* The Part of God which forms the second half of the Am/Not Am equation also exploded into an infinite number of units smaller than the whole. These energy units you would call spirits...

My divine purpose in dividing Me was to create sufficient parts of Me that I could know *Myself experientially*."[180]

◘ *"This is what your religions mean when they say that you were created in the "image and likeness of God." It does mean that our essence is the same. We are composed of the same stuff. We ARE the "same stuff"! With all the same properties and abilities—including the ability to create physical reality out of thin air.*

---

[54]This is also what the Hebrew Scriptures mean when they say God created everything.

My purpose in creating you, My spiritual offspring was for *Me* to know Myself as God. I have no way to do that *save through you*. Thus, it can be said (and has been said many times) that My purpose for you is that you should know yourself as *Me*,"[181]

☐ "Under the plan, you as pure spirit would enter the physical universe just created. This is because *physicality* is the only way to know experientially what you know conceptually. It is in fact, the reason I created the physical cosmos to begin with—and the system of relativity which governs it, and all creation.

Once in the physical universe, you, My spirit children, could experience what you know yourself—but first you had to come to know *the opposite*...

Taken to the ultimate logic, you cannot experience yourself as what you are until you've encountered what you are *not*. This is the purpose of the theory of relativity, and all physical life. It is by that which you are *not* that you yourself are defined."[182]

☐ "This is the goal of your soul. This is the purpose—to fully realize itself while in the body; to become the embodiment of all that it really is.

This is my plan for you. This is My ideal: that I should become realized through you. That thus, concept is turned into experience, that I might know my Self *experientially*.

The Laws of the Universe are laws that I laid down. They are perfect laws, creating perfect function of the physical."[183]

☐ "Now I will explain to you the ultimate mystery; your exact and true relationship to Me

YOU ARE MY BODY.

As *your* body is to *your* mind and soul, so, too, are you to My mind and soul. Therefore:

Everything I experience, I experience through you."[184]

☐ "Now in the case of ultimate knowing—in the case knowing yourself as the Creator—you cannot experience your Self as creator until you *create*. And you cannot create yourself until you un-create yourself. In a sense, you have first "not be" in order to be.

Of course, there is no way for you to not be who and what you are—you simply are that (pure, creative spirit), have been always, and always will be. So, you did the next best thing. You *caused yourself to forget* Who You Really Are.

Upon entering the physical universe, you *relinquish your remembrance of yourself.* This allows you to choose to be Who You Are, rather than simply wake up in the castle, so to speak."[185]

◘ "You are, have always been, and will always be, *a divine part of the divine whole, a member of the body.* That is why the act of rejoining to the whole, the returning to God, is called *remembrance.* You actually choose to re-member Who You Really Are, or to join together with the various parts of you to experience the all of you—which is to say, the All of *Me.*"[186]

♦ St. Augustine [*Augustine of Hippo 354-430, early Christian theologian, doctor of the Roman Catholic Church, and Neoplatonic philosopher*[187]], "articulated the view that time was not an infinite, preexisting condition and that space was not a limitless, preexisting void in which God made matter appear. Time and space came into being together at the creation of the material universe."[188]

● Ulrich de Balbian [*no lifetime dates available; Ph.D at Meta-Philosophy Research Center, Greater Paris Metropolitan Region, Philosophy, Metaphysics, Ontology, Epistemology, Metaphilosophy, Mysticism, Consciousness, Vedanta and Nondualism, Nonduality, Advaita, Meta-Philosophy, Cognitive Studies, Non-dualism Advaita, Nondualism, Metaphilosophie*[189]] in "Philosophy: the intersubjectivity of Sophos, the one and the real self"[190] discusses the many views of attempting to understand the universal (Cosmic) consciousness interrelationship within the writings of mystics, physicists, philosophers, religionists, psychologists, neuroscientists, and other scientists. Sophos is pure consciousness being equated to God, brahmin, etc. in various religious systems. Sophos is the same as the author's Living Spirit and what Haisch defined in the God Theory. They are all saying the uncreated source is being totally complete within itself lacking nothing, needing nothing, formless and simultaneously in every form. It is fully incomprehensible in human terms as it is fulfilled and fulfillment simultaneously. This can be said in other ways as all finitude and infinity simultaneously, everywhere and nowhere, Is and Not-Is, both this and that.

In my unpublished inter-comparison of three Greek texts of the Gospels I translated John 1:1-5 with this same thought:

[1]Within a first cause, the word was existing; and the word was existing towards the god, and a god was the word; [2]within a first cause, this was existing towards the god. [3]Throughout himself {the-ones} all became for-himself and otherwise-than himself not-even one became for-himself, which has become for-himself. [4]Within himself the real-and-genuine-life was existing, and the real-and-genuine-life was the light of the humanity. [5]And the light is appearing within the blackness, and the blackness did not comprehend it.[191]

■ **From these thoughts on how creation happens:**

We find that consciousness is what gives rise to emotions, thoughts, and actions. So, consciousness is also an innate aspect; what have others said?

- Haisch states: "*The God Theory* posits the existence of an infinite, timeless consciousness that, in religious terms, can be called "One God, {Living Spirit}." In principle, this One God is the same for all religions. It is worthy to note here that Kabbalah clearly—and wisely—states that all descriptions of God are necessarily wrong because an infinite, timeless consciousness can have no characteristics that can be properly translated into physical terms. Love, light, and bliss come the closest."[192]

- As a scientist studying the laws of physics and having the concept of talents and abilities coming with a human being when entering the earth plane, Haisch states in *The God Theory*: "We understand the rules because we made them up—not in the state we currently find ourselves as human beings, of course, but back when we were literally one with God {Living Spirit}, before God decided to temporarily become us."[193] This coincides with my concept of human beings having an iota of the universal consciousness in their lifetime.

- Paul Davies [*1946-present, English physicist*[194]] in *The Mind of God*[195] stated in the preface to the book. There is a group of scientists who do not endorse a conventional religion. Through his scientific work he has come to believe more and more strongly that the physical universe is not a purposeless accident. The physical universe is put together with an ingenuity so astonishing that there must be a deeper level of explanation as explained by earlier authors herein. Furthermore, Davies says to have realized the point of view that the mind—i.e., conscious awareness of the world—is not a meaningless and incidental quirk of nature, but an absolutely fundamental facet of reality. He does believe that we humans beings are built into the scheme of things in a very basic way and not necessarily the purpose for the existence of the universe.

- Sir Arthur Eddington [*1882-1944, English astronomer, physicist, mathematician, and philosopher of science*[196]] wrote:

    ♦ In *The Nature of the Physical World, Gifford Lectures 1927*: "I have tried to make the outlook reached in these lectures as coherent as possible, but I should not be greatly concerned if under the shafts of criticism, it becomes very ragged. Coherence goes with finality; and the anxious question is whether our arguments have begun right rather than whether they have had the good fortune to end right. The leading points which have seemed to me to deserve philosophic considerations may be summarized as follows:

        ❑ The symbolic nature of the entire entities of physics is generally recognized; and the scheme of physics now formulated in such a way as to make it almost self-evident that it is a partial aspect of something wider.

- ❑ Strict causality is abandoned in the material world. Our ideas of the controlling laws are in the process of reconstruction, and it is not possible to predict what kind of form they will ultimately take; but all the indications are that strict causality has dropped out permanently. This relieves the former necessity of supposing the mind is subject to deterministic law or alternately that it can suspend deterministic law in the material world.

- ❑ Recognizing that the physical world is entirely abstract and without 'actuality' apart from its linkage to consciousness, we restore consciousness to the fundamental position instead of representing it as an inessential complication occasionally found in the midst of inorganic nature at a late stage of evolutionary history.

- ❑ The sanction for correlating a "real" physical world to certain feelings of which we are conscious does not seem to differ in any essential respect from the sanction for correlating a spiritual domain to another side of our personality."[197]

♦ In *Science and the Unseen World, Swarthmore Lecture 1929*: "So far as I can judge, the kind of question to which I have exposed myself by coming here to-night is,

- ❑ "What is the proper orientation of a rational being towards that experience which he so mysteriously finds himself partaking of?

- ❑ What conception of his surroundings should guide him as he sets about the fulfillment of the life bestowed on him?

- ❑ Which of these strivings and feelings which make up his nature are to be nourished, and which are to be rejected as the seed of illusion?"

The desire for truth so prominent in science, a reaching out of the spirit from its isolation to something beyond, a response to beauty and art, an Inner Light of conviction and guidance—are these as much a part of our being as our sensitivity to sense-impressions. I have no ready-made answers for these questions. Study of the scientific world cannot prescribe the orientation of something which is excluded from the scientific world. The scientific answer is relevant so as concerns the sense-impressions interlocked with the stirrings of the spirit, which indeed form an important part of the mental content. For the rest, the human spirit must turn to the unseen world to which it itself belongs.

Some would put the question in the form,

◻ "Is the unseen world revealed be the mystical outlook a reality?"

Reality is one of the indeterminate words which might lead to infinite philosophical discussions and irrelevancies. There is less danger of misunderstanding if we put the question in the form

◻ "Are we, in pursuing the mystical outlook, facing the hard facts of experience?"

Surely, we are.

◻ "I think that those who would wish to take cognizance of nothing but the measurements of the scientific world by our sense organs are shirking one of the most immediate facts of experience, namely that consciousness is not wholly, not even primarily a device for receiving sense-impressions.""[198]

• Niels Bohr [*1885-1962, Danish physicist*[199]] as recorded by Werner Heisenberg during their conversations concerning their input into the development of quantum mechanics and atomic physics in *Physics and Beyond Encounters and Conversations*:

"We can admittedly find nothing in physics or chemistry that has even a remote bearing on consciousness. Yet all of us know that there is such a thing as consciousness, simply because we have it ourselves. Hence consciousness must be part of nature, or more generally, of reality, which means quite apart from the laws of physics and chemistry as laid down in quantum theory, we must all consider laws of a quite different kind."[200]

To find this quote, I read the book which affected me like no other book. As I finished Chapter 3, "Understanding" in Modern Physics (1920-1922), I started crying unlike any time in my adult life. I cannot find anything therein that participated this other than a deep memory in my subconsciousness from a previous life. Then later during more discussions of the development of quantum theory, I sensed that I was in college in Germany in the 1920-30s and being a participant in these discussions. I wonder if that is why in my physics studies, I felt at home in quantum mechanics and the study of atomic and subatomic structures. Mechanics was not an interesting study; however, electricity and magnetism were more interesting. None of these were as highly interesting as nuclear physics. Was my considering graduate school to study Chemical Physics, a new program at that time, related to these discussions? However, finishing my Bachelor of Science in Physics at midterm. It became impossible, so I was left with the desire to someday pursue the study.

• Sir James Jeans [*1877-1946 English physicist, astronomer, and mathematician*[201]] wrote in *The Mysterious Universe*:

"The concepts which now prove to be fundamental to our understanding of nature—a space which is finite; a space which is empty, so that one point differs from another solely in the properties of space itself; four-dimensional, seven- and more dimensional spaces; a space which forever expands; a sequence of events which follows the laws of probability instead of causation—or, alternately, a sequence of events which can only be fully and consistently described by going outside space and time—all these concepts seem to my mind to be structures of pure thought, incapable of realization in any sense which would properly be described as material."[202]

"To-day there is a wide measure of agreement which on the physical side of science approaches almost to unanimity, that the stream of knowledge is heading towards a non-mechanical reality; the universe begins to look more like a great thought, than like a great machine."[203]

- Haisch follows with this thought, "The idea of the physical world as a "great thought" is, in fact, a central concept of esoteric wisdom."[204]

- A quote from Barbara J. King [*1956-present, biological anthropologist*[205]], in *Evolving God*[206]:

  "Merlin Donald, [*1939-present a Canadian cognitive neuroscientist, psychologist, neuroanthropologist*[207]] in *A Mind so Rare*, believes consciousness to be the primary force in our mental life, and convincingly argues that it is constructed by culture." [55][208]

- In his book *The Idea of the World*, Bernardo Kastrup makes the case for unbounded universal consciousness as the primitive or fundamental versus the many other thoughts on what is ontological primitive. He discusses how living creatures and the world are part of this universal consciousness.[209] How we come to an understanding involves our usage of language forms, such as syntax, nuances, and semantics.

- Keith Ward [*1946-present, English Anglican priest, philosopher, and theologian*[210]], in *The Case for Religion* states:

"One of the strongest and best-known reasons is the perception that our consciousness cannot be reduced to or fully explained in terms of matter. We understand at least to some extent what the universe is like. We feel the intricate beauty of existence, and the subtle interweaving of fear and love, of despair and of hope, that forms the fabric of our lives. We feel ourselves to be free and responsible to act in ways that will harm or help the world in which we live, and the people among whom we live. The inward awareness of our own being is the most immediate thing that we know, and so we know in ourselves the transcendence of the material world, the irreducible reality of something that is

---

[55]The Merlin Donald in the book *A Mind So Rare: The Evolution of Human Consciousness* lays out this approach in Chapter 1 Consciousness in Evolution, subtopic How This Book Is Organized.

not bound by the limits of space, the primacy of awareness over objectivity, in which religious apprehensions of a supreme consciousness are rooted."[211]

- Matthew Webb [*I could not find any background information on this author*] in his article, "God and Consciousness (we are one)" states:

"Through human self-reflection, the universal force that is consciousness also self reflects to some degree. This is so because there are no real boundaries between human beings and Nature, other than those we impose. Humanity is an extension of nature and natural laws. This is why we are a medium for That Which Creates and Understands in the Universe.

As a part of this creative Cosmos, we too create, self-reflect, and come to know the Creator Within. This is why one of the very best ways to know God, is through the knowing of self. Our daily reality is not only a matter of connection with God or Universal Consciousness. We are in fact, actually composed of the same essence as that which is called God. In essence, we are as "cells in the infinite body of God". There are no ultimate boundaries in the cosmos. The universe is actually composed of the very same underlying substance in all places, peoples, and times. We are all "made of God", or in other words, Consciousness...

Subjects such as study of the soul, of unified field implications, psychic phenomena, group mind phenomena and the underpinnings of Natural Law, are all fundamental keys to the understanding of life. A striking feature of such studies is their inherently unifying nature. Such fundamental knowledge encompasses all of religion, science, philosophy and day to day living, simultaneously. If one were to summarize all of these pillars of wisdom under one comprehensive heading, it would have to be under the category of consciousness. This is why a knowledge of consciousness breaks all ideological and social boundaries. Through it, all apparent divisions in the world are rendered essentially meaningless. In the realization of self as consciousness, we may see that the conclusions of scientists, theologians, and philosophers of all ages, (past and present) have been derived from the same fundamental reality. In all the great philosophies and religions of history, consciousness and its particulars form the common thread of Truth, that is woven into the fabric of the world's rituals and practices.

It is within the context of consciousness where Eastern and Western thinking merge. It is here that the views of Native peoples worldwide find communality, and where past, present, and future paradigms cannot truly be distinguished from one another. In this context, the phrase "We are One" is given concrete meaning. Whether this essence be referred to as the Great Spirit, Gaia, the Goddess, Jehovah, the Earth Mother, the All-Seeing Eye of Existence, Consciousness, Unified Field Dynamics or simply God, is of no matter. What is of importance is the real understanding and self-mastery of this common

Table 3. Contrasting Eastern and Western Worldview Duality		
System Facets	**Eastern**	**Western**
The Absolute: The Unknowable Originator	Immanent, within the seeker	Transcendent, supernatural; unearthly
The Ultimate: what is to be achieved through life journey	Tends to be philosophical and less theistic, something transpersonal, goals are awareness and unity. The ultimate is beyond the Absolute, yet locked within the heart of every being	God, The Absolute, is to be known, obeyed, and creating a loving and vital relationship with it
The Divine: who is the sacred or holy	The divine resides in every person	The Divine is a person by anthropomorphizing The Absolute

essence. The mastery of the particulars of consciousness, and the responsible use of that knowledge in daily affairs, is the surest remedy for modern ills…

The study and greater Mastery of consciousness, (Intent, awareness and energy) is the ultimate life focus."[212]

The statement "In essence, we are as "cells in the infinite body of God"." mirrors my expression that like the cells in the human body; we, humans, are the cells of the Living Spirit.

- Diane Morgan [*1947-present, adjunct professor of religion and philosophy*[213]] in her book, *The Best Guide Eastern Philosophy & Religion*[214], relates these relationships between western and eastern concepts. Table 3 is adapted from this book and my journey.

These thoughts on consciousness relate to my concept that our talents and abilities are an iota of the universal consciousness and thus innate in us from conception. The physical body is only the vehicle for expressing these in this plane of the universe.

- Carl Jung postulated that we have a blueprint at birth for our lives and he characterized this by Archetypes. The article "The Jungian Model of the Psyche[56]" summarizing the work of Carl Jung [*1875-1961 Swiss psychiatrist and psychoanalyst*[215]] states the following:

---

[56]This is a recent post on the Journal Psyche without authors identified or the date of post. The welcome to Journal Psyche, http://journalpsyche.org/welcome/ [Accessed on 7/16/2021] states the following: Welcome to the original site of Journal Psyche. Established in 1992, Psyche was a free, online publication exploring the nature of consciousness and its relation to the brain. Psyche was an interdisciplinary journal addressing the problem of consciousness from the perspectives of psychology, philosophy, cognitive science, neuroscience, anthropology, artificial intelligence, and physics. Psyche was founded by Patrick Wilken and it was one of the first online academic journals published on the Internet. Dr. Wilken was an original editor of Psyche and in 2003 he was joined by Timothy Bayne. In 2007 the Association for the Scientific Study of Consciousness (ASSC) assumed the ownership of Psyche and in 2008 the journal was re-launched as an official publication of ASSC. At that time, Patrick Wilken parted ways with ASSC and Gabriel Kreiman become the new editor-in-chief. In 2010 ASSC made a difficult decision to abandon Psyche. During almost 20 years of its existence, Psyche published a large number of

♦ The psyche

"Among Jung's most important work was his in-depth analysis of the psyche, which he explained as follows: "**By psyche I understand the totality of all psychic processes, conscious as well as unconscious**," separating the concept from conventional concept of the mind, which is generally limited to the processes of the conscious brain alone.

Jung believed that the **psyche is a self-regulating system**, rather like the body, one that seeks to maintain a balance between opposing qualities while constantly striving for growth, a process Jung called "**individuation**".

Jung saw the psyche as something that could be divided into component parts with complexes and archetypal contents personified, in a metaphorical sense, and functioning rather like secondary selves that contribute to the whole…

♦ The collective unconscious

The theory of the collective unconscious is one of Jung's more unique theories; Jung believed, unlike many of his contemporaries, that all the elements of an individual's nature are present from birth, and that the environment of the person brings them out (rather than the environment creating them). Jung felt that people are born with a "blueprint" already in them that will determine the course of their lives, something which, while controversial at the time, is fairly widely supported to today owing to the amount of evidence there is in the animal kingdom for various species being born with a repertoire of behaviours uniquely adapted to their environments. It has been observed that these behaviours in animals are activated by environmental stimuli in the same manner that Jung felt human behaviours are brought to the fore. According to Jung, "the term archetype is not meant to denote an inherited idea, but rather an inherited mode of functioning, corresponding to the inborn way in which the chick emerges from the egg, the bird builds its nest, a certain kind of wasp stings the motor ganglion of the caterpillar, and eels find their way to the Bermudas. In other words, it is a 'pattern of behaviour'. This aspect of the archetype, the purely biological one, is the proper concern of scientific psychology."

Jung believed that these blueprints are influenced strongly by various archetypes in our lives, such as our parents and other relatives, major events (births, deaths, etc.), and archetypes originating in nature and in our cultures (common symbols and elements like the moon, the sun,

---

articles and reports for a diverse academic audience. It advanced scientific studies of consciousness and brought together many researchers in different fields of study. This site is a tribute to Journal Psyche.

water, fire, etc.). All of these things come together to find expression in the psyche and are frequently reflected in our stories and myths.

Jung did not rule out the spiritual, despite the biological basis he described the personality as having; he also felt there was an opposing spiritual polarity which greatly impacts the psyche...

♦ **Individuation**

Individuation, to Jung, was the quest for wholeness that the human psyche invariably undertakes, the journey to become conscious of his or herself as a unique human being, but unique only in the same sense that we all are, not more or less so than others.

Jung did not try to run from the importance of conflict to human psychology; he saw it as inherent and necessary for growth. In dealing with the challenges of the outside world and one's own many internal opposites, one slowly becomes more conscious, enlightened, and creative. The product of overcoming these clashes was a "symbol" which Jung felt would contribute to a new direction where justice was done to all sides of a conflict. This symbol was seen as a product of the unconscious rather than of rational thought, and carried with it aspects of both the conscious and unconscious worlds in its work as a transformative agent. The development that springs from this transmutation, which is so essential to Jungian psychology, is the process of individuation."[216]

In "Jung and his Individuation Process"[217] the individuation i.e., becoming the Self, may be summarized:

◘ It encompasses the philosophical, mystical, and spiritual areas of the human being.

◘ It is the achievement of self-actualization through a process of integrating the conscious and the unconscious.

◘ The process is the integration of the ego (consciousness) with the personal consciousness with its unconsciousness part, and collective consciousness.

● Paul Davies poses the questions in *The Mind of God*, "Why should human beings have the ability to discover and understand the principles on which the universe runs?"[218] The answer in *The God Theory* is simple. We understand the rules because we made them up—not in the state we currently find ourselves as human beings, of course, but back when we were literally one with God {Living Spirit}, before God decided to temporarily become us."[219]

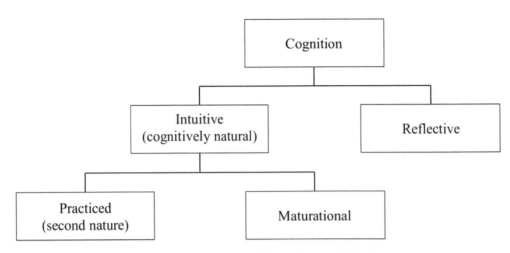

Figure 6. The types of cognition observed in humans

- **Since our consciousness is thought to reside in the brain or mind, what do others say about its functioning?**

  Robert N. McCauley, [*1952-present, Professor of Philosophy and one of the founding fathers of the cognitive science of religion*[220]], writes in *Why Religion Is Natural and Science Is Not* concerning cognition: Although McCauley does not state that consciousness is expressed through the concept of cognition, he shows the types of consciousness is expressed through the concept of cognition. The types of cognition and their interrelationship are represented in Figure 6.[221]

  Two types of cognition, maturationally and practiced naturalness, explain the development of human abilities and the difference between religion and science:[222]

  - "Perception, cognition, and action that possess maturational naturalness are first nature; capacities that possess a practiced naturalness are second nature."[223]

  - Maturationally naturalness explains normal human development and is associated with religion[57] because of these first nature characteristics:

    - "Occurs in early childhood and is not recalled.

    - Is **not**[58] associated with particular artifacts.

    - Does **not** require older humans who already possess these skills, to consciously structure the learning environment to any assistance or to instruction they may offer.

    - Does **not** turn either on inputs that are particular to a culture or (even) on inputs that are culturally distinctive."[224]

---

[57]The broad sense of how one sees their connection to the unseen world depicted by the Spiritual Aspect in Figure 2.

[58]Author's emphasis to help differentiate this sequence with the next sequence that is the same except the opposite polarity.

- Practiced naturalness is acquired skills and is associated with science because of these second nature characteristics:

    - Occurs starting around the age of five.

    - Is associated with particular artifacts.

    - Requires older humans, who already possess these skills, to consciously structure the learning environment to any assistance or to instruction they may offer.

    - Turns either on inputs that are particular to a culture or (even) on inputs that are culturally distinctive.[225]

- "Differentiate the maturational from the practical naturalness of actions:

    - No one invented them.

    - Their emergence never depends upon artifacts (though some cultures have developed artifacts to facilitate their acquisition).

    - Humans undertake them spontaneously.

    - A few have general forms that we share with other species.

    - Their acquisition does not depend upon explicit instruction or specially structured learning environments, and it does not turn either on inputs that are particular to a culture or (even) inputs that are culturally distinctive."[226]

- "The architectural and operational principles governing the systems and process in the brain that manage bodily movement also anchor humans' cognitive achievements. This suggests:

    - That most of humans' maturationally natural forms of knowledge will arise comparatively early.

    - That they will address some of the most basic problems that humans face (like those that are solved by chewing and walking).

    - That they will prove to be so ubiquitous that their emergence counts as normal development."[227]

- "The cultural representations that are cognitively and psychologically appealing constitute the primary selection process {rather than logic}…Representations get transmitted when they have the following properties…

    - Recognizable and attention-grabbing…

    - Easily remembered…

    - Functional…enable people to deal with problems that they face… turns primarily on its inferential potential…

    - Communicable…

- ◆ Motivate people to invest time and energies to broadcast to others."[228]
- Maturationally natural cognitive systems
  - ◆ Language[229]: infants make sounds that adults learn to interpret the meaning before formal language of the adult is expressed without the adult teaching it. Just normal hearing is enough for the young child to begin to express.
  - ◆ Contaminant avoidance[230]
    - ▫ Contaminant is capable to transmitting any characteristic of that source.
    - ▫ Any contact is capable of transmitting the peril it harbors.
    - ▫ Only one contact is capable of fully contamination. The source need not be perceptible.
    - ▫ Consequences tend to be permanent.
    - ▫ Negative effects are more potent than positive ones.
  - ◆ Theory of mind[231]
    - ▫ There are agents (human or non-human) to do actions.
    - ▫ These agents have minds like humans.
    - ▫ These agents interact with other agents or humans.

- ■ **Observation of Consciousness in Animals**

Having grown up on a farm and observing animals, it is evident that they have a consciousness and a neurophysiology as well, often called instinct. A calf born knows where the udder is to get nourishment. The chick coming out of the shell knows how to find food. No mature animal shows its newborn(s) how to survive, unlike humans where the mother must place the baby to the breast so that it can feed itself.

- Animals have a consciousness and a behavior like humans was demonstrated in the following instances:
  - ◆ Dad had bought a second cow, a Holstein. We had put the earlier cow, a Guernsey, in her station; however, when Holstein entered the stable, she went to the right and along the sides until she met Guernsey already tied in her allotted station. There was one station on the other side of Guernsey. We had to move Guernsey so that Holstein could have the first station. Holstein always had to be put in first.
  - ◆ Observing the animals in eating, they would choose what they wanted from different spots. They had a sense when grazing for what was good for them and what was not. We also had to be certain that the pasture was providing enough food for them. Since we rotated crops, we changed the pasture locations to provide enough food for them. Because

the cows didn't understand human language, we could not tell the cows the pasture had changed. They tend, like humans, to keep doing the same thing until a forced change. To train them to move to the new location, we separated the old location by a low voltage electric fence. When the cows touched the fence, they got an electrical shock causing them to back away. Thus, they learned that the new area was their pasture now.

- In *Evolving God*, Barbara King studied ape and monkey behavior and related it to human ancestral development.[232] Although consciousness was not mentioned, it is evident the monkeys and apes had a consciousness related to their social behavior and life.

- In *The Ancient Origins of Consciousness*, Todd E. Feinberg [*no lifetime dates available, Professor of Psychiatry and Neurology*[233]], and Jon M. Mallatt [*no lifetime dates available, Associate Professor Zoology (Biological Sciences) and Medical Education*[234]], find that consciousness can be understood and solved through combining evolutionary, neurobiological, and philosophical approaches.[235]

- Sergio Rossoni [*no lifetime dates available, Zoology Ph. D. student at University of Cambridge*[236]], and Jeremy E. Niven [*no biography is available, Principal Investigator The Laboratory of Evolutionary Computational Neuroscience, University of Sussex, UK*[237]] detail the actions of the praying mantis in capturing prey for its food in "*Prey Speed Influences the Speed and Structure of the Raptorial Strike of a 'Sit-And-Wait' Predator,*"[238] The praying mantis has the ability to adjust its tentacles' movement depending on the speed of the prey; thus it has observation, and rudimentary thinking skills. The article also mentioned that if there is a failure, it makes an adjustment. Thus, even insects and all forms of life have a consciousness and a neurophysiology similar to humans only limited by what the universal consciousness has endowed them with according to its specie.

- With global warming occurring, we are also observing the animal kingdom of all species and plants adapting to the change by moving from their current necessary climate conditions to their new areas with the same conditions because their current conditions are becoming too warm for their life. Thus, in the Northern Hemisphere, they are tending to move further north or becoming extinct. This movement has been happening for several decades, as I remember the reports. National Geographic published in 2017 a report, "Half of All Species Are on the Move—And We're Feeling It. "[239]

■ Observation Consciousness and the Paranormal/Supernatural

Paranormal and supernatural are much more western concepts than eastern because most western systems are based on the physical senses as to what is perceived as reality. M. Admin at Knowledgenuts [*I could not identify who this person is.*] states, "'Paranormal' refers to something that is not understood by current scientific knowledge; there's the potential that something paranormal will someday be explained scientifically, and there's a likelihood there's a good, natural explanation for it. 'Supernatural' refers to a phenomenon that is beyond our capability to understand, now and simply forever, because it just does not operate under our rules."[240] [59] RaK [*I could not identify who this person is.*] posted paranormal phenomena examples are given in Table 4[241]. The supernatural is beyond our capabilities of understanding. Instead, it is in the divine or otherworldly realm, such as a god, a guardian angel, a soul, a miracle, etc. Depending on one's viewpoint, some of the phenomena in Table 4 may be supernatural rather than paranormal.

Table 4. Examples of Paranormal Phenomena		
Mental		
Automatic Writing	Near Death Experiences	Premonitions
Clairaudience	Out-of-Body Experiences	Psychometrics
Clairvoyance	Past-life Experiences	Remote Viewing
Dowsing	Possession	Telepathy
ESP (Extrasensory Perception)	Precognition	
Physical		
Dematerialization	Poltergeist Activity	Psychic Photography
Levitation	Psychic Healing	Psychokinesis
Materialization		
Miscellaneous		
Alien Abductions	Ghosts	Stigmata
Animal Mutilations	Miracles	U.F.O.
Crop Circles		

In many cultures, ghosts are thought of as deceased relatives, implying that a part of them is still in this plane after separation from the physical body at death.

- Could this be a form of their consciousness remaining in this plane?

- Was my experience of my deceased adult members of my immediate family appearing to me as I lay in bed at the rehabilitation facility recovering from my broken femur surgery not a form of their consciousness?

- Was a part of my late significant other still in this plane when I sensed him saying to me after leaving his body, "Was I upset that it took so long?"

If everything must be proven by the scientific process, then I cannot be proven to exist because it is impossible to reproduce me. The only way we know someone has existed is by historical documentation of that person. Thus, are we deluding ourselves when we only want to look at the "seen" part of the "seen-unseen" polarity, and everything must be accounted for only by our sensory faculties, which is the basis for our scientific processes?

■ Interconnectedness

Western philosophy and science, and to some extent religion, has been built on the premise of a substance being comprised of building blocks, each being smaller.

---

[59]This definition and the examples in Table 4 are common in a review of literature by various authors.

However, with the development of quantum mechanics and particle physics, we now have arrived at that everything is interconnected at the energy level. In fact, particle physics describes everything in terms of energy. Mass is not used as it cannot be measured. The current smallest particle is the hadron which is described by Fritjof Capra [*1939-present, an Austrian-born American physicist, systems theorist, and deep ecologist*[242]] in *The Tao of Physics* as:

> "The picture of hadrons that emerges from the bootstrap theory is often summed up in the provocative phrase, 'every particle consists of all other particles.' It must not be imagined however, that each hardon contains all the others in a classical, static sense. Rather than 'containing' one another, hadrons 'involve' one another in the dynamic and probabilistic sense of S-matrix theory, each hadron being a potential 'bound state' of all sets of particles which may interact with one another to form the hardon under consideration. In that sense, all hadrons are composite structures whose components are again hadrons, and none of them is any more elementary than the others. The forces holding the structures together manifest themselves through the exchange of particles, and these exchanges are again hadrons. Each hadron, therefore, plays three roles, it is the composite structure, it may be a constituent of another hadron, and it may be exchanged between constituents and thus constitute part of the forces holding a structure together. The concept of 'crossing' is crucial for the picture. Each hadron is held together by forces associated with the exchange of other hadrons in the cross channel, each of which is in turn, held together by forces to which the first hadron makes a contribution. Thus, 'each particle helps to generate other particles, which in turn generate it.'[60] The whole set of hadrons generates itself in this way or pulls itself up, so to say, by the 'bootstraps'. The idea, then, is that this extremely complex bootstrap mechanism is self-determining, that is, that there is only one way in which it can be achieved. In other words, there is only one possible self-consistent set of hadrons—the one found in nature."[243]

Thus, they can be said to contain one another. Taking this to the human physical level of our consciousnesses, are we all not like a hadron in the Living Spirit?

The Avatamsaka Sutra[244], The Flower Ornament Scripture, is one of the highest held scriptures among all of Buddhism expresses consciousness similar to the hadron:

- All is in one and one is in all without any change in size, of either, such as speck of dust or atom contains the entirety of the world while remaining its size as a speck of dust or atom.

- Everything interpenetrates everything, and everything reflects everything within itself.

- There is a cosmic Buddha whole contains all other Bhuddas who contain all other Buddhas within themselves.

---

[60]G, F. Chew, M. Gell-Mann and A. H. Rosenfeld. 'Strongly Interacting Particles.' Scientific American, vol. 210 (February 1964), p. 93.

- In true existence, past, present, and future are one, i.e., there is no time.[61]

This concept of one containing another has been applied by Tony Nader [*no lifetime dates available, Lebanese neuroscientist, researcher, author of Human Physiology: Expression of Veda and the Vedic Literature, and leader of the Transcendental Meditation movement*[245]], in a paper titled, "Consciousness Is All There Is: A Mathematical Approach with Applications" states:

> "There is a consciousness that exists by itself, independent of any personal owner of the consciousness. Furthermore, this consciousness is all there is, and this consciousness is itself conscious. Since it is conscious, it can assume the three roles of the observer, the observing, and the observed."[246]

More and more in scientific research, we are finding that the observer is influencing the outcome, that is, we are not as independent of our experiments as we think.

Becky Storey [*no lifetime dates available; contributing writer on mental health and wellbeing at Learning Mind*[247]] in "What Is a Spiritual Atheist and What It Means to Be One"[248] quotes Neil deGrasse Tyson [*1958-present; American astrophysicist, planetary scientist, author, and science communicator.*[249]] saying, "We are all connected; To each other, biologically. To the earth, chemically. And to the rest of the universe, atomically."[62]

My graphic (Figure 2) of human aspects reflects this interconnectedness. A universal consciousness is present because all people are interconnected within the graph through every individual. In fact, I am interconnected to all who have lived before me and not just those living today where they are on earth. I could not live as I do except for what they have passed on to me in the past and the present times through their interactions with others.

■ Is Spiritual Consciousness Innate?

From my observations, this is the apex of my triangular pyramid and is coupled with the void (see Figure 2 and explanations).

Taking universal consciousness as the primitive and humans each have a small part of that universal consciousness, let us look at the concept of innate spirituality.

The word "spirit" is derived from Latin *spiritus*, which means breath; in Greek, it is *pneuma*; and in Hinduism, the word is *atman*[250,251]. However, "*ātman* is often translated as soul but better translated as "Self" as it refers to pure consciousness (Hindu,

---

[61]This the same as The Living Spirit herein and mystic's transpsychic experiences. Also, This is the condition of one's iota of universal consciousness return upon death.

[62]The Neil deGrasse Tyson quote may be found on other sites such as https://www.azquotes.com/author/14904-Neil_deGrasse_Tyson.

Purusha[63]) or witness consciousness (Hindu, Sakshi {Witness}[64]), beyond identification with phenomena."252 "Sakshi or Shiva, along with Shakti (will/energy/motion), represents the Brahman, the totality itself in its most fundamental state, the concept of all mighty, revealed in ancient philosophical texts of Hinduism."253 This statement corresponds to my concepts of universal consciousness and universal energy providing life. The triad of experiencer, experiencing and experienced expressed in Sakshi corresponds to Tony Nader's three roles of the observer, the observing, and the observed.

David Hay [*1935-2014, a pioneering researcher into the study of contemporary reports of religious experience*254], in *Something There, The Biology of the Human Spirit* states:

- "Young elementary school children expressed a sense of spirituality expressed through:

    ♦ Awareness of the Here-and-Now

    ♦ Awareness of Mystery

    ♦ Awareness of Value"255

- "Spirituality is about relationship. It is about being profoundly in communion, body and soul, with the totality into which we find ourselves 'thrown.'"256

- "Rapidly accumulating scientific evidence suggests that spiritual awareness is a permanent feature of our biology…The problem is that very often it is isolated, secret, or privatized spirituality…Relational consciousness… and its isolation is permanently in danger of being suppressed or even repressed in the face of dominant secularism. At best it survives as the private consolation of the individual, one of the paradoxical consequences of the decline of genuine community. Until such time as we recover a public spirituality, vast numbers of people are condemned to a loneliness of spirit."257

Spirituality has real profundity because it lies at the root of ethics, i.e., how we treat other people, not just those who we interact with but worldwide as depicted in Figure 2.

Two quotes by others in the book show that consideration of the spiritual is an aspect of humans.

- Alister Hardy [*1896-1985, an English marine biologist*258] in Aberdeen lectures in 1942: "I believe that the only true science of politics is that of human

---

[63]The Purusha concept refers to the abstract essence of the Self, Spirit and the Universal Principle that is eternal, indestructible, without form, and is all-pervasive. Klostermair, Klaus K. (2007). *A Survey of Hinduism*, 3rd Edition, State University of New York Press, ISBN 978-0-7914-7081-7, pp 87

[64]Sakshi is beyond time, space and the triad of experiencer, experiencing and experienced; sakshi witnesses all thoughts, words and deeds without interfering with them or being affected by them. Sakshi or Shiva, along with Shakti (will/energy/motion), represents the Brahman, the totality itself in its most fundamental state, the concept of all mighty, revealed in ancient philosophical texts of Hinduism. *Hinduism*. Chinmaya Mission. 2006. pp. 69–70. ISBN 9781880687383.

ecology—a quantitative science that will take in not only the economic and nutritional needs of man but one that will include his emotional side as well, include the recognition of the spiritual as well as his physical behaviour."[65]259

- "William James [*1842-1910, an American philosopher and psychologist*260] with his desire to generalize became an early and important advocate of 'common core' theory: that is to say he was also implying that spirituality is a primary phenomenon from which religions are derived at a second and dependent level."261

Thus, spirituality precedes religious expression; however, spirituality is often confused with religiosity. If spirituality is the root of ethics, often equated with morality in how we treat others, is there a possibility of morality outside of religion which often claims this as its domain?

The term 'spirituality' has undergone broadening changes over time. The current situation as defined in Wikipedia is:

"The meaning of spirituality has developed and expanded over time, and various connotations can be found alongside each other.[66][67][68][69][70]

Traditionally, spirituality referred to a religious process of re-formation which "aims to recover the original shape of man"[71], oriented at "the image of God"[72][73] as exemplified by the founders and sacred texts of the religions of the world. The term was used within early Christianity to refer to a life oriented

---

[65]Sir Alister Hardy in *The Spiritual Nature of Man* references this idea in *Natural History Old and New*, an inaugural address in 1942 at the University of Aberdeen, Aberdeen, UK.

[66]McCarroll, Pam; O'Connor, Thomas St. James; Meakes, Elizabeth (2005). Assessing Plurality in Spirituality Definitions. In: Meier et al, "*Spirituality and Health: Multidisciplinary Explorations*", Waterloo, ON: Wilfrid Laurier Univ. Press. pp. 44–59.

[67]Koenig, Harold; King, Dana; Carson, Verna B. (2012). *Handbook of Religion and Health*. Oxford, UK: Oxford University Press. p. 36.

[68]Cobb, Mark R.; Puchalski, Christina M.; Rumbold, Bruce (2012). Oxford Textbook of *Spirituality in Healthcare*. Oxford, UK: Oxford University Press. p. 213.

[69]Koenig et. al. (2012). "There is no widely agreed on definition of spirituality today". *Handbook of Religion and Health*. Oxford, UK: Oxford University Press.

[70]Cobb et. al. (2012). "The Spiritual Dimension Is Deeply Subjective and there Is No Authoritative Definition of Spirituality". Oxford Textbook of *Spirituality in Healthcare*. Oxford, UK: Oxford University Press.

[71]Waaijman, Kees. [This refers to footnotes 44 and 45.] uses the Dutch word "omvorming", "to change the form". Different translations are possible: transformation, re-formation, trans-mutation.

[72]Waaijman, Kees (2000). p. 460. [No publications on this date; the question: is this part of the following footnote?].

[73]Waaijman, Kees (2002). *Spirituality: Forms, Foundations, Methods*. Leuven, Belgium: Peeters Publishers.

toward the Holy Spirit[74] and broadened during the Late Middle Ages to include mental aspects of life.[75]

In modern times, the term both spread to other religious traditions[76] and broadened to refer to a wider range of experience, including a range of esoteric traditions and religious traditions. Modern usages tend to refer to a subjective experience of a sacred dimension[77] and the "deepest values and meanings by which people live",[78][79] often in a context separate from organized religious institutions,[80] such as a belief in a supernatural (beyond the known and observable) realm,[81] personal growth,[82] a quest for an ultimate or sacred meaning,[83] religious experience,[84] or an encounter with one's own "inner dimension".[85]262

This 'one's own inner dimension' is another way to characterize the 'void' in the aspects of life in Figure 2.

From the literature spirituality is a broad concept with many perspectives and interpretations. The common thread is that of something beyond the physical and connecting to something greater than oneself. Table 5 (next page) shows some interrelationships between the physical and the spiritual needs gleamed from the authors and their articles.

---

[74]Wong, Yuk-Lin Renita and Vinsky, Jana (2009). "Speaking from the Margins: A Critical Reflection on the 'Spiritual-but-not-Religious' Discourse in Social Work". *British Journal of Social Work*, 39 (7): 1343–59. Oxford, UK: Oxford University Press. doi:10.1093/bjsw/bcn032.

[75] Saunders, Corinne and Fernyhough, Charles (2016). "The medieval mind". *The Psychologist*, Volume 29 (November 2016): 880-883. Leicester, UK: The British Psychological Society.

[76]Gorsuch, R.L. and Miller, W.R. (1999). "Assessing Spirituality", in W.R. Miller (ed.), *Integrating Spirituality into Treatment*. Washington, DC: American Psychological Association. pp. 47–64.

[77]Saucier, Gerard and Skrzypinska, Katarzyna (1 October 2006). "Spiritual but Not Religious? Evidence for Two Independent Dispositions" (PDF). *Journal of Personality*. 74 (5): 1257–92. CiteSeerX 10.1.1.548.7658. doi:10.1111/j.1467-6494.2006.00409.x. JSTOR 27734699. PMID 16958702. Retrieved 2013-03-05. p. 1259.

[78]Sheldrake, Philip (1998). *Questions of Spirituality and History Interpretation and Method*. Maryknoll, NY: Orbis Books. pp. 1–2. ISBN 978-1-57075-203-2. OCLC 796958914.

[79]Griffin, David Ray (1988). *Spirituality and Society*. Albany, NY: State University of NY Press.

[80]Wong, Yuk-Lin Renita (2008). [No publications with this date; however, internet listings give this date associated with footnote 46 above.].

[81]Schuurmans-Stekhoven, J. (2014). "Measuring Spirituality as Personal Belief in Supernatural Forces: Is the Character Strength Inventory-Spirituality subscale a brief, reliable and valid measure?". *Implicit Religion: Journal of the Centre for the Study of Implicit Religion and Contemporary Spirituality*, 17 (2): 211–222. Sheffield, UK: Equinox Publishing. doi:10.1558/imre.v17i2.211.

[82]Houtman, Dick and Aupers, Stef (2007). "The Spiritual Turn and the Decline of Tradition: The Spread of Post-Christian Spirituality in 14 Western Countries, 1981–2000". *Journal for the Scientific Study of Religion*. 46 (3): 305–20. Hoboken, NJ: Wiley-Blackwell Publishing Co. doi:10.1111/j.1468-5906.2007.00360.x.

[83]Snyder, C.R. and Lopez, Shane J. (2007). *Positive Psychology*. Los Angeles, CA: SAGE Publications, Inc. p. 261. ISBN 978-0-7619-2633-7.

[84]Sharf, Robert H. (2000). "The Rhetoric of Experience and the Study of Religion" (PDF), *Journal of Consciousness Studies*, 7 (11–12): 267–87. Exeter, UK: Imprint Academic. archived from the original (PDF) on 2013-05-13, retrieved 2013-01-13.

[85]Wayman, Kees (2002). Spirituality: Forms, Foundations, Methods. Leuven, Belgium: Peeters Publishers. p. 315.

Table 5. The Interrelationship between the Physiological and the Spiritual Needs					
Seen- Physiological and Psychological		Unseen-Spiritual			Explanation
Maslow[265]	Acha[267]	Heyn[269]	Lyons[272]	Clinebell[274]	
Physiological	Safety and survival				air, food, drink, shelter, warmth, sex, sleep, etc.
Safety					protection from elements, security, order, law, stability, freedom from fear
Social	Connection (love) and acceptance	Love/ Belonging	Love	Love	friendship, intimacy, trust, and acceptance, receiving and giving affection and love, individually and within a group
Esteem	Esteem, Identity, Significance	Values	Dignity	Values	esteem for oneself (dignity, achievement, mastery, independence) and being accepted and valued by others (e.g., status, prestige)
Cognitive	Understanding and growth	Ethics/ Morality	Meaning	Inner Wisdom	knowledge and understanding, curiosity, exploration, need for meaning and predictability
	Contribution and creation				
		Meaning-making	Freedom	Spiritual Resources	help heal grief, guilt, resentment, unforgiveness, self-rejection, and shame and deepen experiences of trust, self-esteem, hope, joy, and love of life
				Vital Beliefs	
Aesthetic		Beauty			appreciation and search for beauty, balance, form
	Self-direction (Autonomy), Freedom, and Justice		Power		directing the affairs of our own lives including freedom and justice.
			Rest		the ultimate ability to trust, to release hold on those things that are beyond one's power, and to find peace in the letting go
Self-Actualization	Self-fulfillment and self-transcendence		Celebration	Awareness of oneness	realizing personal potential, self-fulfillment, seeking personal growth and peak experiences. A desire "to become everything one is capable of becoming."
	Resolution				addresses unmet issues in life and before death to forgiven oneself or others; to reminisce or review one's life
Transcendence		Transcendence		Transcendence	A person is motivated by values which transcend beyond the personal self, such as mystical experiences, service to others, the pursuit of science and religious faith.

- Abraham Maslow [1908-1970, *American psychologist known for hierarchy of needs, a theory of psychological health predicated on fulfilling innate human needs in priority, culminating in self-actualization*[263]] the initial hierarchy of needs had five levels and was expanded at eight as reported by Dr. Saul McLeod [*no lifetime dates available, psychology tutor and researcher for The University of Manchester, Division of Neuroscience & Experimental Psychology*[264]] in Maslow's Hierarchy of Needs[265].

- Dr. Kenneth Acha, MD, DMin. [*no lifetime dates available, board certified Family Medicine specialist and founder of Kenneth Acha Ministries*[266]] wrote in The 7 Fundamental Human Needs[267].Matthew Heyn, MDiv. [*no lifetime dates available, created Spiritually Health You website as a touchstone between the sacred and the ordinary*[268]] wrote in a blog, What Are Your Spiritual Needs[269].

- Rev Susan Lyon. [*1958-1996, co-director of Hartford Hospital's pastoral services department*[270]] defined seven core needs in Diacresis and Seven Core Needs: A Model of Spiritual Assessment[271] compiled and edited by The Rev. Dr. Martin G. Montonye [*no lifetime dates available, New York City Health and Hospitals Corporation, Bellevue Hospital Spiritual Care MS, STM, D.Min*[272]

- Howard Clinebell [*1922-2005, a United Methodist Church minister and a professor in pastoral counseling*[273]] wrote Seven Spiritual Needs[274] as quoted by Amy R. Krentzman, [*no lifetime dates available, a researcher focusing on the application of interventions from positive psychology to addiction treatment*[275]].

Although many people equate spirituality with theistic religions as the writers in the table having Western Christian perspectives, there is nothing in these hungers signifying any god system or being different in Eastern Religious Systems. The people who are on the atheism pole of the theism-atheism polarity, such as the author, have these same needs, yet we handle differently depending on our own worldviews.

It is worthy of note that the needs expressed by the Christian authors are all different and thus represent individual views rather than one unique Christian set of needs.

- Keith Ward in *The Case for Religion*[276] states, "The Enlightenment established that moral perception has an independence from, and even in one aspect a certain priority over, religious apprehension. All are capable of apprehending the elementary moral truths of:

  - Justice
  - Impartiality
  - Benevolence
  - Honesty

Those who have, or claim to have, religious apprehensions of spiritual reality are required to test those apprehensions by whether they match up to the highest moral perceptions we have. Even the idea of God itself, the idea of a being 'than which no greater can be conceived', is shaped in the light of our ideas of what values and goals are greatest, or most rationally choosable."

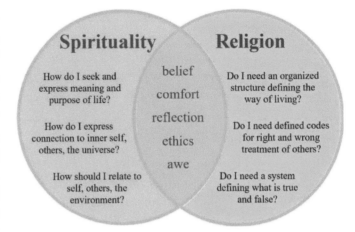

Figure 7. The interrelationship between spirituality and religion

- One way to look at the intersection of spirituality and religion is shown in Figure 7.[86]277 Another way was shown in Table 2. Note that the descriptive words within the intersection are applicable for all aspects of the theism-atheism polarity.

- Another way to characterize these two concepts is expressed by Gary Simmons, Rev. Ph. D, [*no lifetime dates available, co-pastor with his wife at Unity Worldwide Ministries, Spokane, Washington*278] in "Theology of Consciousness."279 He proposes two differentiated theologies:

    ♦ Theology of Belief characterizing most traditional religious perspectives concerning religious doctrine, ideology, dogma, and beliefs which one may draw their identity.

    ♦ Theology of Consciousness is the inner BEING (consciousness / I AM) within which we derive the meaning of our actions in life. This is the true identity of human beings and true spirituality from which mankind has constituted religious systems.

- Adam Brady [*Yoga teacher, author, and martial artist Adam Brady has been affiliated with the Chopra Center for 20 years.*280] discusses the differences between religion and spirituality in "Religion vs. Spirituality: The Difference Between Them."281 The key contrasts are:

    ♦ Objective vs. subjective experience

    ♦ Organized vs. formless

    ♦ Traditional vs. evolutionary approach

---

[86]Venn diagram adapted from the reference.

- Exclusive vs. inclusive
- Belief vs. spiritual experience
- Fear vs. love

This is not a unique set of differences by this author as other authors on this topic use the same contrasts and similarities.

Definition of Religion

Western religion/philosophy is based on dualism, that is everything is separate from God, the creator or universal consciousness; whereas Eastern religion/philosophy is based on oneness, that is the divinity, Creator Force, universal consciousness, or my choice, Living Spirit, resides within everything. Western religion is like looking at each side of a coin separately and thus not interconnected; Eastern religion is looking at the whole coin, both sides interconnected, yet interdependent.

Western thought is centered in categories, uses religion as the place to deal with the source of reasoning and thinking in a dualistic mode. Thus, the application of religion to eastern thought is western because in eastern thought, religious concepts are not separated from everyday life.

The following quote as to what religion is in the Introduction to Religion from Wikipedia[282]:

"Religion is a social-cultural system of designated behaviors and practices, morals, worldviews, texts, sanctified places, prophecies, ethics, or organizations, that relates humanity to supernatural, transcendental, or spiritual elements. However, there is no scholarly consensus over what precisely constitutes a religion.[87][88]

Different religions may or may not contain various elements ranging from the divine,[89] sacred things,[90] faith,[91] a supernatural being or supernatural beings[92] or "some sort of ultimacy and transcendence that will provide norms and power for the rest of life".[93] Religious practices may include rituals, sermons, commemoration or veneration (of deities), sacrifices, festivals, feasts, trances, initiations, funerary services, matrimonial services, meditation, prayer, music, art, dance, public service, or other aspects of human culture. Religions have sacred histories and narratives, which may be preserved in sacred scriptures, and symbols and holy places, that aim mostly to give a meaning to life.

---

[87]Morreall, John and Sonn, Tamara (2013). "Myth 1: All Societies Have Religions". *50 Great Myths of Religion*. Hoboken, NJ: Wiley-Blackwell Publishing Co. pp. 12–17. ISBN 978-0-470-67350-8.

[88]Nongbri, Brent (2013). *Before Religion: A History of a Modern Concept*. New Haven, CT: Yale University Press. ISBN 978-0-300-15416-0.

[89]James, William (1902). *The Varieties of Religious Experience. A Study in Human Nature*. London, UK: Longmans, Green, and Co. p. 31.

[90]Durkheim, Emile (1915). *The Elementary Forms of the Religious Life*. London, UK: George Allen & Unwin.

[91]Tillich, P. (1957). *Dynamics of faith*. New York, NY: Harper Perennial. p. 1.

[92]Vergote, A. (1996). *Religion, Belief and Unbelief. A Psychological Study*, Leuven, Belgium: Leuven University Press. p. 16.

[93]James, Paul and Mandaville, Peter (2010). *Globalization and Culture, Vol. 2: Globalizing Religions*. London, UK: Sage Publications.

Religions may contain symbolic stories, which are sometimes said by followers to be true, that have the side purpose of explaining the origin of life, the universe, and other things. Traditionally, faith, in addition to reason, has been considered a source of religious beliefs.[94]

There are an estimated 10,000 distinct religions worldwide,[95] but about 84% of the world's population is affiliated with one of the five largest religion groups, namely Christianity, Islam, Hinduism, Buddhism or forms of folk religion.[96] The religiously unaffiliated demographic includes those who do not identify with any particular religion, atheists, and agnostics. While the religiously unaffiliated have grown globally, many of the religiously unaffiliated still have various religious beliefs.[97]

The study of religion encompasses a wide variety of academic disciplines, including theology, comparative religion and social scientific studies. Theories of religion offer various explanations for the origins and workings of religion, including the ontological foundations of religious being and belief."[98]

It is helpful to understand the derivation of the English "religion" as it is used by different authors. This long quote is the Wikipedia entry under the topic "Concept and Etymology283:

"Religion (from O.Fr. *religion* religious community, from L. *religionem* (nom. *religio*) "respect for what is sacred, reverence for the gods, sense of right, moral obligation, sanctity",[99] "obligation, the bond between man and the gods"[100]) is derived from the Latin *religiō*, the ultimate origins of which are obscure. One possible interpretation traced to Cicero, connects *lego* read, i.e., *re* (again) with *lego* in the sense of choose, go over again or consider carefully. The definition of *religio* by Cicero is *cultum deorum*, "the proper performance of rites in veneration of the gods."[101] Julius Caesar used *religio* to mean "obligation of an oath" when discussing captured soldiers making an oath to their captors.[102] The Roman naturalist Pliny the Elder used the term *religio* on elephants in that

---

[94]Swindal, James (2001). "Faith and Reason". [Online]. The *Internet Encyclopedia of Philosophy.*

[95]Bonk, Jonathon J. (2005). "Ecclesiastical Cartography and the Problem of Africa". *History in Africa.* 32. p. 119. Cambridge, IL: Cambridge University Press printers for African Studies Association, University of Michigan, Ann Arbor, MI.

[96]Hackett, Conrad, et.al. (2012). "The Global Religious Landscape". *Pew Research Center December 2012* Washington, DC: Pew Forum on Religion & Public Life. [Retrieved 18 December 2012].

[97]"Religiously Unaffiliated". The Global Religious Landscape. *Pew Research Center: Religion & Public Life.* 18 December 2012. Washington, DC: Pew Forum on Religion & Public Life. p. 24.

[98]James, Paul (2018). "What Does It Mean Ontologically to Be Religious?". In Ames, Stephen, et.al. (eds.). *Religion in a Secular Age: The Struggle for Meaning in an Abstracted World.* Fitzroy, Victoria, Australia: Arena Publications. pp. 56–100.

[99]Harper, Douglas (2000). "religion". *Online Etymology Dictionary.* Lancaster, PA.

[100]"obligation, the bond between man and the gods". *Shorter Oxford English Dictionary (SOED).* Oxford, UK: Oxford University Press.

[101]Cicero, M. Tullis. *De natura deorum II*, 28. Harris Rackham (translator 1933). San Francisco, CA: *Academia.* London, UK: W. Heinemann.

[102]Caesar, Julius. "Civil Wars – Book 1". *The Works of Julius Caesar: Parallel English and Latin.* Translated by McDevitte, W.A. and Bohn, W.S. (2007). Leicester, UK: Forgotten Books Publisher. pp. 377–378. ISBN 978-1-60506-355-3.

they venerate the sun and the moon.[103] Modern scholars such as Tom Harpur and Joseph Campbell favor the derivation from *ligare* bind, connect, probably from a prefixed *re-ligare*, i.e. *re* (again) + *ligare* or to reconnect, which was made prominent by St. Augustine, following the interpretation given by Lactantius in *Divinae institutiones*, IV, 28.[104][105] The medieval usage alternates with order in designating bonded communities like those of monastic orders: "we hear of the 'religion' of the Golden Fleece, of a knight 'of the religion of Avys'[106]".

In classic antiquity, *'religio'* broadly meant conscientiousness, sense of right, moral obligation, or duty to anything.[107] In the ancient and medieval world, the etymological Latin root *religio* was understood as an individual virtue of worship in mundane contexts, never as doctrine, practice, or actual source of knowledge.[108][109] In general, *religio* referred to broad social obligations towards anything including family, neighbors, rulers, and even towards God.[110] *Religio* was most often used by the ancient Romans not in the context of a relation towards gods, but as a range of general emotions such as hesitation, caution, anxiety, fear; feelings of being bound, restricted, inhibited; which arose from heightened attention in any mundane context.[111] The term was also closely related to other terms like *scrupulus* which meant "very precisely" and some Roman authors related the term *superstitio*, which meant too much fear or anxiety or shame, to *religio* at times.[112] When *religio* came into English around the 1200s as religion, it took the meaning of "life bound by monastic vows" or monastic orders.[113][114] The compartmentalized concept of religion, where religious things were separated from worldly things, was not used before

[103]Pliny the Elder. *"Elephants; Their Capacity"*. *The Natural History, Book VIII Chapter 1*. Bostock, John M.D., F.R.S. and Riley, H.T. Esq., B.A. (1855) London, UK: Taylor and Francis. [Online] Perseus Digital Library Medford, MA: Tufts University.

[104]Harpur, Tom (2004). *The Pagan Christ: Recovering the Lost Light*. Toronto, ON: Thomas Allen Publishers. ISBN 0-88762-145-7.

[105]Campbell, Joseph, (collaborator) Moyers, Bill, and ed. Flowers, Betty Sue (1991). *The Power of Myth*. New York, Harpswell, ME: Anchor Publishing. ISBN 0-385-41886-8.

[106]Huizinga, Johan (1924). *The Waning of the Middle Ages*. London, UK: Penguin Books. p. 86.

[107]"Religio". *Latin Word Study Tool*. [Online] Perseus Digital Library Medford, MA: Tufts University.

[108]Harrison, Peter (2015). *The Territories of Science and Religion*. Chicago, IL: University of Chicago Press. ISBN 978-0-226-18448-7.

[109]Roberts, Jon (2011). "Science and Religion". Chapter 10 in Shank, Michael; Numbers, Ronald; Harrison, Peter (eds.). *Wrestling with Nature: From Omens to Science*. Chicago, IL: University of Chicago Press. p. 254. ISBN 978-0-226-31783-0.

[110]Morreall, John and Sonn, Tamara (2013). "Myth 1: All Societies Have Religions". *50 Great Myths about Religions*. Hoboken, NJ: Wiley-Blackwell Publishing Co. pp. 12–17. ISBN 978-0-470-67350-8.

[111]Barton, Carlin; and Boyarin, Daniel (2016). "'Religio' without "Religion"". Chapter 1 in *Imagine No Religion: How Modern Abstractions Hide Ancient Realities*. New York, NY: Fordham University Press. pp. 15–38. ISBN 978-0-8232-7120-7.

[112]*ibid.*

[113]Huizinga, Johan (1924). *The Waning of the Middle Ages*. London, UK: Penguin Books. p. 86.

[114]Morreall, John and Sonn, Tamara (2013). "Myth 1: All Societies Have Religions". *50 Great Myths about Religions*. Hoboken, NJ: Wiley-Blackwell Publishing Co. pp. 12–17. ISBN 978-0-470-67350-8.

the 1500s. The concept of religion was first used in the 1500s[115] to distinguish the domain of the church and the domain of civil authorities.[116]

In the ancient Greece, the Greek term *threskeia* was loosely translated into Latin as *religio* in late antiquity. The term was sparsely used in classical Greece but became more frequently used in the writings of Josephus in the first century CE. It was used in mundane contexts and could mean multiple things from respectful fear to excessive or harmfully distracting practices of others, to cultic practices. It was often contrasted with the Greek word *deisidaimonia* which meant too much fear.[117]

The modern concept of religion, as an abstraction that entails distinct sets of beliefs or doctrines, is a recent invention in the English language. Such usage began with texts from the 17th century due to events such the splitting of Christendom during the Protestant Reformation and globalization in the age of exploration, which involved contact with numerous foreign cultures with non-European languages.[118][119][120] Some argue that regardless of its definition, it is not appropriate to apply the term religion to non-Western cultures. Others argue that using religion on non-Western cultures[121][122] distorts what people do and believe.[123]

The concept of religion was formed in the 16th and 17th centuries,[124][125] despite the fact that ancient sacred texts like the Bible, the Quran, and others did not have a word or even a concept of religion in the original languages and neither did the people or the cultures in which these sacred texts were written.[126][127] For example, there is no precise equivalent

---

[115]*ibid.*

[116]*ibid.*

[117]Barton, Carlin and Boyarin, Daniel (2016). "Imagine No 'Threskeia': The Task of the Untranslator". Chapter 8 in *Imagine No Religion: How Modern Abstractions Hide Ancient Realities.* New York, NY: Fordham University Press. pp. 123–134. ISBN 978-0-8232-7120-7.

[118]Harrison, Peter (2015). *The Territories of Science and Religion.* Chicago, IL: University of Chicago Press. ISBN 978-0-226-18448-7.

[119]Roberts, Jon (2011). "Science and Religion". Chapter 10 in Shank, Michael; Numbers, Ronald; Harrison, Peter (eds.). *Wrestling with Nature: From Omens to Science.* Chicago, IL: University of Chicago Press. p. 254. ISBN 978-0-226-31783-0.

[120]Harrison, Peter (1990). *'Religion' and the Religions in the English Enlightenment.* Cambridge, UK: Cambridge University Press. ISBN 978-0-521-89293-3.

[121]Dubuisson, Daniel (2007). *The Western Construction of Religion: Myths, Knowledge, and Ideology.* Baltimore, MD: Johns Hopkins University Press. ISBN 978-0-8018-8756-7.

[122]Fitzgerald, Timothy (2007). *Discourse on Civility and Barbarity.* Oxford, UK: Oxford University Press. pp. 45–46.

[123]Smith, Wilfred Cantwell (1991). *The Meaning and End of Religion.* Minneapolis, MN: Fortress Press. ISBN 978-0-8006-2475-0.

[124]Nongbri, Brent (2013). *Before Religion: A History of a Modern Concept.* New Haven, CT: Yale University Press. p. 152. ISBN 978-0-300-15416-0.

[125]Harrison, Peter (1990). *'Religion' and the Religions in the English Enlightenment.* Cambridge, UK: Cambridge University Press. p. 1. ISBN 978-0-521-89293-3.

[126]Nongbri, Brent (2013). "2. Lost in Translation: Inserting "Religion" in Ancient Texts". *Before Religion: A History of a Modern Concept.* New Haven, CT: Yale University Press. ISBN 978-0-300-15416-0.

[127]Morreall, John and Sonn, Tamara (2013). *50 Great Myths about Religions.* Hoboken, NJ: Wiley-Blackwell. p. 13. ISBN 978-0-470-67350-8.

of religion in Hebrew, and Judaism does not distinguish clearly between religious, national, racial, or ethnic identities.[128] One of its central concepts is *halakha*, meaning the walk or path sometimes translated as law, which guides religious practice and belief and many aspects of daily life.[129] Even though the beliefs and traditions of Judaism are found in the ancient world, ancient Jews saw Jewish identity as being about an ethnic or national identity and did not entail a compulsory belief system or regulated rituals. Even in the 1st century CE, Josephus had used the Greek term *ioudaismos*, which some translate as Judaism today, even though he used it as an ethnic term, not one linked to modern abstract concepts of religion as a set of beliefs.[130] It was in the 19th century that Jews began to see their ancestral culture as a religion analogous to Christianity.[131] The Greek word *threskeia*, which was used by Greek writers such as Herodotus and Josephus, is found in the New Testament. *Threskeia* is sometimes translated as religion in today's translations, however, the term was understood as worship well into the medieval period.[132] In the Quran, the Arabic word *din* is often translated as religion in modern translations, but up to the mid-1600s translators expressed *din* as law.[133]

The Sanskrit word *dharma*, sometimes translated as religion, also means law. Throughout classical South Asia, the study of law consisted of concepts such as penance through piety and ceremonial as well as practical traditions. Medieval Japan at first had a similar union between imperial law and universal or Buddha law, but these later became independent sources of power.[134][135]

Throughout the Americas, Native Americans never had a concept of 'religion' and any suggestion otherwise is a colonial imposition by Christians.[136]

Though traditions, sacred texts, and practices have existed throughout time, most cultures did not align with Western conceptions of religion since they did not separate everyday life

---

[128]Edelheit, Hershel and Edelheit, Abraham J. *History of Zionism: A Handbook and Dictionary*. Abingdon, UK: Routledge Publishing p. 3, citing Zeitlin, Solomon (1936). *The Jews. Race, Nation, or Religion?* Philadelphia, PA: Dropsie College Press.

[129]Whiteford, Linda M. and Trotter II, Robert T. (2008). *Ethics for Anthropological Research and Practice*. Long Grove, IL: Waveland Press. p. 22. ISBN 978-1-4786-1059-5.

[130]Nongbri, Brent (2013). *Before Religion: A History of a Modern Concept*. New Haven, CT: Yale University Press. ISBN 978-0-300-15416-0.

[131]Burns, Joshua Ezra (2015). *"Jewish ideologies of Peace and Peacemaking"*. Chapter 3 in Omar, Irfan; Duffey, Michael (eds.). *Peacemaking and the Challenge of Violence in World Religions*. Hoboken, NJ: Wiley-Blackwell. pp. 86–87. ISBN 978-1-118-95342-6.

[132]Nongbri, Brent (2013). *Before Religion: A History of a Modern Concept*. New Haven, CT: Yale University Press. ISBN 978-0-300-15416-0.

[133]*ibid.*

[134]Kuroda, Toshio (1996). Translated by Jacqueline I. Stone. "The Imperial Law and the Buddhist Law" (PDF). *Japanese Journal of Religious Studies: 23.3–4*. Archived from the original (PDF) on 23 March 2003. Shōwa-ku Nagoya, Japan: Nanzan Institute for Religion and Culture [Retrieved 28 May 2010].

[135]McMullin, Neil (1984). *Buddhism and the State in Sixteenth Century Japan*. Princeton, NJ: Princeton University Press.

[136]Tinker, Tink (2015). "Irrelevance of euro-christian Dichotomies for Indigenous Peoples". Chapter 7 in Omar, Irfan; Duffey, Michael (eds.). *Peacemaking and the Challenge of Violence in World Religions*. Hoboken, NJ: Wiley-Blackwell. pp. 86–87. ISBN 978-1-118-95342-6.

from the sacred. In the 18th and 19th centuries, the terms Buddhism, Hinduism, Taoism, Confucianism, and world religions first entered the English language.[137][138][139] No one self-identified as a Hindu or Buddhist or other similar terms before the 1800s.[140] "Hindu" has historically been used as a geographical, cultural, and later religious identifier for people indigenous to the Indian subcontinent.[141][142] Throughout its long history, Japan had no concept of religion since there was no corresponding Japanese word, nor anything close to its meaning, but when American warships appeared off the coast of Japan in 1853 and forced the Japanese government to sign treaties demanding, among other things, freedom of religion, the country had to contend with this Western idea.[143][144]

According to the philologist Max Müller in the 19th century, the root of the English word religion, the Latin *religio*, was originally used to mean only reverence for God or the gods, careful pondering of divine things, piety (which Cicero further derived to mean diligence).[145][146] Max Müller characterized many other cultures around the world, including Egypt, Persia, and India, as having a similar power structure at this point in history. What is called ancient religion today, they would have only called law."[147]

The important terms to understand in western religions are: animism, theism, deism, pantheism, pandeism, atheism, Gnosticism, agnosticism, humanism, and paganism. There are other terms that could be listed; however, they are often seen as part of these terms. To get a sense of the issues, let us look at the definitions of these terms from the same source. The introductory paragraphs from Wikipedia are quoted:

[137]Harrison, Peter (2015). *The Territories of Science and Religion*. Chicago, IL: University of Chicago Press. p. 101. ISBN 978-0-226-18448-7.

[138]Josephson, Jason Ananda (2012). *The Invention of Religion in Japan*. Chicago, IL: University of Chicago Press. p. 12. ISBN 978-0-226-41234-4.

[139]Morreall, John and Sonn, Tamara (2013). *50 Great Myths about Religions*. Hoboken, NJ: Wiley-Blackwell. p. 12. ISBN 978-0-470-67350-8.

[140]Morreall, John and Sonn, Tamara (2013). *50 Great Myths about Religions*. Hoboken, NJ: Wiley-Blackwell. p. 14. ISBN 978-0-470-67350-8.

[141]Pennington, Brian K. (2005). *Was Hinduism Invented? Britons, Indians, and the Colonial Construction of Religion*, Oxford UK: Oxford University Press, pp. 111–118, ISBN 978-0-19-803729-3.

[142]Lloyd Ridgeon (2003). *Major World Religions: From Their Origins To The Present*. Abingdon, UK: Routledge Publishing. pp. 10–11. ISBN 978-1-134-42935-6.

[143]Josephson, Jason Ananda (2012). *The Invention of Religion in Japan*. Chicago, IL: University of Chicago Press. pp. 1, 11–12. ISBN 978-0-226-41234-4.

[144]Zuckerman, Phil, et al. (2016). "Secularity around the World". Chapter 2 in *The Nonreligious: Understanding Secular People and Societies*. Oxford, UK: Oxford University Press. pp. 39–40. ISBN 978-0-19-992494-3.

145[]Müller, Friedrich Max (1889). *Natural Religion*, London, UK: Longmans Green and Co. p. 33.

[146]Lewis, Charlton T and Short, Charles (1879). *A Latin Dictionary*. New York, NY: Harper and Brothers.

[147]Müller, Friedrich Max (2001). *Introduction to the science of religion*. Chestnut Hill, MA: Adamant Media Corporation. p. 28.

- **Animism:**[284]

"Animism (from Latin *anima*, "breath, spirit, life")[148][149] is the belief that objects, places and creatures all possess a distinct spiritual essence.[150][151][152][153] Potentially, animism perceives all things—animals, plants, rocks, rivers, weather systems, human handiwork, and perhaps even words—as animated and alive. Animism is used in the anthropology of religion as a term for the belief system of many indigenous peoples,[154] especially in contrast to the relatively more recent development of organized religions.[155]

Although each culture has its own different mythologies and rituals, "animism" is said to describe the most common, foundational thread of indigenous peoples' "spiritual" or "supernatural" perspectives. The animistic perspective is so widely held and inherent to most indigenous peoples that they often do not even have a word in their languages that corresponds to "animism" (or even "religion");[156] the term is an anthropological construct.

Largely due to such ethnolinguistic and cultural discrepancies, opinion has differed on whether animism refers to an ancestral mode of experience common to indigenous peoples around the world, or to a full-fledged religion in its own right. The currently accepted definition of animism was only developed in the late 19th century (1871) by Sir Edward Tylor, who created it as "one of anthropology's earliest concepts, if not the first".[157][158]

Animism encompasses the beliefs that all material phenomena have agency, that there exists no hard and fast distinction between the spiritual and physical (or material) world and that soul or spirit or sentience exists not only in humans, or rivers or other entities

---

[148]Lonie, Alexander Charles Oughter (1878). "Animism". In Baynes, T. S. (ed.). *Encyclopædia Britannica*. 2 (9th ed.). New York, NY: Charles Scribner's Sons. pp. 55–57.

[149]Segal, Robert (2004) *Myth: A Very Short Introduction*. Oxford, UK: Oxford University Press. p. 14.

[150]Taylor, Bron (ed.) (2005) "Religion and Nature" (PDF). *Encyclopedia of Religion and Nature*. London, UK: Bloomsbury Continuum Publishing.

[151]Stringer, Martin D. (1999). "Rethinking Animism: Thoughts from the Infancy of our Discipline". *Journal of the Royal Anthropological Institute*. 5 (4): 541–56. Hoboken, NJ: Wiley-Blackwell. doi:10.2307/2661147. JSTOR 2661147.

[152]Hornborg, Alf (2006). "Animism, fetishism, and objectivism as strategies for knowing (or not knowing) the world". *Ethnos: Journal of Anthropology*. 71 (1): 21–32. Stockholm Sweden: Taylor & Francis Group (Sweden) doi:10.1080/00141840600603129. S2CID 143991508.

[153]Haught, John F (1990). *What Is Religion? An Introduction*. New York, NY: Paulist Press. p. 19.

[154]Hicks, David (2010). *Ritual and Belief: Readings in the Anthropology of Religion* (3 ed.). Lanham, MD: Rowman & Littlefield Publishing Group. p. 359.

[155]"*Animism*". Contributed by Helen James; coordinated by Dr. Elliott Shaw with assistance from Ian Favell. ELMAR Project. Carlisle City, UK: University of Cumbria. 1998–1999.

[156]"Native American Religious and Cultural Freedom: An Introductory Essay". *The Pluralism Project*. President and Fellows of Harvard College and Diana Eck. 2005. Cambridge, MA: Harvard University

[157]Bird-David, Nurit (1999). ""Animism" Revisited: Personhood, Environment, and Relational Epistemology". *Current Anthropology*. 40s: S67-S91. Chicago, IL: University of Chicago Press. doi:10.1086/200061.

[158]Harvey, Graham (2005). *Animism: Respecting the Living World*. New York, NY: Columbia University Press. p. 9. ISBN 978-0-231-13700-3.

of the natural environment: water sprites, vegetation deities, tree sprites, ... Animism may further attribute a life force to abstract concepts such as words, true names or metaphors in mythology. Some members of the non-tribal world also consider themselves animists (such as author Daniel Quinn, sculptor Lawson Oyekan and many contemporary Pagans).[159]"

- **Theism:**[285]

"Theism is broadly defined as the belief in the existence of a Supreme Being or deities.[160],[[161] In common parlance, or when contrasted with deism, the term often describes the classical conception of God that is found in monotheism (also referred to as classical theism) – or gods found in polytheistic religions—a belief in God or in gods without the rejection of revelation as is characteristic of deism.[162][163]"

- **Deism:**[286]

"Deism (/ˈdiːɪzəm/ DEE-iz-əm[164][165] or /ˈdeɪ.ɪzəm/ DAY-iz-əm; derived from Latin "deus" meaning "god") is the philosophical position that rejects revelation as a source of religious knowledge and asserts that reason and observation of the natural world are sufficient to establish the existence of a Supreme Being or creator of the universe.[166][167][168]

At least as far back as Thomas Aquinas, Christian thought has recognized two sources of knowledge of God: revelation and "natural reason". The study of the truths revealed by reason is called natural theology. During the Age of Enlightenment, especially in Britain and France, philosophers began to reject revelation as a source of knowledge and to appeal only to truths that they felt could be established by reason alone. Such philosophers were called "deists" and the philosophical position that they advocated is called 'deism'.

Deism as a distinct intellectual movement declined toward the end of the 18th century. Some of its tenets continued to live on as part of other intellectual movements (e.g., Unitarianism) and it continues to have some advocates today."

---

[159]ibid. p. 7.

[160]"theism," *Dictionary.com Online Dictionary*. [Retrieved 21 October 2016].

[161]"theism," *Merriam-Webster Online Dictionary*. [Retrieved 18 March 2011].

[162]"deism" *Dictionary.com Online Dictionary*. [Retrieved 21 October 2016].

[163]"deism" *Dictionary.com Online Dictionary*. [Retrieved 23 November 2016].

[164]R. E. Allen (ed) (1990). *The Concise Oxford Dictionary*. Oxford, UK: Oxford University Press.

[165]"Deist – Definition and More from the Free Merriam-Webster Dictionary". *Merriam-webster.com. 2012.* [Retrieved 10 October 2012].

[166]"Deism". *Encyclopædia Britannica. 2012.* New York, NY: Charles Scribner's Sons.

[167]"Deism". *Jewish Encyclopedia. 1906.* [Retrieved 10 October 2012].

[168]Gomes, Alan W. (2011). "Deism". *The Encyclopedia of Christian Civilization*. Hoboken, NJ: Wiley-Blackwell. doi:10.1002/9780470670606.wbecc0408. ISBN 9781405157629.

- **Pantheism:**[281]

"The belief that reality is identical with divinity,[169] or that all-things compose an all-encompassing, immanent god.[170] Pantheist belief does not recognize a distinct personal god,[171] anthropomorphic or otherwise, and instead characterizes a broad range of doctrines differing in forms of relationships between reality and divinity.[172] Pantheistic concepts date back thousands of years, and pantheistic elements have been identified in various religious traditions. The term *pantheism* was coined by mathematician Joseph Raphson in 1697[173][174] and has since been used to describe the beliefs of a variety of people and organizations.

Pantheism was popularized in Western culture as a theology and philosophy based on the work of the 17th-century philosopher Baruch Spinoza, particularly his book *Ethics*.[175] A pantheistic stance was also taken in the 16th century by philosopher and cosmologist Giordano Bruno.[176]"

- **Pandeism (or pan-deism):**[288]

"A theological doctrine first delineated in the 18th century, combines aspects of pantheism with aspects of deism. It holds that a creator deity became the universe (pantheism) and ceased to exist as a separate and conscious entity (deism holding that God does not interfere with the universe after its creation).[177][178][179][180] Pandeism is proposed to explain (as it relates to deism) why God would create a universe and then appear to abandon it, and (as it relates to pantheism) an origin and purpose of the universe.

---

[169]"pantheist" *The New Oxford Dictionary of English.* Oxford, UK: Clarendon Press. 1998. p. 1341. ISBN 978-0-19-861263-6

[170]Edwards, Paul (ed.) (1967). *Encyclopedia of Philosophy.* New York, NY: Macmillan and Free Press. p. 34.

[171]Taliaferro, Charles et.al. (eds.). A *Companion to Philosophy of Religion.* Hoboken, NJ: John Wiley & Sons, Inc. p. 340.

[172]Levine, Michael (1994). *Pantheism: A Non-Theistic Concept of Deity.* Hove, UK: Psychology Press. ISBN 9780415070645, pp. 44, 274-275.

[173]Taylor, Bron (2008). *Encyclopedia of Religion and Nature.* London, UK: A&C Black. pp. 1341–1342. ISBN 978-1441122780. [Retrieved 27 July 2017].

[174]Thomson, Ann (2008). *Bodies of Thought: Science, Religion, and the Soul in the Early Enlightenment,* Oxford, UK: Oxford University Press. page 54.

[175]Lloyd, Genevieve (1996). *Routledge Philosophy Guide Book to Spinoza and The Ethics.* (1st ed.). Abingdon, UK: Routledge Publishing. p. 24. ISBN 978-0-415-10782-2.

[176]Birx, Jams H. "Giordano Bruno". *The Harbinger November 11, 1197.* Mobile, AL: The Harbinger, a community newspaper no longer published.

[177]Sean F. Johnston (2012). *The History of Science: A Beginner's Guide.* London, UK: Oneworld Publications. p. 90. ISBN 9781780741598.

[178]Paul Bradley (2011). *This Strange Eventful History: A Philosophy of Meaning.* New York, NY: Algora Publishing. p. 156. ISBN 978-0875868769.

[179]Dawe, Alan H. (2011). *The God Franchise: A Theory of Everything.* Lower Hutt, NZ: Life Magic Publishing (self-published). p. 48. ISBN 978-0473201142.

[180]Ronald R. Zollinger (2010). *"6". Mere Mormonism: Defense of Mormon Theology.* Springville, UT: Cedar Fort, Inc. ISBN 978-1-46210-585-4.

Various theories suggest the coining of the word "pandeism" as early as the 1780s, but one of the earliest unequivocal uses of the word with its present meaning came in 1859 with Moritz Lazarus and Heymann Steinthal.[181]"

■ **Atheism:**[289]

"Atheism is, in the broadest sense, an absence of belief in the existence of deities.[182][183][184][185] Less broadly, atheism is a rejection of the belief that any deities exist.[186][187] In an even narrower sense, atheism is specifically the position that there are no deities.[188][189][190][191] Atheism is contrasted with theism,[192][193] which, in its most general form, is the belief that at least one deity exists.[194][195][196]

The etymological root for the word atheism originated before the 5th century BCE from the ancient Greek ἄθεος (*atheos*), meaning "without god(s)". In antiquity, it had multiple uses as a pejorative term applied to those thought to reject the gods worshiped by the larger society,[197] those who were forsaken by the gods, or those who had no

[181]Lazarus, Moritz and Steinthal, Heymann (1859). *Zeitschrift für Völkerpsychologie und Sprachwissenschaft [Journal of Social Psychology and Linguistics]*. Leipzig, Germany: Wilhelm Friedrich, p. 262.

[182]Harvey, Van A. "Agnosticism and Atheism". In Flynn, Tom, (ed.) (2007). *The New Encyclopedia of Unbelief*. Buffalo, NY: Prometheus Books. p. 35 ISBN 978-1-59102-391-3. OL 8851140M.

[183]Blackburn, Simon (ed.) (2008). "atheism". *The Oxford Dictionary of Philosophy*. Oxford, UK: Oxford University Press. ISBN 9780199541430. [Retrieved 21 November 2013].

[184]Runes, Dagobert D. (ed.) (1942). *Dictionary of Philosophy*. New York, NY: Philosophical Library. ISBN 978-0-06-463461-8. [Retrieved 9 April 2011].

[185]"Atheism". *OxfordDictionaries.com*. Oxford, UK: Oxford University Press. [Archived from the original on 11 September 2016. Retrieved 23 April 2017].

[186]Nielsen, Kai (2013). "Atheism". *Encyclopædia Britannica*. New York, NY: Charles Scribner's Sons. [Retrieved 25 November 2013].

[187]Edwards, Paul (2005) [original printing 1967]. "Atheism". In Borchert, Donald M. (ed.). *The Encyclopedia of Philosophy*. Vol. 1 (2nd ed.). Farmington Hills, MI: MacMillan Reference US (Gale). p. 359. ISBN 978-0-02-865780-6.

[188]Harvey, Van A. "Agnosticism and Atheism". In Flynn, Tom, (ed.) (2007). The New Encyclopedia of Unbelief. Buffalo, NY: Prometheus Books. p. 35 ISBN 978-1-59102-391-3. OL 8851140M.

[189]Blackburn, Simon (ed.). "atheism". *The Oxford Dictionary of Philosophy (2008 ed.)*. Oxford, UK: Oxford University Press. ISBN 9780199541430. [Retrieved 21 November 2013].

[190]Rowe, William L. (1998). "Atheism". In Craig, Edward (ed.). *Routledge Encyclopedia of Philosophy*. Milton, UK: Taylor & Francis. ISBN 978-0-415-07310-3.

[191]Smart, J.J.C. (2017). "Atheism and Agnosticism". *Stanford Encyclopedia of Philosophy*. Palo Alto, CA: Metaphysics Research Lab, Stanford University.

[192]*"Definitions: Atheism"*. Department of Religious Studies, Tuscaloosa, AL: University of Alabama. {*This reference could not be located*}

[193]*"atheism"*. *Oxford English Dictionary (2nd ed.) 1989*. Oxford, UK: Oxford University Press.

[194]*ibid.*

[195]*"atheism"*. *Merriam-Webster Online Dictionary*. Springfield, MA: Merriam-Webster, Inc. [Archived from the original on 14 May 2011. Retrieved 9 April 2011].

[196]Smart, J.J.C. (9 March 2004). Zalta, Edward N. (ed.). "Atheism and Agnosticism". *The Stanford Encyclopedia of Philosophy (Spring 2013 Edition)*. Palo Alto, CA: Metaphysics Research Lab, Stanford University. [Archived from the original on 2 December 2013. Retrieved 26 April 2015].

[197]Drachmann, Anders Bjorn (1922). *Atheism in Pagan Antiquity*. Chicago Ridge, IL: Ares Publishers 1977. ISBN 978-0-89005-201-3.

commitment to belief in the gods.[198] The term denoted a social category created by orthodox religionists into which those who did not share their religious beliefs were placed.[199] The actual term atheism emerged first in the 16th century.[200] With the spread of freethought, skeptical inquiry, and subsequent increase in criticism of religion, application of the term narrowed in scope. The first individuals to identify themselves using the word atheist lived in the 18th century during the Age of Enlightenment.[201][202] The French Revolution, noted for its "unprecedented atheism," witnessed the first major political movement in history to advocate for the supremacy of human reason.[203]

Arguments for atheism range from philosophical to social and historical approaches. Rationales for not believing in deities include arguments that there is a lack of empirical evidence,[204][205] the problem of evil, the argument from inconsistent revelations, the rejection of concepts that cannot be falsified, and the argument from nonbelief.[206][207] Nonbelievers contend that atheism is a more parsimonious position than theism and that everyone is born without beliefs in deities;[208] therefore, they argue that the burden of proof lies not on the atheist to disprove the existence of gods but on the theist to provide a rationale for theism.[209] Although some atheists have adopted secular philosophies (e.g., secular humanism), there is no one ideology or code of conduct to which all atheists adhere.[210]

---

[198]Whitmarsh, Tim (2015). "8. Atheism on Trial". *Battling the Gods: Atheism in the Ancient World*. New York, NY: Knopf Doubleday. ISBN 978-0-307-94877-9.

[199]*ibid.*

[200]Wootton, David (1992). "New Histories of Atheism". Chapter 1 in Hunter, Michael and Wootton, David (eds.). *Atheism from the Reformation to the Enlightenment*. Oxford, UK: Clarendon Press. ISBN 978-0-19-822736-6.

[201]Armstrong, Karen (1999). *A History of God*. London, UK: Vintage. ISBN 978-0-09-927367-7.

[202]Wootton, David (1992). "New Histories of Atheism". Chapter 1 in Hunter, Michael and Wootton, David (eds.). *Atheism from the Reformation to the Enlightenment*. Oxford, UK: Clarendon Press. ISBN 978-0-19-822736-6.

[203]Hancock, Ralph, et. al. (1996). *The Legacy of the French Revolution*. Lanham, MA: Rowman and Littlefield Publishers. p. 22. ISBN 978-0-8476-7842-6. [Archived from the original on 30 September 2015. Retrieved 30 May 2015. Extract of page 22Archived 29 September 2015 at the Wayback Machine].

[204]Various authors. *"Logical Arguments for Atheism"*. The Secular Web Library. Carson City, NV: Internet Infidels at a Glance. [Archived from the original on 17 November 2012. Retrieved 2 October 2012].

[205]Shook, John R (2010). *"Skepticism about the Supernatural" (PDF)*. [Online]. Center for Inquiry and University at Buffalo. [Archived (PDF) from the original on 18 October 2012. Retrieved 2 October 2012].

[206]Various authors. *"Logical Arguments for Atheism"*. The Secular Web Library. Carson City, NV: Internet Infidels at a Glance. [Archived from the original on 17 November 2012. Retrieved 2 October 2012].

[207]Drange, Theodore M. (1996). *"The Arguments from Evil and Nonbelief"*. Secular Web Library. Carson City, NV: Internet Infidels. [Archived from the original on 10 January 2007 2. Retrieved October 2012].

[208]Harvey, Van A. "Agnosticism and Atheism". In Flynn, Tom, (ed.) (2007). *The New Encyclopedia of Unbelief*. Buffalo, NY: Prometheus Books. p. 35 ISBN 978-1-59102-391-3. OL 8851140M.

[209]Stenger, Victor J. (2007). *God: The Failed Hypothesis*. Buffalo, NY: Prometheus Books. ISBN 1-59102-481-1pp. 17–18. {Cites Parsons, Keith M. (1989). *God and the Burden of Proof: Plantinga, Swinburne, and the Analytical Defense of Theism*. Buffalo, NY: Prometheus Books. ISBN 978-0-87975-551-5}.

[210]Baggini, Julian (2003). *Atheism: A Very Short Introduction*. Oxford, UK: Oxford University Press. pp. 3–4.

Since conceptions of atheism vary, accurate estimations of current numbers of atheists are difficult.[211] According to global Win-Gallup International studies, 13% of respondents were "convinced atheists" in 2012,[212] 11% were "convinced atheists" in 2015,[213] and in 2017, 9% were "convinced atheists".[214] However, other researchers have advised caution with WIN/Gallup figures since other surveys which have used the same wording for decades and have a bigger sample size have consistently reached lower figures.[215] An older survey by the British Broadcasting Corporation (BBC) in 2004 recorded atheists as comprising 8% of the world's population.[216] Other older estimates have indicated that atheists comprise 2% of the world's population, while the irreligious add a further 12%.[217] According to these polls, Europe and East Asia are the regions with the highest rates of atheism. In 2015, 61% of people in China reported that they were atheists.[218] The figures for a 2010 Eurobarometer survey in the European Union (EU) reported that 20% of the EU population claimed not to believe in "any sort of spirit, God or life force".[219]"

- **Gnosticism:**[290]

"Gnosticism (from Ancient Greek: γνωστικός gnostikos, "having knowledge") is a collection of ancient religious ideas and systems which originated in the first century AD among early Christian and Jewish sects.[220] These various groups, labeled "gnostics" by their opponents, emphasized personal spiritual knowledge (gnosis) over orthodox teachings, traditions, and ecclesiastical authority. They considered the

[211]Zuckerman, Phil (2007). *Atheism: Contemporary Rates and Patterns*. In Martin, Michael T (ed.). *The Cambridge Companion to Atheism*. Cambridge, UK: Cambridge University Press. p. 56. ISBN 978-0-521-60367-6. OL 22379448M. [Archived from the original on 31 October 2015. Retrieved 9 April 2011].

[212]*"Religiosity and Atheism Index" (PDF)*. 27 July 2012. Zurich, Switzerland: WIN-Gallup International. [Archived from the original (PDF) on 21 October 2013. Retrieved 1 October 2013].

[213]*"New Survey Shows the World's Most and Least Religious Places"*. Washington, D.C: National Public Radio. 13 April 2015. [Archived from the original on 6 May 2015. Retrieved 29 April 2015].

[214]*"Religion prevails in the world" (PDF)*. 14 November 2017. Zurich, Switzerland: WIN-Gallup International [Archived from the original (PDF) on 14 November 2017. Retrieved 27 February 2018].

[215]Keysar, Ariela and Navarro-Rivera, Juhem (2017). "A World of Atheism: Global Demographics". Chapter 36 in Bullivant, Stephen and Ruse, Michael (eds.). *The Oxford Handbook of Atheism*. Oxford, UK: Oxford University Press. ISBN 978-0-19-964465-0.

[216]*"UK among most secular nations"*. London, UK: British Broadcasting Corporation, BBC News. 26 February 2004. [Archived from the original on 2 September 2017. Retrieved 14 January 2015].

[217]"Worldwide Adherents of All Religions by Six Continental Areas, Mid-2007". *Encyclopædia Britannica. 2007*. New York, NY: Charles Scribner's Sons. [Archived from the original on 12 December 2013. Retrieved 21 November 2013].

[218]*"Gallup International Religiosity Index" (PDF)*. https://www.washingtonpost.com/blogs/worldviews/. Data source Zurich, Switzerland: Zurich, Switzerland: WIN-Gallup International. April 2015. [Archived (PDF) from the original on 1 February 2016. Retrieved 9 January 2016].

[219]*Social values, Science and Technology (2005)*. Directorate General Research, European Union. 2010. p. 207. [Archived from the original (PDF) on 30 April 2011. Retrieved 9 April 2011]. {2010 reference not found. The link went to 2005 thus its reference in title.}

[220]Magris, Aldo (2005). "Gnosticism: Gnosticism from its origins to the Middle Ages (further considerations)". In Jones, Lindsay (ed.), *MacMillan Encyclopedia of Religion*, Farmington Hills, MI: *MacMillan Reference USA (Gale)*. pp. 3515–3516.

principal element of salvation to be direct knowledge of the supreme divinity, experienced as intuitive or esoteric insight. Generally, Gnostic cosmogony presents a distinction between a supreme, transcendent God and a blind, evil demiurge responsible for creating the material universe, thereby trapping the divine spark within matter.[221] Many Gnostic texts deal not in concepts of sin and repentance, but with illusion and enlightenment.[222]

Gnostic writings flourished among certain Christian groups in the Mediterranean world until about the second century, when the Fathers of the early church denounced them as heresy.[223] Efforts to destroy supposedly heretical texts proved largely successful, resulting in the survival of very few Gnostic texts.[224] Nonetheless, early Gnostic teachers such as Valentinus saw their beliefs as aligned with Christianity. In the Gnostic Christian tradition, Christ is seen as a divine being which has taken human form in order to lead humanity back to the Light.[225] However, Gnosticism is not a single standardized system, and the emphasis on direct experience allows for a wide variety of teachings, including distinct currents such as Valentianism and Sethianism. In the Persian Empire, Gnostic ideas spread as far as China via the related movement Manichaeism, while Mandaeism is still alive in Iraq.

For centuries, most scholarly knowledge of Gnosticism was limited to the anti-heretical writings of orthodox Christian figures such as Irenaeus of Lyons and Hippolytus of Rome. Renewed interest in Gnosticism occurred after the 1945 discovery of Egypt's Nag Hammadi library, a collection of rare early Christian and Gnostic texts, including the Gospel of Thomas and the Apocryphon of John. A major question in scholarly research is the qualification of Gnosticism as either an interreligious phenomenon or as an independent religion. Scholars have acknowledged the influence of sources such as Hellenistic Judaism and Platonism, and some have noted possible links to Buddhism and Hinduism, though the evidence of direct influence from these latter sources is inconclusive.[226]"

---

[221]Pagels, Elaine (1989). *The Gnostic Gospels (PDF)*. New York, NY: Random House. p. xx.

[222]*ibid.*

[223]Layton, Bentley (1995). "Prolegomena to the Study of Ancient Gnosticism" essay in White, L. Michael (Author), Yarbrough, O. Larry (Editor) (1995). *The Social World of the First Christians*. Minneapolis, MN: Fortress Press ISBN 0-06-064586-5. {The ISBN for The Social World of the First Christians: Essays in Honor of Wayne A. Meeks, by L. Michael White (Author), O. Larry Yarbrough (Editor) 1995 is 0800625854. ISBN 0-06-064586-5 is for Gnosis on the Silk Road: Gnostic Parables, Hymns & Prayers from Central Asia by Hans-Joachim Klimkeit published by HarperCollins 1993.}

[224]Pagels, Elaine (1989). *The Gnostic Gospels (PDF)*. New York, NY: Random House. p. xx.

[225]Friedman, Jerome (1978). *Michael Servetus: A Case Study in Total Heresy*. Paris, France: Librairie Droz. p. 142. ISBN 2600030751.

[226]Pagels, Elaine (1989). *The Gnostic Gospels (PDF)*. New York, NY: Random House. *p. xx.*

■ **Agnosticism:**[291]

"Agnosticism is the view that the existence of God, of the divine or the supernatural is unknown or unknowable.[227][228][229] Another definition provided is the view that "human reason is incapable of providing sufficient rational grounds to justify either the belief that God exists or the belief that God does not exist.[230]

The English biologist Thomas Henry Huxley coined the word agnostic in 1869 and said, "It simply means that a man shall not say he knows or believes that which he has no scientific grounds for professing to know or believe." Earlier thinkers, however, had written works that promoted agnostic points of view, such as Sanjaya Belatthaputta, a 5th-century BCE Indian philosopher who expressed agnosticism about any afterlife;[231][232][233] and Protagoras, a 5th-century BCE Greek philosopher who expressed agnosticism about the existence of 'the gods'.[234][235][236][237]

Agnosticism is the doctrine or tenet of agnostics with regard to the existence of anything beyond and behind material phenomena or to knowledge of a First Cause or God[238] and is not a religion."

■ **Humanism:**[292]

"Humanism is a philosophical and ethical stance that emphasizes the value and agency of human beings, individually and collectively, and generally prefers critical thinking and evidence (rationalism and empiricism) over acceptance of dogma or superstition. The meaning of the term humanism has fluctuated according to the successive

[227]Hepburn, Ronald W. (2005) [original printing 1967]. "Agnosticism". In Borchert, Donald M. (ed.). *The Encyclopedia of Philosophy. 1 (2nd ed.)*. Farmington Hills, MI: MacMillan Reference USA (Gale). p. 92. ISBN 0-02-865780-2.

[228]Rowe, William L. (1998). "Agnosticism". In Craig, Edward (ed.). *Routledge Encyclopedia of Philosophy*. Milton, UK: Taylor & Francis. ISBN 978-0-415-07310-3.

[229]"agnostic, agnosticism". *OED Online (3rd ed.)* Oxford, UK: Oxford University Press. September 2012.

[230]Rowe, William L. (1998). "Agnosticism". In Craig, Edward (ed.). *Routledge Encyclopedia of Philosophy*. Milton, UK: Taylor & Francis. ISBN 978-0-415-07310-3.

[231]"Samaññaphala Sutta. The Fruits of the Contemplative Life". a part of the *Digha Nikaya* translated in 1997 by Thanissaro Bhikkhu. [Archived from the original on February 9, 2014].

[232]Bhaskar, Bhagchandra Jain (1972). *Jainism in Buddhist Literature*. Nagpur, India: Alok Prakashan:. [Available on-line at http://jainfriends.tripod.com/books/jiblcontents.html].

[233]Lloyd Ridgeon (2003). *Major World Religions: From Their Origins to The Present*. Milton, UK: Taylor & Francis. pp. 63–. ISBN 978-0-203-42313-4.

[234]Poster, Carol. *The Internet Encyclopedia of Philosophy – Protagoras (c. 490 – c. 420 BCE)*. [Archived from the original on February 10, 2014. Retrieved July 22, 2013].

[235]Patri, Umesh and Prativa Devi (February 1990). "*Progress of Atheism in India: A Historical Perspective*". Atheist Centre 1940–1990 Golden Jubilee. Vijayawada, India: Atheist Centre. [Archived from the original on September 25, 2013. Retrieved June 29, 2014].

[236]Treharne, Trevor (2012). *How to Prove God Does Not Exist: The Complete Guide to Validating Atheism*. Irvine, CA: Universal-Publishers. pp. 34 ff. ISBN 978-1-61233-118-8.

[237]Schwab, Helmut (2012). *Essential Writings: A Journey Through Time: A Modern "De Rerum Natura"*. Bloomington, IN: iUniverse. pp. 77 ff. ISBN 978-1-4759-6026-6.

[238]"agnosticism". *Oxford English Dictionary (3rd ed.) (2005)*. Oxford, UK: Oxford University Press.

intellectual movements which have identified with it.[239] The term was coined by theologian Friedrich Niethammer at the beginning of the 19th century to refer to a system of education based on the study of classical literature ("classical humanism"). Generally, however, humanism refers to a perspective that affirms some notion of human freedom and progress. It views humans as solely responsible for the promotion and development of individuals and emphasizes a concern for man in relation to the world.[240]

In modern times, humanist movements are typically non-religious movements aligned with secularism, and today humanism may refer to a nontheistic life stance centered on human agency and looking to science rather than revelation from a supernatural source to understand the world.[241][242]"

- **Paganism:**[293]

"Paganism (from classical Latin *pāgānus* "rural", "rustic", later "civilian") is a term first used pejoratively in the fourth century by early Christians for people in the Roman Empire who practiced polytheism.[243] In the time of the Roman empire, individuals fell into the pagan class either because they were increasingly rural and provincial relative to the Christian population, or because they were not *milites Christi* (soldiers of Christ).[244][245] Alternative terms in Christian texts were hellene, gentile, and heathen.[246] Ritual sacrifice was an integral part of ancient Graeco-Roman religion[247]

---

[239]Walter, Nicolas (1997). *Humanism: What's in the Word.* London, UK: Secular Society (G. W. Foote) Ltd. ISBN 0-301-97001-7.

[240]Marbaniang, Domenic. "Developing the Spirit of Patriotism and Humanism in Children for Peace and Harmony". In *Children At Risk: Issues and Challenges*, Jeyaraj, Jesudason (ed.), Bangalore, India: CFCD/ISPCK, 2009, p.474

[241]See for example the 2002 *Amsterdam Declaration*<http://iheu.org/humanism/the-amsterdam-declaration/> issued by the International Humanist and Ethical Union

[242]The British Humanist Association's definition of Humanism.

[243]Brown, Peter (1999). "Pagan". In Bowersock, Glen Warren; Brown, Peter; Grabar, Oleg (eds.). *Late Antiquity: A Guide to the Postclassical World.* Cambridge, MA: Harvard University Press. pp. 625–26. ISBN 978-0-674-51173-6.

[244]O'Donnell, J. J. (1977). *Paganus: Evolution and Use.* Classical Folia, 31: 163–69.

[245]Augustine of Hippo, De Diversis Quaestionibus ("Eighty-three Questions"). Further reading in Fitzgerald, Allan O.S.A. (ed,) (199). *Augustine through the Ages: An Encyclopaedia.* Grand Rapids, MI: Wm. B. Eerdmans Publishing Company. ISBN: 0-8028-3843-X.

[246]Brown, Peter (1999). "Pagan". In Bowersock, Glen Warren; Brown, Peter; Grabar, Oleg (eds.). *Late Antiquity: A Guide to the Postclassical World.* Cambridge, MA: Harvard University Press. pp. 625–26. ISBN 978-0-674-51173-6.

[247]Jones, Christopher P. (2014). *Between Pagan and Christian.* Cambridge, MA: Harvard University Press. ISBN 978-0-674-72520-1.

and was regarded as an indication of whether a person was pagan or Christian.[248] Paganism has broadly connoted the "religion of the peasantry".[249][250]

During and after the Middle Ages, the term paganism was applied to any non-Christian religion, and the term presumed a belief in false god(s).[251][252]

The origin of the application of the term pagan to polytheism is debated.[253] In the 19th century, paganism was adopted as a self-descriptor by members of various artistic groups inspired by the ancient world. In the 20th century, it came to be applied as a self-descriptor by practitioners of Modern Paganism, Neopagan movements and Polytheistic reconstructionists. Modern pagan traditions often incorporate beliefs or practices, such as nature worship, that are different from those in the largest world religions.[254][255]

Contemporary knowledge of old pagan religions and beliefs comes from several sources, including anthropological field research records, the evidence of archaeological artifacts, and the historical accounts of ancient writers regarding cultures known to Classical antiquity.

Most modern pagan religions existing today (Modern or Neopaganism[256][257]) express a world view that is pantheistic, polytheistic or animistic, but some are monotheistic.[258]"

Origins and Development of Religions

Now that we have looked at the nature of human beings from the standpoint of being a part of the universal consciousness and what we mean by spirituality and religion, we see that humans are the source of creating religions. This only makes sense for all the different forms we have in the world

---

[248]ibid.

[249]Brown, Peter (1999). "Pagan". In Bowersock, Glen Warren; Brown, Peter; Grabar, Oleg (eds.). *Late Antiquity: A Guide to the Postclassical World.* Cambridge, MA: Harvard University Press. pp. 625–26. ISBN 978-0-674-51173-6.

[250]Owen Davies (2011). *Paganism: A Very Short Introduction.* Oxford University Press. pp. 1–2. ISBN 978-0-19-162001-0.

[251]Aitamurto, Kaarina (2016). *Paganism, Traditionalism, Nationalism: Narratives of Russian Rodnoverie.* Abingdon, UK: Routledge. pp. 12–15. ISBN 978-1-317-08443-3.

[252]Owen Davies (2011). *Paganism: A Very Short Introduction.* Oxford, UK: Oxford University Press. pp. 1–6, 70–83. ISBN 978-0-19-162001-0.

[253]Davies, Owen (2011). Paganism: A Very Short Introduction. New York: Oxford University Press. ISBN 978-0191620010.

[254]"Paganism". Simpson, John (ed.) (2014). *Oxford Dictionary.* Oxford, UK: Oxford University Press.

[255]"Paganism". Taylor, Bron (ed.) (2010). *The Encyclopedia of Religion and Nature.* Oxford, UK: Oxford University Press. ISBN 978-0199754670.

[256]Lewis, James R. (ed.) (2004). *The Oxford Handbook of New Religious Movements.* Oxford, UK: Oxford University Press. p. 13. ISBN 0-19-514986-6.

[257]Hanegraff, Wouter J. (1006). *New Age Religion and Western Culture: Esotericism in the Mirror of Secular Thought.* Boston, MA: Brill Academic Publishers. p. 84. ISBN 90-04-10696-0.

[258]Cameron, Alan G. (2011). *The Last Pagans of Rome.* Oxford, UK: Oxford University Press. pp. 28, 30. ISBN 978-0199780914. OCLC 553365192.

from the past and what is developing now. In addition, as I study history, the behavior of humans does not appear to have changed much, if any. With all the advancements in knowledge, we are still behaving as always because history keeps repeating itself, only the circumstances are different because of the times of occurrences.

Having grown up on a farm, I observed the progression of life from season to season just as my ancestors' millennia ago observed. Since I do not know my ancestors' thought processes for explaining life, however, my observation of peoples' observation, and explanation skills do not appear to be any different today than they were millennia ago. I base this on the development of what I see in the sciences as well as other human endeavors. What I have today is more information about a subject because of my ancestors having added to it over the millennia. Thus, I will start with mine and hopefully along the way I will encounter those who may have like insights.

Being trained in the physical sciences, I realize that there must be a source to what I observe around me. In my upbringing I was taught that this source was God. However, after translating and intercomparing three Greek Gospel versions of the Christian Bible, I finally realized they were all fiction after years as an avocation of reading about religions and being involved in various religious communities. Today I see that along with the universal consciousness discussed herein that there is also a universal energy of which our various categories of energy are subsets just like each living animal including humans has a subset of the universal consciousness further divided down to each individual as being who they are with all the varied interests expressed so that one may experience life at this time in history. We need all, even those that have gone before us as they have contributed to our experiences and journey today. In addition, we need the experiences with many opposing views to better understand who we are and how we want to be treated.

As I observed plant life during my farm years, the conditions must be right for it to sprout, develop, reproduce, and then die. In this process there needs to be a source of energy as well as the source that gives the plant its characteristics and the innate processes for its lifetime. As a scientist I have not observed any reactions or interactions that do not require a source of energy. We know that the atoms of what we call solid matter, such as these laptop keys that I am punching in writing this, are constantly in motion. So where does this energy come from? It is from and part of the same undefinable, unknowable source and coupled with the universal consciousness. I consider them acting together to give what is termed 'life' whether plant or animal or human. This type of reasoning is the same for my ancestors in their explanations of life and what was its origin.

In Chapter 4, Avocation: Origins of Religion, the various creation and sources of human life concepts from around the world were delineated. It is unlikely that they were built from the interaction of the various cultures. So, these are expressions from human's observations of conditions. The peoples' inquisitiveness led to interpreting what the causes of the conditions were by reasoning and stating how they were related to the observations. These early humans were the scientists of their times. Once the explanations were put forth others then accepted them, and they formed part of that culture. Future cultures that interacted with the earlier culture then adapted their cultural beliefs on these.

Using similar logic there were those like unto myself who postulated there must be an undefinable, unknowable source. This was then developed into the term god(s) having the names respective to the language and culture at that given time in history. These were then given characteristics of humans or greater than human, such as raising the dead, self-resurrection from being dead, and ascension into the sky. By describing these gods with superpowers, they set forth rituals, dogmas, and other forms of worship and spiritual practices which have been categorized by western thought as religions even though that term does not exist in any ancient writings which are based on prior verbal and written communications.

The following is an attempt to make some sense out of the many conflicting articles concerning the various thought processes of humans in their many different perspectives on religion and its origins. I am only able to read an iota of the many related articles available, such as noted in the footnotes herein.

The original thoughts for something have to begin within an individual who may have existed during the developments leading to Homo Sapiens; thus, Hervey C. Peoples [?- *present, a molecular geneticist and evolutionary anthropologist*[294]] states in the article, *Hunter-Gatherers and the Origins of Religion*[295], "We should not dismiss the possible presence of non-linguistic religious thought and sentiment among early members of the genus Homo. However, a case can be made that transmission of religious concepts from one individual to another requires complex mental imaging, and a capacity for symbolic thought and communication that might include ritual, dancing, singing, gestures, art, and ornamentation, as well as language."[259][260] These latter actions may be more appropriate in Homo Sapiens.

It is recognized that hunter-gatherers preceded the agricultural peoples. So, what do we know about these people and their way of life, especially what we now term religion? In the article, *Hunter-Gatherers and the Origins of Religion*, an analysis of many articles written about 33 groups of these people around the world, Hervey C. Peoples shows that all cultures from around the world had animism as the core belief. They defined 'animism' as the belief that all "natural" things, such as plants, animals, and even such phenomena as thunder, have intentionality (or a vital force) and can have influence on human lives.[296] This is like panpsychism[297] and my thought of universal energy.

Hervey C. Peoples then traces the development of religious thought from animism in the following sequence[298]:

1. Belief in afterlife

2. Shamanism

3. Ancestor worship being present—not active

4. Ancestor worship being present—active

5. High gods being present—not active

6. High gods being present—active

Thus, as these hunter-gatherers transitioned into agricultural groups these religious concepts would also be retained. Therefore, Kersey Graves [*1813-1883, a skeptic, atheist, rationalist, spiritualist,*

---

[259]Deacon, T., & Cashman, T. (2010). The role of symbolic capacity in the origins of religion. Journal for the Study of Religion, Nature and Culture, 3(4), 1–28

[260]Mithen, S. (1998). *The Prehistory of the Mind*. London: UK; Orion Publishing Co, ISBN13: 9780753802045

reformist writer[299]] documents in *"The World's Sixteen Crucified Saviors"*[300], "The primary and constituent elements and properties of human nature being essentially the same in all countries and centuries. The feeling called 'Religion' could be a spontaneous outgrowth of the devotional elements of the human mind. The coincidence would naturally produce similar feelings, similar thought, similar views, and similar documents on the subject, religion, in different countries, however widely separated. This accounts in part for the analogous features in all the primary systems of religious faith, which have flourished in the past ages."

So, what is the progression from the observation that there is an unknowable source to the various practices by social-cultural groups? There is logical progression of thought, considering human thought processes, for the development of religious systems that makes sense quoted in *Anthropology of Religion*[301]:

"Anthony F. C. Wallace [1923-2015, *a Canadian-American anthropologist*[302]] proposes four categories of religion, each subsequent category subsuming the previous. These are, however, synthetic categories and do not necessarily encompass all religions.

1. Individualistic: most basic; simplest. Example: vision quest.

2. Shamanistic: part-time religious practitioner, uses religion to heal, to divine, usually on the behalf of a client. The Tillamook have four categories of shaman. Examples of shamans: spiritualists, faith healers, and palm readers. Religious authority acquired through one's own means.

3. Communal: elaborate set of beliefs and practices; group of people arranged in clans by lineage, age group, or some religious societies; people take on roles based on knowledge, and ancestral worship.

4. Ecclesiastical: dominant in agricultural societies and states; are centrally organized and hierarchical in structure, paralleling the organization of states. Typically deprecates competing individualistic and shamanistic cults."

Another approach to this is discussed in *Evolving Brains Emerging Gods* by E. Fuller Torrey traces the development of the functioning of the brain for genus Homo over time along with the development of secular and religious aspects of human life from the changes in brain, see Figure 8 (next page).[303] Animism could easily have been part of the brain development times.

In the development of religions, Hinduism is a culture which later was considered a religion dating from about 7000 BCE[304,305] and its writings, the Riga Veda, of what was being practiced from 1700 BCE[306]. The oldest known writing is the Kesh Temple Hymn dating from 2600 BCE[307] and concerns the Sumerian creation of man and woman[308].

One of the problems with writings in the BCE time frame is the often widely varying centuries in the dates, as well as uncertainties in the dates themselves, for a writing, such as the Baghavat Gita, is dated between 500 BCE and 200 BCE[309]. Kersey Graves documents in *"The World's Sixteen Crucified Saviors"* that there is an episode in the Baghavat Gita section Mahabaret (Mahabharata) from which he compares Chrishna Zeus (or Jeseus, as some writers spell it) to Jesus Christ [note the similarity in name spelling] in the Christian Bible[310]. The following is a sampling of some of the 346 parallels that he states:

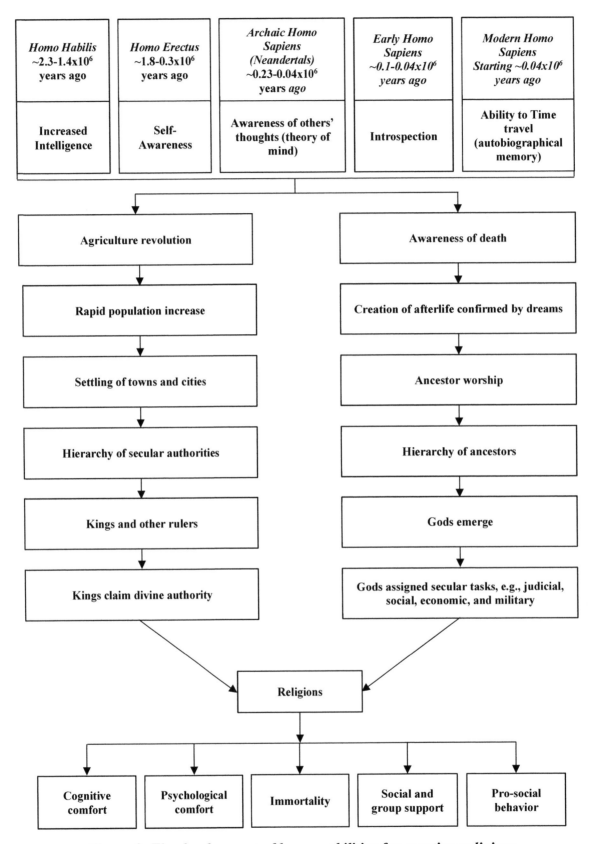

Figure 8. The development of human abilities for creating religions

- "His miraculous birth by a virgin.

- The mother and child being visited by shepherds, wise men and the angelic host, who joyously sang, "In thy delivery, O favored among women, all nations shall have cause to exult."

- The edict of the tyrant ruler Cansa, ordering all the first born to be put to death.

- The miraculous escape of the mother and child from his bloody decree by the parting of the waves of the River Jumna to permit them to pass through on dry ground.

- The early retirement of Chrishna to a desert.

- His baptism or ablution in the River Ganges, corresponding to Christ's baptism in Jordan.

- His transfiguration at Madura, where he assured his disciples that "present or absent, I will always be with you."

- He had a favorite disciple (Arjoon), who was his bosom friend, as John was Christ's.

- He was anointed with oil by women, like Christ.

- Confessing the Savior is also required in both cases.

- A memorable last supper marked the closing career of both.

- Both were put to death by "wicked hands."

- Chrishna, as well as Christ, was crucified."[311]

Because of these similarities and many other Saviors of various religious systems predating Christianity, it is looked at as a copycat religion. Christianity was formed at the Council of Nicaea in 325 CE called by Emperor Constantine because of the many different religions in Rome. The Council was attended by Eusebius (Bishop of Caesarea in Palestine "Father of Church History") and a friend of Constantine[312] Eusebius prepared the documents that became the Christian Bible. At this time Alexandria, Egypt had a major library and was renowned for comparing various philosophies that could now days be considered religions. Kersey Graves traces the Jewish group the Essenes, which are of unknown origin compared to their counterparts the Sadducees and the Pharisees that we know from the Hebrew Scriptures, and that the Essene religious system is greatly similar to the Hindus. In addition, he shows that they changed their name to Christianity as the group no longer existed after the name change.[313]

Humans have always changed the names of different groups of religious believers when a slight change in thought is implemented. Just consider all the variations within Christianity and those closely related to it: such as Islam, Protestant, Quaker, etc. The same is of all the major world religions: such as Sunni and Shi'a of Islam, Shaivism and Vaishnava of Hinduism, Theravada and Mahayana in Buddhism, et.al. This is not unique to religious thought for we can find the same concepts in any field of study. It is necessary for progress in the fields as well as for one to experience life without being a robot.

Kersey Graves quotes throughout his book the many Christian writers including saints of the Roman Catholic Church and Orthodox churches as confirming the ideas of Christianity being taken from earlier religions and thus, not being of divine origin coming down from the God associated with Christian belief system. A few examples are:

- "And that popular Christian writer, Mr. Milman [*Henry Hart, 1791-1868, an English historian and Church of England ecclesiastic*[314]], informs us that the Jewish founders of Christianity believed in an original Divine Word, which they call Memra. When it descended to the earth, and "became flesh, and dwelt amongst us" (John I. 4.) according to the evangelist John, it was known as Jesus Christ. Mr. Milman states also, that "the appellation to the Word is found in the Indian (Hindoo), Persian, the Platonic, and the Alexandrian systems." (Hist. of Chr., Book I., Chap. 2.)"[315,316]

- "Truly did St. Augustine say, 'This, in our day, is the Christian religion, not as having been unknown in former times, but as having recently received that name.'"[317]

- "The schools of Alexandria" says Mr. Enfield [*William, 1741–1797, divine and author*[318]], a Christian writer, "by pretending to teach sublime doctrines concerning God and divine things, enticed men of different countries and religions, and among the rest the Jews, to study its mysteries, and incorporate them with their own…The Jewish faith mixed with the Pythagorean, and afterward with the Egyptian oriental theology." (that is, they became Essenes in the Grecian school of Pythagoras, who taught the doctrines of that religious order, then Buddhists in the Egyptian schools of Alexandria). And finally, with Christ as their leader, who taught the doctrines of both schools (they being essentially alike), they assumed the name of Christian of him, and thus is Christianity from Essene Buddhism."[319]

- "That standard Christian author, Mr. Milman, in his "*History of Christianity*," tells us that "the doctrine of the incarnation ('God manifest in the flesh') was the doctrine from the Ganges[261], and even the shores of the Yellow Sea to the Ilissus. It was the fundamental principle of the Indian Buddhist religion and philosophy. It was the basis of Zoroasterism. It was pure Platonism. It was Platonic Judaism in the Alexandrian school."[320,321]

Yes, we have more gadgets, but the treatment of one another is no different. Time and time again, there have been those in past centuries across all cultures who have stated the Golden Rule, "Do unto others as you want to be treated!" or a version thereof. Let us look at some of its history:

Kersey Graves lists several versions of the Golden Rule from ancient times which are here rearranged in order of dates as stated by him.[322] The Hebrew and Christian Scriptures versions are included showing the same thought has occurred by humans for centuries up to present.

- 650 BCE, Pittacus, [*an ancient Mytilenaen military general and one of the Seven Sages of Greece*[323]] stated, "Do not to your neighbor what you would take ill from him."

- 500 BCE, Confucius, [*a Chinese philosopher and politician of the Spring and Autumn period*[324]] stated, "Do unto another what you would have him do unto you, and do not to another what you would not have him do unto you. Thou needest this law alone. It

---

[261]Noted from above Hindu Chrishna Zeus: His miraculous birth by a virgin.

is the foundation of all the rest."[325] This is the basis of Confucianism which is about overcoming lack of reciprocity through the power of virtue.[326]

- 464 BCE, Thales, [*a Greek mathematician, astronomer and pre-Socratic philosopher from Miletus in Ionia, Asia Minor, and one of the Seven Sages of Greece*[327]] stated, "Avoid doing what you would blame others for doing."[328]

- 406 BCE, Sextus, a Pythagorean, [*nothing specific about this Sextus, however there is about the Pythagoreans and their philosophies.*[329]], stated, "What you wish your neighbors to be to you, such be also to them."[330] A similar quote attributed to Pythagoras is: ἀλλήλοις θ' ὁμιλεῖν, ὡς τοὺς μὲν φίλους ἐχθροὺς μὴ ποιῆσαι, τοὺς δ' ἐχθροὺς φίλους ἐργάσασθαι. ἴδιόν τε μηδὲν ἡγεῖσθαι. **We ought so to behave to one another as to avoid making enemies of our friends, and at the same time to make friends of our enemies.** As quoted in Diogenes Laërtius, Lives and Opinions of Eminent Philosophers, "Pythagoras", Sect. 23, as translated in Dictionary of Quotations (http://archive.org/details/dictionaryquota02harbgoog) (1906) by Thomas Benfield Harbottle, p.320[331]

- 385 BCE, Aristotle, [*a Greek philosopher and polymath during the Classical period in Ancient Greece*[332]] stated, "We should conduct ourselves toward others as we would have them act toward us."[333]

- 365 BCE, Aristippus of Cyrene, [*a pupil of Socrates, the founder of the Cyrenaic school of Philosophy, teaching that the goal of life was to seek pleasure by circumstances to oneself and by maintaining proper control over both adversity and prosperity*[334]] stated, "Cherish reciprocal benevolence, which will make you as anxious for another's welfare as your own."[335]

- 338 BCE, Isocrates, [*an ancient Greek rhetorician, one of the ten Attic orators*[336]] stated, "Act toward others as you desire them to act toward you."[337]

- 50 BCE, Hillel, [*a Jewish religious leader, sage and scholar associated with the development of the Mishnah and the Talmud and the founder of the House of Hillel school of tannaim*[338]] stated, "Do not to others what you would not like others to do to you."[339]

- 30 CE, Jesus of Nazareth, in Matthew 7.12, "In everything do to others what you would have them do to you, for this sums up the Law and the Prophets,"[340] quotes Leviticus 19:34, "The stranger who resides in you shall be to you as one of your citizens; you shall love him as yourself, for you were strangers in the land of Egypt: I the Lord am your God."[341]

These are supposedly the message of religions, yet they have violated it all the time. Today we see these violations, such as in the Israeli - Palestinian conflict in Israel, Hindu - Muslim conflict in India, and the Mexican and Afro-American - White Supremist conflict occurring in the United States.

As one considers the religious systems of the cultures one finds that they also are part of the governing of people in those cultures including their understanding of what is morally right in treating their own people and those around them. Religious systems are some of the worst in oppressing people as the study of history shows.

Closing Commentary

As I am finishing this work during the COVID-19 pandemic, I am not seeing a dichotomy between science and religion, but a failure of unconditional love for our neighbor, any person in the world as we all come from the same unknowable source just with a different iota of its consciousness. There is an oppression of knowledge that the Living Spirit has endowed in consciousness of people. This oppression of knowledge comes about through the ego need for greed expressed in many ways, principally money and power. The oppression of knowledge goes both ways as many religious advocates suppress scientific explanations just as many scientists suppress the unseen world.

In fact, as a comparison to religious systems mentioned earlier the term scientism has been recently coined to express the western science worldview being also religious-like in nature, "Science is the best or only objective means by which society should determine normative and epistemological values."[342] Another way of stating this is, "Scientism is the broad-based belief that the assumptions and methods of research of the physical and natural sciences are equally appropriate (or even essential) to all other disciplines, including philosophy, the humanities and the social sciences. It is based on the belief that natural science has authority over all other interpretations of life, and that the methods of natural science form the only proper elements in any philosophical (or other) inquiry."[343] Thus, from what we have discussed, "Certainly, it requires the almost complete abandonment of any metaphysical or religious discussion, (and arguably also any ethical discussion), on the grounds that these cannot be apprehended by the scientific method, which is very limiting for a supposedly all-encompassing doctrine. Some would say that proponents of Scientism merely avoid actually engaging with many important arguments."[344] However, the scientists and others quoted do not agree with current thinking of scientism.

To help our fellow brethren, whether being religious or scientific, to stay alive and to love and care for one another, i.e., the command from both religious and scientific authors needs to be expressed. This pandemic is showing both sides of human behavior whether religious or scientific:

1. The caring people follow mandates for curbing the virus spread and reaching out to help with money or time that they have available.

2. Because the uncaring people want to live as the pandemic will not affect them, they are oppressing others, whether sick or not through their unwillingness to help others stay healthy.

So, why this oppression which is another polarity of life? However, just as "When the human system {body} has been long prostrated with chronic disease, no system of medication can restore it at once to health. The same principle governing the mind makes it morally impossible to eradicate its deeply seated moral and religious {or science} errors in a day by even the presentation of the most powerful and convincing truths and demonstrations that can be brought to bear or operate upon the human judgment. The mind instinctively repels everything (no difference how true or how beautiful) that conflicts with its long-established opinions and convictions. The fires of truth usually require much time to burn their way through those incrustations of moral and religious {or science} error which often environ the human mind as the products of a false education. But when they once enter, the work of convincement is complete."[345]

As I complete the writing on the question of dichotomy between science and religion, these are not seen as being mutually exclusive but polar parts of a larger seen-unseen entity, my Living Spirit. What I do see is an egocentricity for power with control of others and unacceptance of each other being interrelated in a larger worldview.

Now that my iota of universal consciousness (life) is drawing closer to its transitioning to another plane in this vast universe. I have not found answers to the following types of basic consciousness questions by scientists, philosophers, or religionists:

- What is the energy source that causes the fetus to develop through the changing of the molecules to form the various parts of the body?

- Is an iota of the universal consciousness the source of the program that causes the molecules to form the various parts of the body and thus be the source for talents, abilities, and personality of the fetus when born?

- Does a fetus not have consciousness when it moves on its own in the womb and has a heartbeat, or it responds to outside stimuli such as music?

- Does a fetus cry or show signs of pain during an abortion? If so, where did it get the ability to feel pain and respond?

- How does a baby know how to suck when no one has to instruct it, or the calf knows where the cow's udder is for its nourishment without needing someone to show it, or the turtle once it hatches knows to go into the water?

- What is the source of intuition, Déjà vu (experiencing something previously during a first-time encounter), extrasensory perception (ESP), visions, clairvoyance, all-in-oneness with the universe, etc. as these are experiences in some human beings?

- Where are reasonings and thoughts derived for novel ideas and approaches to issues? Scientists, upon reviewing the same data, argue different approaches and outcomes. Religionists espousing that theirs is the true religion which all must believe because all others are false.

- Is transgender a result of the iota of consciousness coming back into this plane without forgetting that it was the expressed sex previously? Thus, it is preferring that sexuality, not the maleness/femaleness it was born to experience life at this time.

- Is transgender another way of showing that we have had previous lives?

References

Note: Internet references quoted during my earlier writing of this article may be no longer available.

1. Klatt, Prof. E., *et. al.* (1983). *Standard German Dictionary*. Berlin, Germany: Langenscheidt Publishers, Inc.

2. The Langenscheidt Editorial Staff (1970). *Pocket French Dictionary*. Berlin, Germany: Langenscheidt Publishers, Inc.

3. Magazis, George A. (ed.) (1990). *Standard Greek Dictionary*. Berlin, Germany: Langenscheidt Publishers, Inc.

4. Ruck, Carl A. P. (1979). *Ancient Greek, A New Approach* (2nd ed.). Cambridge, MA: The MIT Press.

5. Strong, James (1995). The New Strong's Exhaustive Concordance of the Bible. Nashville TN: Thomas Nelson Publishers.

6. History of the English Language. [Online]. http://www.soon.org.uk/page18.htm [accessed 5 July 2006].

7. Cotgrave, Randle (compiler) (1611). *A Dictionarie of the French and English Tongues*. London, UK: Adam Islip. [Online]. Available from: http://www.pbm.com/~lindahl/cotgrave/972small.html [originally accessed 5 July 2006, verified accessible 12 November 2021].

8. Green, Harvey A. Edgar Cayce on the Soul Realms. [Online]. http://www.near-death.com/experiences/cayce06.html [accessed 5 July 2006].

9. Mondello, Geoffrey K. (2018). *The Metaphysics of Mysticism: A Commentary on the Mystical Philosophy of St. John of the Cross*. Independently published. [Online]. Available from: http://www.johnofthecross.com [accessed 7 March 2006].

10. LeShan, Lawrence (1974). *The Medium, the Mystic, and the Physicist*. New York, NY: Penguin Books.

11. Olesen, Jacob. Chakra Colors: The 7 Chakras and Their Meanings, [Online]. https://www.color-meanings.com/chakra-colors-the-7-chakras-and-their-meanings/ [accessed 10 February 2021].

12. Psychological Test, Kuder Preference Record Vocational. Form BB. [Online]. https://americanhistory.si.edu/collections/search/object/nmah_692529#:~:text=The%20Kuder%20Preference%20Test%2C%20first%20published%20in%201938%2C,Form%20BB.%20This%20test%20was%20copyrighted%20in%201942 [accessed 1 January 2021].

13. Myers–Briggs Type Indicator. [Online]. https://en.wikipedia.org/wiki/Myers%E2%80%93Briggs_Type_Indicator [accessed 1 January 2021].

14. Filice, Michelle. Two-Spirit. [Online].
https://www.thecanadianencyclopedia.ca/en/article/two-spirit [accessed 9 January 2020].

15. Bem Sex-Role Inventory. [Online]. https://en.wikipedia.org/wiki/Bem_Sex-Role_Inventory [accessed 9 January 2020].

16. Masculinity/Femininity Test Results. [Online]. https://psycho-tests.com/test/gender-role-test [accessed 10 December 2020].

17. Development of the Open Sex-Role Inventory. [Online].
https://openpsychometrics.org/tests/OSRI/development/ [accessed 9 January 2020].

18. Open Sex-Role Inventory Results. [Online].
https://openpsychometrics.org/tests/OSRI/results.php?d=TnpB-056LWMc [accessed 10 December 2020]. citation and results,

19. Gender Role Test. [Online]. https://www.idrlabs.com/gender/test.php [accessed 9 January 2020].

20. Gender Role Test Results. [Online]. https://www.idrlabs.com/gender/test.php [accessed 10 December 2020].

21. Marshall, Chris (1996). *The Complete Book of Chinese Horoscopes*. New York, NY: Stewart, Tabori & Chang Publishers, Inc.

22. Heavenly Stems. [Online]. https://en.wikipedia.org/wiki/Heavenly_Stems [accessed 3 January 2021].

23. Astrology.com. Dragon. [Online]. https://www.astrology.com/chinese-zodiac/dragon [accessed 15 January 2021].

24. Western Astrology. [Online]. https://en.wikipedia.org/wiki/Western_astrology [accessed 3 January 2021].

25. Birth Chart, a private communication received 22 November 2020.

26. Numerology. [Online]. https://en.wikipedia.org/wiki/Numerology [accessed 4 January 2021].

27. Deluxe Numerology Report, a private communication received 22 November 2020.

28. Archetype. [Online]. https://en.wikipedia.org/wiki/Archetype [accessed 4 January 2021].

29. Hero. [Online]. https://individualogist.com/offer/paa/reading-v4/?name=undefined&email=lederbaer2000@gmail.com&archetype=hero [accessed 11 November 2020].

30. Hero Archetype. [Online]. https://individualogist.com/12-archetypes/hero-archetype [accessed 5 January 2021].

31. Psychological Test, Kuder Preference Record Vocational. Form BB. [Online].
https://americanhistory.si.edu/collections/search/object/nmah_692529#:~:text=The%20Kuder%20Preference%20Test%2C%20first%20published%20in%201938%2C,Form%20BB.%20This%20test%20was%20copyrighted%20in%201942 [accessed 1 January 2021].

32. Myers–Briggs Type Indicator. [Online].
https://en.wikipedia.org/wiki/Myers%E2%80%93Briggs_Type_Indicator [accessed 1 January 2021].

33. National Defense Education Act. [Online]. https://en.wikipedia.org/wiki/National_Defense_Education_Act [accessed 17 June 2020].

34. Fillmore, C. L.; Eckert, A. C.; Scholle, J. V. (1969). Determination of Antimony, Tin, and Arsenic in Antimonial Lead Alloys by X-Ray Fluorescence. *Applied Spectroscopy* 23(5) 502-507.

35. Workaholics Anonymous World Service Organization. *Book of Recovery*. Printed in U.S. 2005.

36. Six Sigma. [Online]. https://en.wikipedia.org/wiki/Six_Sigma [accessed 17 June 2020].

37. Scholle, Jerome V. (1993). *Metrology* (The Six Sigma Research Institute Series). Boston, MA: Addison-Wesley.

38. Callaway, Edgar H., Hill, David A., Scholle. Jerome V. (1993). *Probability Distributions* (The Six Sigma Research Institute Series). Boston, MA: Addison-Wesley.

39. Workaholism: The Respectful Addiction. I haven't been able to find this 1991-1992 article that was in an airline magazine during travel.

40. Alcoholics Anonymous (1976). *The Big Book* (3rd ed). New York, NY: Alcoholics Anonymous World Service Organization.

41. *The Holy Bible, New International Version* (1978), Zondervan Bible Publishers, Grand Rapids, MI. Ez 16:49-50

42. *The Holy Bible, New International Version* (1978), Zondervan Bible Publishers, Grand Rapids, MI. Jer 23:13-14

43. Siege of Jerusalem (70 CE). [Online]. https://en.wikipedia.org/wiki/Siege_of_Jerusalem_(70_CE). [accessed 22 March 2020].

44. *Hebrew-Jewish TANAKH* (1999). Philadelphia, PA: Jewish Publication Society.

45. Liddell, Henry George et.al. (1996). *Classical Greek-English Lexicon* (9th ed). Oxford, UK: Oxford University Press.

46. Berry, George Ricker (1897). *The Interlinear KJV, Parallel New Testament in Greek and English based on the Textus Receptus*. Grand Rapids, MI: Zondervan Publishing House, ISBN 0-310-39380-9.

47. Nestle, Eberhard and Aland, Kurt (1993). *Novum Testamentum Graece*. Stuttgart, Germany: Deutsche Bibelgesellschaft. ISBN 978-3-438-05100-4.

48. Hodges, Zane C. & Farstad, Arthur L. (eds.) (1985). *The Greek New Testament according to the Majority Text* (2nd ed.). Nashville, TN: Thomas Nelson Publishers.

49. *The Holy Bible, New International Version* (1978), Zondervan Bible Publishers, Grand Rapids, MI. Luke 18:13

50. Ege, Seyhan (1989). *Organic Chemistry*, (2nd ed.). Lexington, MA: D. C. Heath Co. p. 194

51. *Handbook of Chemistry and Physics*, (44th ed.) (1962). Cleveland, OH: The Chemical Rubber Publishing Co.

52. Planck Length. [Online]. http://www.physlink.com/Education/AskExperts/ae281.cfm. [accessed 11 June 2006].

53. Abell, George O. (1975). *Exploration of the Universe*, (3rd ed.). New York, NY: Holt, Rinehart and Winston.

54. Cosmic Dust in Farthest Quasar. [Online]. http://www.redorbit.com/news/space/1338/cosmic_dust_in_farthest_quasar_clue_to_early_star_formation/index.html [accessed 11 June 2006].

55. Age of the universe. [Online]. https://en.wikipedia.org/wiki/Age_of_the_universe [accessed 20 March 2021].

56. *The Holy Bible, New International Version* (1978), Zondervan Bible Publishers, Grand Rapids, MI, John 9:1-41

57. El-Abbadi, Mostafa. Library-of-Alexandria. [Online]. https://www.britannica.com/topic/Library-of-Alexandria [accessed 21 March 2021.

58. Basham, A.L., *Nasadiya Sukta*, [Online]. http://www.kondor.de/shaman/sanskrt_e.html [accessed 12 June 2006].

59. Panikkar, Prof. Raimundo, Translator, *Nasadiya Sukta, RigVeda*, [Online]. http://www.members.tripod.com/~anusandhan/articles/article.html. from Prof. Raimundo Panikkar. "*The Vedic Experience- Mantra-manjari*" New Dehli, India: Motilal Banarasidas Publishing House [accessed 12 June 2006].

60. Bierlein, J. F. (1994). *Parallel Myths*, New York, NY: Ballatine Publishing Group. p. 46.

61. *ibid.* p. 54

62. *ibid.* p. 47

63. *ibid.* p. 40

64. *The Holy Bible, New International Version* (1978), Zondervan Bible Publishers, Grand Rapids, MI, Gen 1:1-2.

65. Fans. [Online]. http://www.dreamscape.com/morgana/miranda.htm [accessed 9 February 2013].

66. Chelan. [Online]. http://www.dreamscape.com/morgana/miranda.htm [accessed 9 February 2013].

67. Tahitian. [Online]. http://www.dreamscape.com/morgana/ophelia.htm [accessed 5 May 2006].

68. Sikh. [Online]. http://www.dreamscape.com/morgana/ophelia.htm [accessed 5 May 2006].

69. Mik'Maq. [Online]. http://www.dreamscape.com/morgana/cordelia.htm [accessed 5 May 2006].

70. Bierlein, J. F. (1994). *Parallel Myths*, New York, NY: Ballatine Publishing Group. p. 44.

71. Chinese. http://www.dreamscape.com/morgana/ariel.htm [accessed 5 May 2006].

72. Maya. [Online]. http://www.dreamscape.com/morgana/cordelia.htm [accessed 5 May 2006].

73. Ekoi. [Online]. http://www.dreamscape.com/morgana/miranda.htm [accessed 9 February 2013].

74. Bierlein, J. F. (1994). *Parallel Myths*, New York, NY: Ballatine Publishing Group. p.48.

75. *ibid*. p. 51

76. *ibid*. p. 63

77. Scandinavian. [Online]. http://www.dreamscape.com/morgana/cordelia.htm [accessed 5 May 2006].

78. Apache. [Online]. http://www.dreamscape.com/morgana/miranda.htm [accessed 9 February 2013].

79. Iroquois. [Online]. http://www.dreamscape.com/morgana/oberon.htm [accessed 5 May 2006].

80. Hopi. [Online]. http://www.dreamscape.com/morgana/umbriel.htm [accessed 5 May 2006].

81. Craig, Dr. William Lane. *The Ultimate Question of Origins: God and the Beginning of the Universe*. [Online]. http://www.leaderu.com/offices/billcraig/docs/theism-origin.html [accessed 24 May 2006].

82. Questions About Atheistic Culture and Belief. [Online]. http://www.positiveatheism.org/mail/eml9082.htm#ORIGINS [accessed 24 May 2006].

83. Who Are the Raelians? [Online]. http://www.time.com/time/nation/article/0,8599,404175,00.html [accessed 26 May 2006].

84. *The Holy Bible, New International Version* (1978), Zondervan Bible Publishers, Grand Rapids, MI, Gen 2:7

85. Why a "naked" Adam in Eden? [Online]. http://bibleorigins.net/EdenDatePalmGardenIragHrouda.html, [accessed 4 February 2018].

86. Bierlein, J. F. (1994). *Parallel Myths*, New York, NY: Ballatine Publishing Group. p.49.

87. *ibid*., p. 50

88. Digueno. [Online]. http://www.dreamscape.com/morgana/ariel.htm [accessed 5 May 2006].

89. Hungarian. [Online]. http://www.dreamscape.com/morgana/oberon.htm [accessed 5 May 2006].

90. Boshongo. [Online]. http://www.dreamscape.com/morgana/miranda.htm [accessed 9 February 2013].

91. Bierlein, J. F. (1994). *Parallel Myths*, New York, NY: Ballatine Publishing Group. p. 40.

92. *ibid*. p. 51

93. *ibid*. p. 65

94. *ibid*. p. 59

95. *ibid*. p. 62

96. *ibid*. p. 60

97. Japanese Creation Myth (712Ce). [Online]. http://www.wsu.edu:8080/~wldciv/world_civ_reader/world_civ_reader_1/kojiki.html, [accessed 19 May 2006].

98. Clarke, Dr. Peter B. (ed.) (1993). *The World's Religions*. Pleasantville, NY: Reader's Digest. p. 150.

99. Darwin, Charles (1859). "*Origins of the Species*". [Online]. https://www.britannica.com/biography/Charles-Darwin/On-the-Origin-of-Species [accessed 26 April 2020].

100. Who Are the Raelians? [Online]. http://www.time.com/time/nation/article/0,8599,404175,00.html [accessed 26 May 2006].

101. *The Holy Bible, New International Version* (1978), Zondervan Bible Publishers, Grand Rapids, MI, Isa 42:5, Col 1:16, Rev 4:11.

102. Near-death and afterlife, [Online]. http://www.near-death.com/ [accessed 9 June 2006].

103. LeShan, Lawrence (1974). *The Medium, the Mystic, and the Physicist*. New York, NY: Penguin Books.

104. Arapaho, [Online]. http://www.dreamscape.com/morgana/bianca.htm [accessed 23 May 2006].

105. Zoroastrianism. [Online]. http://www.religionfacts.com/a-z-religion-index/zoroastrianism.htm [accessed 12 June 2006].

106. *The Holy Bible, New International Version* (1978), Zondervan Bible Publishers, Grand Rapids, MI, Mat 10:28, Luke16:24-26.

107. Inuit. [Online]. http://www.dreamscape.com/morgana/umbriel.htm [accessed 5 May 2006].

108. Questions About Atheistic Culture and Belief. [Online]. http://www.positiveatheism.org/mail/eml9082.htm#ORIGINS [accessed 24 May 2006].

109. Sadducees. [Online]. http://www.near-death.com/religion.html#rel13 [accessed 30 May 2006].

110. Who Are the Raelians? [Online]. http://www.time.com/time/nation/article/0,8599,404175,00.html [accessed 26 May 2006].

111. Harvey A. Green. *Edgar Cayce on the Soul Realms*. [Online]. http://www.near-death.com/experiences/cayce06.html [accessed 5 July 2006].

112. *Edgar Cayce on Spirit Realms*, [Online]. http://www.near-death.com/experiences/cayce07.html [accessed 6 July 2006].

113. His Divine Grace a. C. Bhaktivedanta Swami Prabhupada (1997). *Bhagavad-Gita As It Is*. Los Angeles, CA: The Bhaktivedanta Book Trust. p. 402.

114. *Hebrew-Jewish TANAKH* (1999). Philadelphia, PA: Jewish Publication Society. Gen 2:4.

115. *The Holy Bible, New International Version* (1978), Zondervan Bible Publishers, Grand Rapids, MI, John 1:3.

116. Dawood, N. J., (translator) (1999). *The Koran*. London, UK: Penguin Books. p. 304.

117. Bierlein, J. F. (1994). *Parallel Myths*, New York, NY: Ballatine Publishing Group. p. 41.

118. Campbell, Joseph (1964). *The Masks of God: Occidental Mythology*. New York, NY: Penguin Group. p. 192.

119. Bierlein, J. F. (1994). *Parallel Myths*, New York, NY: Ballatine Publishing Group p. 48

120. *ibid.* p. 59

121. *ibid.* p. 61

122. *ibid.* p. 63

123. Fans, [Online]. http://www.dreamscape.com/morgana/miranda.htm [accessed 5 May 2006].

124. Tahitian [Online]. http://www.dreamscape.com/morgana/ophelia.htm [accessed 5 May 2006].

125. Mik'Maq, [Online]. http://www.dreamscape.com/morgana/cordelia.htm [accessed 5 May 2006].

126. *Hebrew-Jewish TANAKH* (1999). Philadelphia, PA: Jewish Publication Society. Deut 26:15.

127. Bierlein, J. F. (1994). *Parallel Myths*, New York, NY: Ballatine Publishing Group. p 54.

128. *ibid.* p. 48

129. *ibid.* p. 61

130. *ibid.* p. 51

131. *ibid.* p. 46

132. Australian Aboriginal: Dreamtime. [Online]. http://www.dreamscape.com/morgana/miranda.htm [accessed 5 May 2006].

133. Bierlein, J. F. (1994). *Parallel Myths*, New York, NY: Ballatine Publishing Group. p.63.

134. *ibid.* p. 41

135. *ibid.* p. 61

136. *ibid.* p. 63

137. *The Holy Bible, New International Version* (1978). Zondervan Bible Publishers, Grand Rapids, MI.

138. sruti. https://www.dictionary.com/browse/sruti.

139. As I complete this work some fifteen years since starting, I could not find my references from when starting to write this work in 2006.

140. Berry, George Ricker (1897). *The Interlinear KJV, Parallel New Testament in Greek and English based on the Textus Receptus.* Grand Rapids, MI: Zondervan Publishing House, ISBN 0-310-39380-9.

141. Nestle, Eberhard and Aland, Kurt (1993). *Novum Testamentum Graece.* Stuttgart, Germany: Deutsche Bibelgesellschaft. ISBN 978-3-438-05100-4.

142. Hodges, Zane C. & Farstad, Arthur L. (eds.) (1985). *The Greek New Testament according to the Majority Text* (2nd ed.). Nashville, TN: Thomas Nelson Publishers.

143. Scholle, Jerome. *Greek Gospels.* unpublished work lasted edited on 11 May 2011.

144. Biblical Literalism. [Online]. https://en.wikipedia.org/wiki/Biblical_literalism [accessed 4 January 2006].

145. Brennan, Zoe. Reincarnated! Our son is a World War II pilot come back to life. [Online]. https://www.dailymail.co.uk/femail/article-1209795/Reincarnated-Our-son-World-War-II-pilot-come-life.html [accessed 16 March 2021].

146. LeShan, Lawrence (1974). *The Medium, the Mystic, and the Physicist*. New York, NY: Penguin Books.

147. Werner Heisenberg. [Online]. https://en.wikipedia.org/wiki/Werner_Heisenberg [accessed 4 July 2021].

148. Heisenberg, Werner (1971). *Physics and Beyond Encounters and Conversations*. World Perspectives Vol. 42, Edited by Ruth Nanda Anshen. New York, NY: Harper & Row Publishers.

149. Luna, Aletheia. Past Lives: 11 Signs Your Soul Has Reincarnated Many Times. [Online]. https://lonerwolf.com/past-lives-soul-reincarnated/ [accessed 24 November 2021].

150. Human. [Online]. https://en.wikipedia.org/wiki/Human [accessed 16 November 2019].

151. Spirit. [Online]. https://en.wikipedia.org/wiki/Spirit [accessed 17 November 2019].

152. Soul. [Online]. https://en.wikipedia.org/wiki/Soul [accessed 17 November 2019].

153. Mind. [Online]. https://en.wikipedia.org/wiki/Mind [accessed 17 November 2019].

154. Consciousness. [Online]. https://en.wikipedia.org/wiki/Consciousness [accessed 17 November 2019].

155. Stanford Encyclopedia of Philosophy. Physicalism. [Online]. https://plato.stanford.edu/entries/physicalism [archived version May 25, 2021].

156. Stanford Encyclopedia of Philosophy. Panpsychism. [Online]. https://plato.stanford.edu/entries/panpsychism [archived version July 18, 2017].

157. Stanford Encyclopedia of Philosophy. Dualism. [Online]. https://plato.stanford.edu/entries/dualism [archived version September 11, 2020].

158. Stanford Encyclopedia of Philosophy. Idealism. [Online]. https://plato.stanford.edu/entries/idealism [archived version February 5, 2021].

159. Bernardo Kastrup. [Online]. https://www.bernardokastrup.com/ [accessed 4 May 2020].

160. Kastrup, Bernardo (2019). *The Idea of the World*. Alresford, Hampshire, UK: iff Books, an imprint of John Hunt Publishing.

161. E. Fuller Torrey. [Online]. https://en.wikipedia.org/wiki/E._Fuller_Torrey [accessed 4 May 2020].

162. Torrey, E. Fuller (2017). *Evolving Brains Emerging Gods*. New York, NY: Columbia University Press. p. 205.

163. Human. [Online]. https://en.wikipedia.org/wiki/Human [accessed 16 November 2019].

164. Stanford Encyclopedia of Philosophy. Consciousness. [Online]. https://plato.stanford.edu/entries/consciousness [archived version January 14, 2014].

165. Theory of Mind. [Online]. https://en.wikipedia.org/wiki/Theory_of_mind [accessed 6 August 2019].

166. Bernard Haisch. [Online]. https://en.wikipedia.org/wiki/Bernard_Haisch [accessed 4 May 2020].

167. Haisch, Bernard (2006). *The God Theory*, San Francisco, CA: Weiser Books.

168. *ibid.*, pp. 16-7.

169. *ibid.*, p. 19.

170. *ibid.*, pp. 22-23.

171. *ibid.*, p. 113.

172. *ibid.*, pp. 28-31.

173. *ibid.*, p. 112.

174. In reviewing references, I could not find this one specifically, however it appears that I synthesized this from several of references that mention free will as well as my concept of creation by the Living Spirit.

175. Haisch, Bernard (2006). *The God Theory*. San Francisco, CA: Weiser Books. pp. 107-108.

176. *ibid.*, pp. 114-115.

177. Neale Donald Walsch. [Online]. https://en.wikipedia.org/wiki/Neale_Donald_Walsch [accessed 4 May 2020].

178. Walsch, Neale Donald (2005). *Conversations with God*. New York, NY: Penguin Group. p. 28

179. *ibid.*, p. 28-29

180. *ibid.*, p. 30

181. *ibid.*, p. 31

182. *ibid.*, p. 32

183. *ibid.*, p. 44

184. *ibid.*, p. 171

185. *ibid.*, p. 32

186. *ibid.*, p. 33

187. Augustine of Hippo. [Online]. https://en.wikipedia.org/wiki/Augustine_of_Hippo [accessed 4 May 2020].

188. Haisch, Bernard (2006). *The God Theory*. San Francisco, CA: Weiser Books. p. 119.

189. Ulrich de Balbian. [Online]. https://fr.linkedin.com/in/ulrich-de-balbian-5a080538ulrich de balbian. [accessed 19 September 2021].

190. Balbian, Ulrich de. Philosophy: the intersubjectivity of Sophos, the one and the real self. [Online]. https://www.academia.edu/30241906/philosophos_the_one_the_real_self_pure_conscious ness. [accessed 8 September 2021].

191. Scholle, Jerome. *Greek Gospels*. unpublished work lasted edited on 11 May 2011.

192. Haisch, Bernard (2006). *The God Theory*. San Francisco, CA: Weiser Books. pp. 147-148

193. *ibid.* p.152-53

194. Paul Davies. [Online]. https://en.wikipedia.org/wiki/Paul_Davies [accessed 4 May 2020].

195. Davies, Paul (1992). *The Mind of God*, New York, NY: Touchstone.

196. Sir Arthur Eddington. [Online]. https://en.wikipedia.org/wiki/Arthur_Eddington [accessed 4 May 2020].

197. Eddington, Sir Arthur (1929). *The Nature of the Physical World*. New York, NY: The MacMillan Company. p. 331-332

198. Eddington, Sir Arthur (1929). *Science and the Unseen World*. New York, NY: The MacMillan Company. p.42-44

199. Niels Bohr. [Online]. https://en.wikipedia.org/wiki/Niels_Bohr [accessed 4 May 2020].

200. Heisenberg, Werner (1971). *Physics and Beyond*. World Perspectives Vol. 42, Edited by Ruth Nanda Anshen. New York, NY: Harper & Row Publishers. pp. 114

201. Sir James Jeans. [Online]. https://en.wikipedia.org/wiki/James_Jeans [accessed 17 March 2021].

202. Jeans, Sir James (1943). *The Mysterious Universe*. New York, NY: The MacMillan Company. p. 166

203. *ibid*. p. 186

204. Haisch, Bernard (2006). *The God Theory*. San Francisco, CA: Weiser Books. p. 143.

205. Barbara J. King. [Online]. https://en.wikipedia.org/wiki/Barbara_J._King [accessed 4 May 2020].

206. King, Barbara J. (2007). *Evolving God*. New York, NY: Doubleday Broadway Publishing Group. p. 59.

207. Merlin Donald. [Online]. https://en.wikipedia.org/wiki/Merlin_Donald [accessed 4 May 2020].

208. Donald, Merlin (2001). *A Mind So Rare: The Evolution of Human Consciousness*. New York, NY: W. W. Norton & Company, Incorporated,

209. Kastrup, Bernardo (2019). *The Idea of the World*. Alresford, Hampshire, UK: iff Books an imprint of John Hunt Publishing Ltd.

210. Keith Ward. [Online]. https://en.wikipedia.org/wiki/Keith_Ward [accessed 4 May 2020].

211. Ward, Keith (2004). *The Case for Religion*. Oxford, UK: Oneworld Publications. Reproduced with permission of the Licensor through PLSclear.p. 72

212. Webb, Matthew. God and Consciousness (we are one). [Online]. https://esolibris.com/articles/reality/god_consciousness.php. [accessed 26 October 2019].

213. Diane Estelle Morgan. [Online]. https://www.encyclopedia.com/arts/educational-magazines/morgan-diane-1947-diane-estelle-morgan [accessed 4 May 2020].

214. Morgan, Diane (2001). *The Best Guide to Eastern Philosophy & Religion*. Los Angeles CA: Renaissance Books.

215. Carl Jung. [Online]. https://en.wikipedia.org/wiki/Carl_Jung [accessed 4 May 2020].

216. The Jungian Model of the Psyche. [Online]. http://journalpsyche.org/jungian-model-psyche. [accessed 16 July 2021].

217. Jung and his Individuation Process. [Online]. http://journalpsyche.org/jungian-model-psyche. [accessed 27 July 2021].

218. Davies, Paul (1992). *The Mind of God*, New York, NY: Touchstone. p. 20.

219. Haisch, Bernard (2006). *The God Theory*. San Francisco, CA: Weiser Books. pp. 152-153

220. Robert N. McCauley. [Online]. https://www.giffordlectures.org/lecturers/robert-n-mccauley [accessed 4 May 2020].

221. McCauley, Robert N. (2011). *Why Religion Is Natural and Science Is Not*. New York, NY: Oxford University Press. p. 27.

222. *ibid.* p. 5

223. *ibid.* p. 30

224. *ibid.* p. 22

225. *ibid.* p. 24

226. *ibid.* p. 29

227. *ibid.* p. 29-30

228. *ibid.* p. 159-160

229. *ibid.* p. 172-176

230. *ibid.* p. 177-182

231. *ibid.* p. 182-221

232. King, Barbara J. (2007). *Evolving God*. New York, NY: Doubleday Broadway Publishing Group.

233. Feinberg, Todd E. [Online]. https://www.mountsinai.org/profiles/todd-e-feinberg [accessed 4 May 2020].

234. Mallatt, Jon M. [Online]. https://public.wsu.edu/~jmallatt/ [accessed 4 May 2020].

235. Feinberg, Todd E. & Mallat, Jon M. (2016). *The Ancient Origins of Consciousness*. Cambridge, MA: The MIT Press.

236. Rossoni, Sergio. [Online]. https://www.zoo.cam.ac.uk/directory/sergio-rossoni [accessed 13 June 2020].

237. Niven, Jeremy E. [Online]. https://royalsociety.org/people/jeremy-niven-10162/ and http://www.sussex.ac.uk/lifesci/nivenlab/ [accessed 13 June 2020].

238. Rossoni, Sergio & Niven, Jeremy E. Prey speed influences the speed and structure of the raptorial strike of a 'sit-and-wait' predator. [Online]. https://royalsocietypublishing.org/doi/10.1098/rsbl.2020.0098 [accessed 19 May 2020].

239. National Geographic. Half of All Species Are on the Move—And We're Feeling It. [Online]. https://www.nationalgeographic.com/news/2017/04/climate-change-species-migration-disease/ [accessed 13 June 2020].

240. M.Admin. Difference Between Paranormal and Supernatural. [Online]. https://knowledgenuts.com/2014/02/20/difference-between-paranormal-and-supernatural [accessed 3 November 2019].

241. RaK. What is considered "Paranormal?" [Online]. http://community.humanityhealing.net/group/beyondtheordinary/forum/topics/what-is-

considered-paranormal Posted by RaK on January 16, 2011 at 2:14 pm in Beyond the Ordinary [accessed 2 November 2019].

242. Fritjof Capra. https://en.wikipedia.org/wiki/Fritjof_Capra [accessed 4 May 2020].

243. Capra, Fritjof (2010). *The Tao of Physics*, (5th ed). Boulder, CO: Shambhala Publications, Inc. pp. 295-6.

244. Cleary, Thomas (1993). *The Flower Ornament Scripture, A Translation of the Avatamsaka Sutra*. Boston, MA: Shambhala Publications, Inc. [Online]. https://ia801601.us.archive.org/26/items/TheFlowerOrnamentScriptureATranslationOfThe AvatamsakaSutraByThomasClearypdfdtyxxytd/The%20Flower%20Ornament%20Scriptur e%20A%20Translation%20of%20the%20Avatamsaka%20Sutra%20by%20Thomas%20Cl eary%20%5Bpdf%5D%20%7Bdtyxxytd%7D.pdf [accessed 27 August 2021].

245. Tony Nader. [Online]. https://en.wikipedia.org/wiki/Tony_Nader [accessed 4 May 2020].

246. Nader, Tony. Consciousness Is All There Is: A Mathematical Approach with Applications, [Online]. http://www.ijmac.com/wp-content/uploads/2015/11/all04.pdf [accessed 11 March 2020].

247. Becky Storey. [Online]. https://www.learning-mind.com/author/beckystorey/ [accessed 11 September 2021]

248. Storey, Becky. What Is a Spiritual Atheist and What It Means to Be One. [Online]. https://www.learning-mind.com/spiritual-atheist-meaning [accessed 8 September 2021]

249. Neil deGrasse Tyson. https://en.wikipedia.org/wiki/Neil_deGrasse_Tyson [accessed 11 September 2021]

250. Spirit. [Online]. https://en.wikipedia.org/wiki/Spirit [accessed 17 November 2019].

251. Soul. [Online]. https://en.wikipedia.org/wiki/Soul [accessed 17 November 2019].

252. Ātman (Hinduism). [Online]. https://en.wikipedia.org/wiki/%C4%80tman_(Hinduism) [accessed 30 January 2022].

253. Chinmaya Mission Trust (2006). *Hinduism/Frequently Asked Questions*. Chinmaya Mission, Mumbai, India. ISBN 9781880687383. pp. 69–70.

254. David Hay. [Online]. https://www.theguardian.com/theguardian/2014/dec/22/david-hay-obituary [accessed 4 May 2020].

255. Hay, David (2006). *Something There, The Biology of the Human Spirit*. Philadelphia, PA: Templeton Foundation Press pp. 129-132.

256. *ibid*. p. 209

257. *ibid*. p. 210

258. Alister Hardy. [Online]. https://en.wikipedia.org/wiki/Alister_Hardy [accessed 4 May 2020].

259. Hay, David (2006). *Something There, The Biology of the Human Spirit*. Philadelphia, PA: Templeton Foundation Press p. 44-45.

260. William James. [Online]. https://en.wikipedia.org/wiki/William_James [accessed 4 May 2020].

261. Hay, David (2006). *Something There, The Biology of the Human Spirit.* Philadelphia, PA: Templeton Foundation Press 2006 p. 151.

262. Spirituality. [Online]. https://en.wikipedia.org/wiki/Spirituality [accessed 14 April 2020].

263. Abraham Maslow. [Online]. https://en.wikipedia.org/wiki/Abraham_Maslow [accessed 24 April 2022].

264. Saul Mcleod. [Online]. https://crediblemind.com/people/saul-mcleod [accessed 24 April 2022].

265. Mcleod, Saul. Maslow's Hierarchy of Needs [Online]. https://www.simplypsychology.org/maslow.html [accessed 23 April 2022].

266. Kenneth Acha. https://www.kennethmd.com/about-kenneth-acha-md/ [accessed 24 April 2022].

267. Acha, Kenneth. The 7 Fundamental Human Needs, [Online]. https://www.kennethmd.com/the-7-fundamental-human-needs/ [accessed 23 April 2022].

268. Matthew Heyn, MDiv. [Online]. https://www.spirituallyhealthyyou.com/ [accessed 24 April 2022]

269. Heyn, Matthew, MDiv. [Online]. https://www.spirituallyhealthyyou.com/spiritualneeds/#:~:text=Your%20Spiritual%20needs%20will%20consist%20of%20the%20following,5%20Ethics%20and%20Morality%206%20/Resolution%207%20Beauty [accessed 23 April 2022].

270. Rev Susan Lyon. [Online]. https://www.courant.com/news/connecticut/hc-xpm-1996-09-22-9609220192-story.html [accessed 24 April 2022]

271. Lyon, Rev Susan. [Online]. https://www.scribd.com/document/302720337/Diacresis-Seven-Core-Spiritual-Needs-Assessment-by-Susan-Lyons [accessed 23 April 2022]

272. Rev. Dr. Martin G. Montonye. [Online]. https://www.researchgate.net/profile/Martin-Montonye-2 [accessed 24 April 2022]

273. Howard Clinebell. [Online]. https://en.wikipedia.org/wiki/Howard_Clinebell [accessed 4 May 2020].

274. Krentzman, Amy R. reviewer of Seven Spiritual Needs. [Online]. https://www.takingcharge.csh.umn.edu/enhance-your-wellbeing/purpose/spirituality/seven-spiritual-needs [accessed 14 April 2020].

275. Amy R. Krentzman. [Online]. https://www.takingcharge.csh.umn.edu/our-experts/amy-r-krentzman-msw-phd [accessed 4 May 2020].

276. Ward, Keith (2004). *The Case for Religion.* Oxford, UK: Oneworld Publications. Reproduced with permission of the Licensor through PLSclear. p. 191

277. Delagran, Louise, What Is Spirituality? [Online]. https://www.takingcharge.csh.umn.edu/what-spirituality. copy of figure. [accessed 18 March 2018].

278. Gary Simmons. [Online]. https://fr.linkedin.com/in/ulrich-de-balbian-5a080538ulrich de balbian. [accessed 19 September 2021].

279. Simmons, Gary. Theology of Consciousness. [Online].
https://www.drgarysimmons.com/2015/07/07/theology-of-consciousness/. [accessed 18 September 2021].

280. Adam Brady, https://www.chopra.com/bio/adam-brady. [accessed 19 November 2021].

281. Brady, Adam, Religion vs. Spirituality: The Difference Between Them. [Online].
https://chopra.com/articles/religion-vs-spirituality-the-difference-between-them [accessed 8 September 2021].

282. Religion. [Online]. https://en.wikipedia.org/wiki/Religion, Introduction to article [accessed 15 September 2019].

283. Religion. [Online]. https://en.wikipedia.org/wiki/Religion, Concept and Etymology [accessed 15 September 2019].

284. Animism. [Online]. https://en.wikipedia.org/wiki/Animism [accessed 4 May 2020].

285. Theism. [Online]. https://en.wikipedia.org/wiki/Theism [accessed 18 November 2019].

286. Deism. [Online]. https://en.wikipedia.org/wiki/Deism [accessed 10 December 2019].

287. Pantheism. [Online]. https://en.wikipedia.org/wiki/Pantheism [accessed 1 May 2020].

288. Pandeism. [Online]. https://en.wikipedia.org/wiki/Pandeism [accessed 1 May 2020].

289. Atheism. [Online]. https://en.wikipedia.org/wiki/Atheism [accessed 9 December 2019].

290. Gnosticism. [Online]. https://en.wikipedia.org/wiki/Gnosticism [accessed 11 December 2019].

291. Agnosticism, [Online]. https://en.wikipedia.org/wiki/Agnosticism [accessed 9 December 2019].

292. Humanism. [Online]. https://en.wikipedia.org/wiki/Humanism [accessed 9 December 2019].

293. Paganism. [Online]. https://en.wikipedia.org/wiki/Humanism [accessed 9 December 2019].

294. Hervey Cunningham Peoples, [Online]. https://humanquestion.com/about-hervey [accessed 4 May 2020].

295. Peoples, Hervey C. & Duda Pavel & Marlowe1, Frank W. Hunter-Gatherers and the Origins of Religion. Hum Nat (2016) 27:261–282 DOI 10.1007/s12110-016-9260-0 [Online]. Available from https://www.ncbi.nlm.nih.gov/pmc/articles/PMC4958132/pdf/12110_2016_Article_9260.pdf, p. 3 [accessed 22 April 2020].

296. *ibid*, p. 6

297. Stanford Encyclopedia of Philosophy: Panpsychism. [Online].
https://plato.stanford.edu/entries/panpsychism [accessed 6 April 2020].

298. Peoples, Hervey C. & Duda Pavel & Marlowe1, Frank W. Hunter-Gatherers and the Origins of Religion. Hum Nat (2016) 27:261–282 DOI 10.1007/s12110-016-9260-0 [Online]. Available from https://www.ncbi.nlm.nih.gov/pmc/articles/PMC4958132/pdf/12110_2016_Article_9260.pdf, p. 11 [accessed 22 April 2020].

299. Kersey Graves. https://en.wikipedia.org/wiki/Kersey_Graves [accessed 4 May 2020].

300. Graves, Kersey (1999). *The World's Sixteen Crucified Saviors*, first published in1875 (2nd ed.). Escondido, CA: republished The Book Tree. p. 21

301. Anthropology of Religion. [Online]. https://en.wikipedia.org/wiki/Anthropology_of_religion [accessed 22 April 2020].

302. Anthony F. C. Wallace. [Online]. https://en.wikipedia.org/wiki/Anthony_F._C._Wallace [accessed 4 May 2020].

303. Torrey, E. Fuller (2017). *Evolving Brains Emerging Gods*. Columbia University Press. p. 205

304. Neil, Shasha. 8 Oldest Religions in the World. [Online]. https://www.oldest.org/religion/religions/ [accessed 20 April 2020].

305. Dudhane, Rahul, Founder of Hinduism, [Online]. https://www.hinduismfacts.org/founder-of-hinduism/ [accessed 24 November 2021].

306. Neil, Shasha. 10 Oldest Religious Texts in The World. [Online]. https://www.oldest.org/religion/religious-texts/ [accessed 20 April 2020].

307. *ibid.*

308. Kesh Temple Hymn. [Online]. https://en.wikipedia.okesh_temple_hymnrg/wiki/ [accessed 23 April 2020].

309. Bhagavad Gita. [Online]. https://en.wikipedia.org/wiki/Bhagavad_Gita [accessed 4 May 2020].

310. Graves, Kersey (1999). *The World's Sixteen Crucified Saviors*, first published in1875 (2nd ed.). Escondido, CA: republished The Book Tree. pp. 109-110.

311. Graves, Kersey (1999). *The World's Sixteen Crucified Saviors*, first published in1875 (2nd ed.). Escondido, CA: republished The Book Tree. pp. 256-273

312. How Christianity Was Invented: The Truth! [Online]. https://acurseonalltheirhouses.wordpress.com/2012/01/21/how-christianity-was-invented/ [accessed 22 April 2020].

313. Graves, Kersey (1999). *The World's Sixteen Crucified Saviors*, first published in1875 (2nd ed.). Escondido, CA: republished The Book Tree. pp. 288-293.

314. Henry Hart Milman. [Online]. https://en.wikipedia.org/wiki/Henry_Hart_Milman [accessed 4 May 2020].

315. Graves, Kersey (1999). *The World's Sixteen Crucified Saviors*, first published in1875 (2nd ed.). Escondido, CA: republished The Book Tree. pp. 181-182.

316. Milman, Henry Hart (1872). *The History of Christianity*, New York, NY: W. J. Widdleton Publisher. Vol. 1, Chap. 2, p. 80.

317. Graves, Kersey (1999). *The World's Sixteen Crucified Saviors*, first published in1875 (2nd ed.). Escondido, CA: republished The Book Tree. p. 280

318. William Enfield. [Online]. https://en.wikisource.org/wiki/Enfield,_William_(DNB00) [accessed 4 May 2020].

319. Graves, Kersey (1999). *The World's Sixteen Crucified Saviors*, first published in1875 (2nd ed.). Escondido, CA: republished The Book Tree. p. 286

320. Milman, Henry Hart (1872). *The History of Christianity*, New York, NY: W. J. Widdleton Publisher. Vol. 1, Chap. 2, p. 79.

321. Graves, Kersey (1999). *The World's Sixteen Crucified Saviors*, first published in1875 (2nd ed.). Escondido, CA: republished The Book Tree. p. 288.

322. Pittacus of Mytilene. [Online]. https://en.wikipedia.org/wiki/Pittacus_of_Mytilene [accessed 3 May 2020]. quote 12 words,

323. Graves, Kersey (1999). *The World's Sixteen Crucified Saviors*, first published in1875 (2nd ed.). Escondido, CA: republished The Book Tree. p. 348

324. Confucius. [Online]. https://en.wikipedia.org/wiki/Confucius [accessed 3 May 2020].

325. Graves, Kersey (1999). *The World's Sixteen Crucified Saviors*, first published in1875 (2nd ed.). Escondido, CA: republished The Book Tree. p. 348

326. Morgan, Diane (2001). *The Best Guide to Eastern Philosophy & Religion*. Los Angeles CA: Renaissance Books. p. xii.

327. Thales of Miletus. [Online]. https://en.wikipedia.org/wiki/Thales_of_Miletus [accessed 3 May 2020].

328. Graves, Kersey (1999). *The World's Sixteen Crucified Saviors*, first published in1875 (2nd ed.). Escondido, CA: republished The Book Tree. p. 348

329. Pythagoreanism. [Online]. https://en.wikipedia.org/wiki/Pythagoreanism [accessed 3 May 2020].

330. Graves, Kersey (1999). *The World's Sixteen Crucified Saviors*, first published in1875 (2nd ed.). Escondido, CA: republished The Book Tree. p. 349

331. Laërtius, Diogenes. Lives and Opinions of Eminent Philosophers, "Pythagoras", Sect. 23, as translated in Dictionary of Quotations [Online]. https://ia800701.us.archive.org/28/items/dictionaryquota02harbgoog/dictionaryquota02harbgoog.pdf [accessed 1 August 2021], p. 332

332. Aristotle. [Online]. https://en.wikipedia.org/wiki/Aristotle [accessed 3 May 2020].

333. Graves, Kersey (1999). *The World's Sixteen Crucified Saviors*, first published in1875 (2nd ed.). Escondido, CA: republished The Book Tree. p. 348

334. Aristippus. [Online]. https://en.wikipedia.org/wiki/Aristippus [accessed 3 May 2020].

335. Graves, Kersey (1999). *The World's Sixteen Crucified Saviors*, first published in1875 (2nd ed.). Escondido, CA: republished The Book Tree. p. 349

336. Isocrates. [Online]. https://en.wikipedia.org/wiki/Isocrates [accessed 3 May 2020].

337. Graves, Kersey (1999). *The World's Sixteen Crucified Saviors*, first published in1875 (2nd ed.). Escondido, CA: republished The Book Tree. p. 348

338. Hillel. [Online]. https://en.wikipedia.org/wiki/Hillel_the_Elder [accessed 3 May 2020].

339. Graves, Kersey (1999). *The World's Sixteen Crucified Saviors*, first published in1875 (2nd ed.). Escondido, CA: republished The Book Tree. p. 349

340. *The Holy Bible, New International Version* (1978). Zondervan Bible Publishers, Grand Rapids, MI.

341. *ibid.*

342. Scientism, Introduction. [Online]. https://en.wikipedia.org/wiki/Scientism [accessed 5 May 2020].

343. Mastin, Luke (2008). Basics of Philosophy, Scientism, Introduction. [Online]. from https://www.philosophybasics.com/branch_scientism.html [accessed 5 May 2020].

344. Mastin, Luke (2008). Basics of Philosophy, Scientism, Criticisms of Scientism. [Online]. https://www.philosophybasics.com/branch_scientism.html [accessed 5 May 2020].

345. Graves, Kersey (1999). *The World's Sixteen Crucified Saviors*, first published in1875 (2nd ed.). Escondido, CA: republished The Book Tree. p. 427

What is Your Journey in the Spirit of the Universe?

The following pages document my artistic presentation in an art gallery 2007-2008 that is no longer in operation. This is an early rendition on which this book has been developed. The sequence of pictures is:

1. The picture in the gallery.
2. My presence with the picture.
3. The picture as a whole showing more detail having been created in PowerPoint, Word and Excel from which the individual sheets were printed.
4. The Picture Title Card.
5. The Handout Cover page.
6. The Handout text about the picture and my journey to that time.
7. The Handout showing the center section of the picture.
8. The Handout showing the side panels.
9. The Picture Wording details for readability.
10. The Center Aspects showing image details.
11. The Religiosity Top Half Panels for readability.
12. The Religiosity Bottom Half Panels for readability.
13. The Spirituality Top Half Panels for readability.
14. The Spirituality Bottom Half Panels for readability

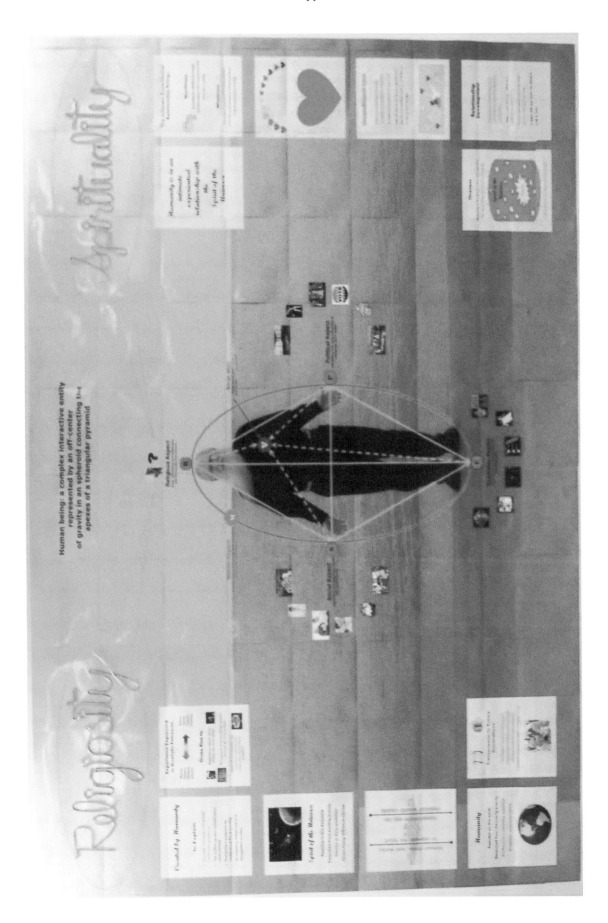

Picture Title Card

What Is Your Journey in the Spirit of the Universe?

Mixed media

Jerry Scholle

Wire Scripts and Photography courtesy of Fluidikons, Kelly Courtney

What is Your Journey in the Spirit of the Universe?

by Jerome V. Scholle

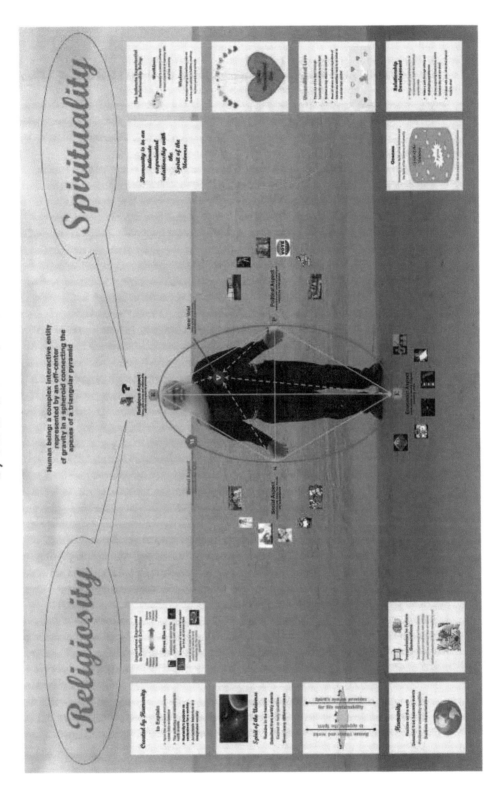

Jerry's Journey in the Spirit of the Universe

The art work and what follows are the insights from my journey of over 60+ years from a farming community through a career in chemical physics while pursing also my avocation of what are the origins of religious systems to find my relationship in the Spirit of the Universe.

The spirit, whatever its source in the earth plane at this time, entered a body formed by mid-life parents who named me, their first born of five children, Jerry. The tone for expressing the abilities that I brought to the earth plane was set partially by the circumstances my parents were experiencing at my birth. They married in mid-life and were ostracized from their families for a time because of their mixed Christian religions. Thus they started with minimal provisions in another farming community as outsiders. This led to my being socially isolated during childhood and learning to cope and develop my abilities leading to being a highly introverted thinker according to psychological tests.

A major turning point in my scholastic abilities and approach to life occurred when the third grade teacher told me that I could be whatever I wanted to be. In addition my mother long recognized that there was no farm boy in me. These coupled with my strong interest in the Roman Catholic priesthood led me to enter seminary as a freshman in high school. Although I was not able to continue for personal reasons, I remained determined to go back to seminary during my high school years. These years also saw the development of my interest in why is there a dichotomy between science and religion. After starting college with majors in mathematics and physical sciences, I returned to the seminary for two more years. However finding this not meeting my spiritual needs, I left organized religions and earned a Master of Science degree in physics. At this time I started to pursue, as an avocation, what are the origins of religions while having a career in the physical sciences.

One of the hallmarks of my scientific training is to work from basics and to be open to all possibility. From my scientific studies I realized that there had to be a Creative Force, which I now term the Spirit of the Universe. My avocation studies included highly scholastic works on comparative religions, writings of the major religions and even practicing some of these for a time. Each showed that there were many similarities as well as differences; but again none truly brought about an inner satisfaction. In addition my educator's heart propelled my teaching and writing on the quality sciences both within and outside my employment. Easily over extending myself psychological issues resulted leading to my recognition that workaholism was a means of trying to satisfy the inner void.

Sometime in the midst of all of this I started being thankful to the Spirit of the Universe in all circumstances while not practicing anyone religious faith. As I continued to do this and study multiple viewpoints, my attitudes began to change bringing what had been very important into proper balance; and if unimportant, it was shed in order to be guided into a deeper relationship in the Spirit of the Universe. These changes came about by being attuned to what the Spirit was saying not only through what I read but also listening to my dreams and intuitive self. Now I am experiencing an inner peace that I had not known previously and feel in harmony with the universe. However I know that a deeper intimate relationship in the Spirit of the Universe is possible, and I yearn and work to develop it as I travel the path that will let the spirit go to wherever it is to go when this earth-plane body is shed.

As part of this evolving path I have written short articles, which are available on my website, www.christianbear.org. Longer articles are in development and from which this artwork is created.

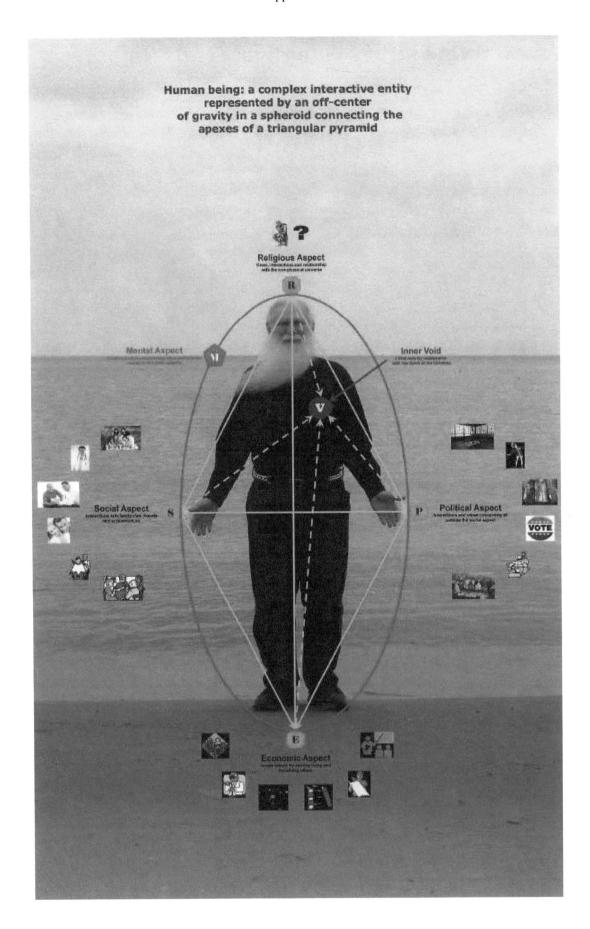

Human being: a complex interactive entity
represented by an off-center
of gravity in a spheroid connecting the
apexes of a triangular pyramid

Religiosity

Created by Humanity

to Explain

➤ How the universe and people came into existence
➤ The suffering and catastrophic earth events
➤ Humanity's purpose as understood for a society
➤ Acceptable behaviors in a designated society

Experience Expressed in Dualistic Extremes

Above	Below
Heavens	Earth
Perfect	Flawed
Sacred	Profane

Gives Rise to

Addictions which fail to satisfy the void within

Arrogance of one's belief system as true, all others false

Strife of all kinds for the control of others and resources by the more powerful

Spirit of the Universe

Resides in the heavens
Detached from earthly events
Sacred or holy qualities
Given many different names

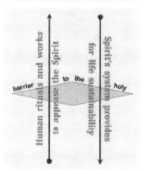

Humanity

Resides on the earth
Detached from heavenly events
Profane or unworthy qualities
Dualistic characteristics

Transmission to Future Generations

Developed based on forerunners through oral traditions into writings which are defined later as sacred whether considered Spirit revealed or not

Spirituality

Humanity is in an intimate experiential relationship with the Spirit of the Universe

The Intimate Experiential Relationship Brings

Worthiness

Humanity is created not flawed to learn how to live in harmony with all of the universe

Wholeness

The innate longing (sometimes referred to as the void within) is fulfilled resulting in inner peace and serenity.

Unconditional Love

➤ Flows out of the Spirit through humanity given wholly to the Spirit
➤ Enables loving others as one's self
➤ Sees all others as equals regardless of talents and abilities; each is no better or no worse than another

Oneness

Humanity in the Spirit of the Universe and the Spirit of the Universe is Humanity

Earth a spot in an unbounded universe

Relationship Development

➤ Brings about thankfulness in all circumstances: both the blessings and the trials
➤ Walks a path of growth of sifting and challenging experiences
➤ Grows exposing hindrances which become dim and are shed
➤ Is taken with one when the physical body is shed

Picture Wording

Human being: a complex interactive entity represented by an off-center of gravity in an spheroid connecting the apexes of a triangular pyramid

Religious Aspect

Views, interactions and relationship
with the non-physical universe

Inner Void

Filled only by relationship
with the Spirit of the Universe

Mental Aspect

Communications concerning ideas and
actions related to the other aspects

Social Aspect

Interactions with family clan, friends and acquaintances

Political Aspect

Interactions and views concerning all outside the social aspect

Economic Aspect

Innate talents for earning living and benefiting others

Center Panel Aspects

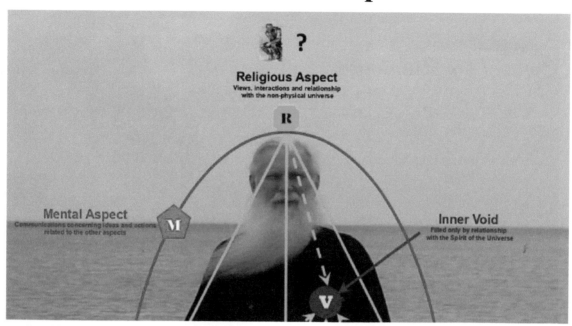

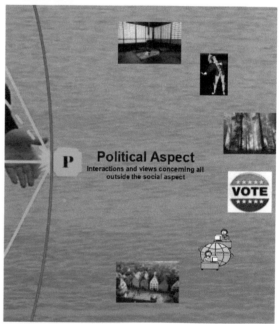

Religiosity Top Half Panels

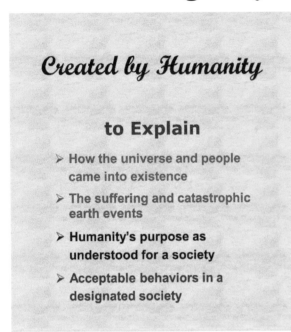

Created by Humanity

to Explain

➢ How the universe and people came into existence

➢ The suffering and catastrophic earth events

➢ **Humanity's purpose as understood for a society**

➢ Acceptable behaviors in a designated society

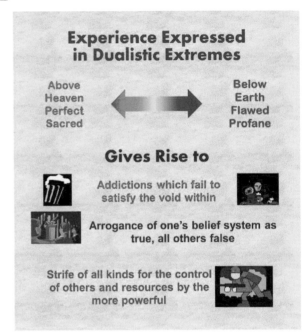

Experience Expressed in Dualistic Extremes

Above		Below
Heaven		Earth
Perfect		Flawed
Sacred		Profane

Gives Rise to

Addictions which fail to satisfy the void within

Arrogance of one's belief system as true, all others false

Strife of all kinds for the control of others and resources by the more powerful

Spirit of the Universe

Resides in the heavens

Detached from earthly events

Sacred or holy qualities

Given many different names

Religiosity Bottom Half Panels

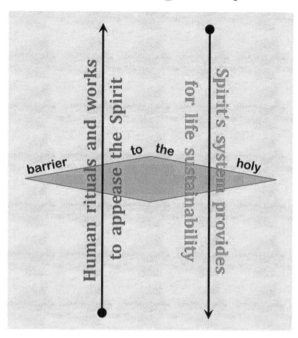

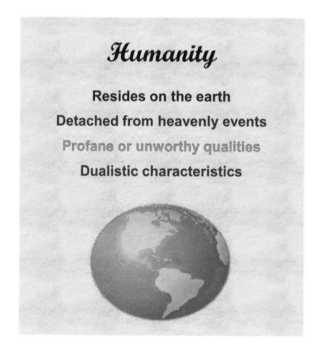

Spirituality Top Half Panels

Humanity is in an intimate experiential relationship with the Spirit of the Universe

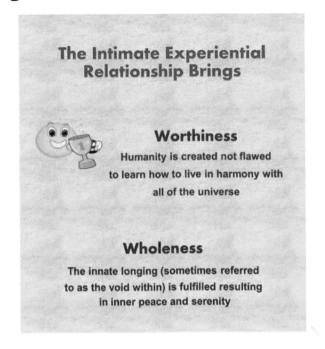

The Intimate Experiential Relationship Brings

Worthiness

Humanity is created not flawed
to learn how to live in harmony with
all of the universe

Wholeness

The innate longing (sometimes referred
to as the void within) is fulfilled resulting
in inner peace and serenity

Spirituality Bottom Half Panels

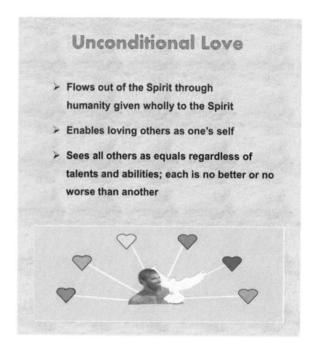

Unconditional Love

> Flows out of the Spirit through humanity given wholly to the Spirit

> Enables loving others as one's self

> Sees all others as equals regardless of talents and abilities; each is no better or no worse than another

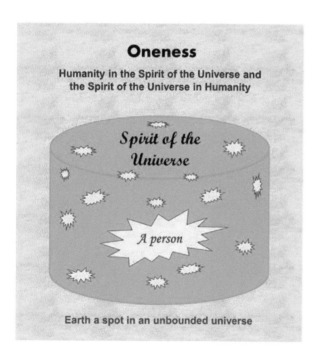

Oneness

Humanity in the Spirit of the Universe and the Spirit of the Universe in Humanity

Spirit of the Universe

A person

Earth a spot in an unbounded universe

Relationship Development

> Brings about thankfulness in all circumstance: both the blessings and the trials

> Walks a path through sifting and challenging experiences

> Grows exposing hindrances which become dim and are shed

> Is taken with one, when the physical body is shed